THE GALLIPOLI CAMPAIGN

The war against the Ottomans, on Gallipoli, in Palestine and in Mesopotamia was a major enterprise for the Allies with important long-term geo-political consequences. The absence of a Turkish perspective, written in English, represents a huge gap in the historiography of the First World War. This timely collection of wide-ranging essays on the campaign, drawing on Turkish sources and written by experts in the field, addresses this gap. Scholars employ archival documents from the Turkish General Staff, diaries and letters of Turkish soldiers, Ottoman journals and newspapers published during the campaign, and recent academic literature by Turkish scholars to reveal a different perspective on the campaign, which should breathe new life into English-language historiography on this crucial series of events.

Major (Ret.) Metin Gürcan is a visiting research fellow at the Changing Character of War (CCW) programme in Oxford University and a PhD candidate at Bilkent University, Turkey, studying change in the Turkish military and the changing nature of warfare in the twenty-first century.

Dr Robert Johnson is the Director of the Changing Character of War programme at Oxford University. He is currently finishing his book *The Great War in the Middle East*, to be published in 2016.

The Gallipoli Campaign
The Turkish perspective

Edited by

METIN GÜRCAN AND ROBERT JOHNSON

Routledge
Taylor & Francis Group
LONDON AND NEW YORK

First published 2016
by Routledge
2 Park Square, Milton Park, Abingdon, Oxon OX14 4RN

and by Routledge
711 Third Avenue, New York, NY 10017

Routledge is an imprint of the Taylor & Francis Group, an informa business

British Library Cataloguing in Publication Data
A catalogue record for this book is available from the British Library

Library of Congress Cataloging-in-Publication Data
Names: Gürcan, Metin, editor. | Johnson, Robert, 1967—editor.
Title: The Gallipoli Campaign : the Turkish perspective / edited by Metin Gürcan and Robert Johnson.
Series: Routledge studies in First World War history | Includes bibliographical references and index.
Identifiers: LCCN 2015038118
Subjects: LCSH: World War, 1914–1918–Campaigns–Turkey–Gallipoli Peninsula. World War, 1914–1918–Campaigns–Turkey–Gallipoli Peninsula–Sources.
Classification: LCC D568.3. G29 2016 | DDC 940.4/26–dc23
LC record available at http://lccn.loc.gov/2015038118

ISBN: 9781472450609 (hbk)
ISBN: 9781315557847 (ebk)

Typeset in Times New Roman
by Apex CoVantage, LLC

MIX
Paper from responsible sources
FSC® C013985

Printed in the United Kingdom
by Henry Ling Limited

Contents

List of figures

List of tables

Contributors

Captain Ferhat Çalışkan is a serving officer of the Turkish Armed Forces at the Military Staff College.

Major (retd) Dr Metin Gürcan, formerly of the Turkish General Staff, holds a PhD from Bilkent University.

Şafak Horzum is a Research Associate of the Faculty of Letters, Department of English Language and Literature at Hacettepe University, Ankara.

Robert Johnson is the Director of the Changing Character of War programme at Oxford University and author of the forthcoming *The Great War in the Middle East* (Oxford University Press, 2016).

Alev Karaduman is a member of the Department of English Language and Literature at Hacettepe University, Ankara.

Captain Hilmi Kendircioğlu is a serving officer of the Turkish Armed Forces at the Military Staff College.

Mehmet Akif Okur is a member of the Department of International Relations, Gazi University.

Hülya Toker works at the Archives of the General Staff Military History and Strategic Studies Department (ATASE).

Kahraman Şakul is a member of Sehir University, Istanbul.

Captain Hasan Tahsin Vanlı is a serving officer of the Turkish Armed Forces at the Military Staff College.

Those heroes that shed their blood and lost their lives . . .
You are now lying in the soil of a friendly country.
Therefore, rest in peace.
There is no difference between the Johnnies
And the Mehmets to us where they lie side by side
Here in this country of ours . . .
You, the mothers,
Who sent their sons from faraway countries
Wipe away your tears,
Your sons are now lying in our bosom
And are in peace.
After having lost their lives on this land they have
Become our sons as well.

Mustafa Kemal Atatürk, 1934

Chapter 1
Introduction

Robert Johnson and Metin Gürcan

> Stop wayfarer! . . . Bend down and lend your ear, for this silent mound / Is the place where the heart of a nation sighs.

With its evocative azure blue colour, the Dardanelles Strait connects the Sea of Marmara to the Aegean Sea and separates two ranges of hills, both of which are surmounted by narrow plateaux. On the upper bluffs, close to the city of Çanakkale, there is a pale brown hill on which a contrasting white crescent and star are drawn. Beneath them are large white numbers, which are best seen from the ferry that heads for Eceabat on the Gallipoli peninsula. It boldly announces: '18 March 1915'. Further away, across the straits and also clearly visible from the Gallipoli Peninsula, is the ancient castle guarding the region known locally as Kilitbahir [the Lock of the Sea]. Above this fortress, on a hilltop to the north, is a huge silhouette of a 1915 Turkish soldier carved in white. In one hand he holds a rifle, while his other arm is outstretched towards a Turkish inscription, a verse taken from the poem of Necmettin Halil Onan, entitled *To a Traveller.* It states: 'Stop wayfarer! Unbeknownst to you this ground / You come and tread on, is where an epoch lies; / Bend down and lend your ear, for this silent mound / Is the place where the heart of a nation sighs'. The word 'epoch' in these verses does not simply refer to the defeat of the Allied forces in a campaign that took place in 1915 within the context of the First World War. For some, it suggests that the old colonial empires of Britain and France were somehow brought to an end, here, at the hands of '*Mehmetçik*', the ordinary Turkish soldiers, and ushered in a new beginning for the nation-state of Turkey. This interpretation seems more plausible if the whole of Necmettin Halil Onan's poem is recalled:

> To the left of this deserted shadeless lane
> The Anatolian slope now observes you well;
> For liberty and honour, it is, in pain,
> Where wounded Mehmetçik laid down his life and fell.
> This very mound, when violently shook the land,
> When the last bit of homeland passed from hand to hand,
> And when Mehmetçik drowned the enemy in flood,
> Is the spot where he added his own pure blood.
> Think, the consecrated blood and flesh and bone
> That make up this mound, is where a whole nation,

After a harsh and pitiless war, alone
Tasted the joy of freedom with elation.

In light of these lines, the inscription on the hillside has a more profound sense. Necmettin Halil Onan commands us to stop and reflect on the mass of earth called the Gallipoli Peninsula, since, here, he maintains, beats the heart of whole 'epoch' of Turkish national life. It was here in 1915 that *Mehmetçik* voluntarily laid down his life for the freedom of Turkey. For Turks, he paid for that freedom with his own blood. Onan's poem is as well known in Turkey as a hymn of patriotic praise to those who defended the Ottoman Empire from the invaders of 1915. For Turks, it is only necessary to quote the first two lines on the Kilitbahir memorial for the sentiments of the whole poem to be recalled. '*Stop wayfarer!*' is the motto which reminds everyone of the price the Ottoman Empire paid for victory at Gallipoli: some 49,882 dead and over 164,000 wounded.[1] For many Turks, the date of 18 March 1915 also marked the end of the Royal Navy's dominance as a force with global reach. That is why, in Turkey, there are many scholars who tend to present the motto of '*Stop wayfarer!*' as the first check, by the Eastern world, on Western imperialist domination in spite of its overwhelming technological superiority.[2] Taking this symbolic significance of the motto of 'stop wayfarer!' in Gallipoli one step further, by not limiting it to the Eastern world, Edward J. Erickson, the eminent American scholar of the Ottoman Empire, suggests that this 'spirit' is of huge psychological importance, not only for Turkey but for Australia and New Zealand, as it represents 'a coming of age of a people about to test themselves against the currents of the twentieth century'.[3]

During the preparations for the campaign, if the decision-makers in the Allied army under General Sir Ian Hamilton's command, who attempted to seize the Gallipoli Peninsula with insufficient forces, could have read Onan's poem symbolising the resilience of Turkish soldiers, and if they had known that they would have to test their strength against these Turkish soldiers yard by yard in the battles of Krithia, Kereves Dere, Gully Ravine, Achi Baba Nullah, Sari Bair, Lone Pine, Chunuk Bair, Suvla,

1 Along with the Ottoman soldiers killed in the campaign, all the prisoners of war, deserters, missing and the soldiers who lost their lives due to disease are included in this death toll.

Gnkur. ATASE Bşk. lığı Yay., Birinci Dünya Harbinde Türk Harbi; V. Cilt, Çanakkale Cephesi, III. Kitap, p. 500.

2 This presentation of the Gallipoli Campaign as the first check on Western imperialism has been embraced both Turkish Islamist and Turkish leftist discourse.

For the Islamist discourse, please see: Ramazan Hurç, 'Çanakkale Savaşının Manevi Yönü (The Religious Side of the Gallipoli Campaign) – Turkish', *The Journal of Theological Studies*, Firat University, Vol. IV (1999), pp. 61–96.

For the leftist discourse, please see the interview of Erol Mütercimler (Turkish) http://www.turksolu.com.tr/80/soylesi80.htm (accessed 16 May 2014).

3 Edward J. Erickson, *Ordered To Die: A History of the Ottoman Army in the First World War* (Westport: Greenwood Press, 2001), p. 76.

Anafarta and Scimitar Hill, would they have changed their initial operational plans? We do not know the answer to this counter-factual question of course, although there is empirical evidence to show that the British underestimated the Ottoman Army. After defeats in the Balkans in 1912–13, the Ottoman armed forces were undergoing extensive reorganisation just before the war broke out. In late 1914, British and Indian formations had driven the Ottomans out of Basra in Mesopotamia, and the Ottomans had been defeated in the Sinai and in the Caucasus. All the indications were that the Ottomans were riven with political disunity and military inefficiency.

What we know for sure is that orthodox Anglocentric discourse would now prefer to suggest that the campaign's failure was the result of incompetence in the Allied forces at the strategic-political level. This conceptualisation of the Gallipoli Campaign as the Allies' 'strategic failure' does not seem, however, to recognise that it was an Ottoman victory. While it is true to highlight the Allies' strategic and operational mistakes, this should not automatically imply that, had they not made these mistakes, the Allies would have won. In much of the Anglophone discussions, the main research question, which has directed scholars for decades, is: 'what was the causal mechanism that led to a strategic failure in the Gallipoli Campaign?' To seek answers to this question, starting with the famous British Dardanelles Commission in 1917, many scholarly works reflect the orthodox Anglocentric perspective of Allied failure. This volume offers the opportunity to reformulate the old question as: 'what was the causal mechanism that led to the victory of the Ottoman army in the Gallipoli Campaign?' In the Turkish literature, there are five explanatory approaches to answer this question.

First is the 'Atatürkist' discourse which emphasises the agency of Mustafa Kemal's skills as a commander as the crucial factor in the Ottoman victory, especially his foresight and charismatic leadership. Hakan Uzun asserts that, for the Turks, inspired by the heroic act of Lieutenant Colonel Mustafa Kemal, soldiers voluntarily rushed to defend their country and formed a heroic human shield to make it impossible for the Allies to pass through the straits or traverse the Peninsula.[4] Uzun tends to describe the Gallipoli Campaign as an 'unusual context' that gave birth to a hero who, following the Turkish War of Independence (or Turkish National Struggle), laid the foundations of modern Turkey. Mustafa Kemal's successful operation confined the Allies to a narrow strip of shore and eventually put a halt to the Allies' advance up the Peninsula. Uzun's central question is whether Mustafa Kemal came to be known as 'the hero of Gallipoli' because he was 'Atatürk' or whether his heroic acts at Ariburnu and Suvla Bay paved the way for him to *become* 'Atatürk'.[5] It is also worth mentioning that Uzun

---

4 Hakan Uzun, (Turkish) 'Bir Savaş ve Bir Liderin Doğuşu: Mustafa Kemal Paşa'nın Çanakkale Savaşı'na, Çanakkale Savaşı'nın Mustafa Kemal Paşa'nın Yaşamına Etkileri', 3. Uluslararası Gelibolu Sempozyumu, Bağlarbaşı Kültür ve Kongre Merkezi, İstanbul 20–21 Nisan 2012.

5 Ibid.

develops his argument only by examining Mustafa Kemal's former career, his role at Gallipoli, various quotations from memoirs and the reports of those who had participated in the campaign, including those of Mustafa Kemal himself. On the other hand, İsmet Görgülü, a retired colonel who has studied many of the academic works on the campaign, asserts that the land battles of the Gallipoli Campaign, which lasted almost eight months, could have ended within a day if the Ottoman soldiers had been commanded properly. Dismissing the senior command, he places the emphasis on the agency of Mustafa Kemal.[6] For him, during the campaign, Kemal saved İstanbul, the capital of the Ottoman Empire, no less than five times. Görgülü argues:

> The first time Mustafa Kemal saved İstanbul was on 25 April 1915, the first day of the battle. As the Allied forces landed troops on the shore of Arıburnu, also known as Anzac Cove, the Turkish forces were quantitatively outnumbered by the enemy forces. They were unable to stop the Allies. The enemy was well on the way to Chunuk Bair. If Chunuk Bair was captured by the Allies, the defence in Çanakkale would be impossible and our forces there would be eliminated, and eventually both the land and the sea route to İstanbul would be wide open; and thus İstanbul would fall. At that vital moment, Lieutenant Colonel Mustafa Kemal divined the crucial attack upon the enemy landing at Arıburnu and asked the corps commander's permission to execute his plan. The corps commander was unable to decide by himself as Mustafa Kemal's division was the reserve of the army. For the assault, permission had to be given by the army general. At the same time, there came the news of the enemy's simultaneous landing in three different areas. If Mustafa Kemal's 19th Division was to be committed at Arıburnu, there would be no force left to be used in case of emergency in any of the other areas. It was then learned that the army general had gone to the Gulf of Saros, which could mean the enemy was probably landing its troops there too. There was no certain knowledge about any of the landings. Therefore, the corps commander first tried to reach the general via telephone and then decided to go to the Saros region himself, which, being some 40km away, would take two hours. Yet the Allied forces would not wait for his return that afternoon for their attacks. At that exact moment, Mustafa Kemal decided to make an assault on the enemy without waiting for the order from the corps commander or the army general, and thus he alone changed the fortunes of the Battle of Çanakkale.

After this critical decision, Görgülü continued:

> The second time Mustafa Kemal saved İstanbul was 7 August, when he was the commander of the 19th Division. The enemy was making an assault on the front

6 İsmet Görgülü, Çanakkale Bir Günde Biterdi, (Bilgi Yayınevi, Ankara, 2000), pp. 96–7.

> line, and one wing of the Allies was surrounding Chunuk Bair. There were only 30 or 40 Turkish [Ottoman] soldiers there and it was clear that they would be insufficient to stop the enemy. In addition, this area was totally out of Mustafa Kemal's responsibility. Despite this fact, and the attack on his own front, Kemal sent all his remaining forces (about 1.5 battalions) to Chunuk Bair. He, thus, prevented the fall of Chunuk Bair for the second time, and, therefore, he saved İstanbul for a second time.
>
> The third occasion Mustafa Kemal saved İstanbul was 9 August. Upon having had no concrete results from three months of assaults, the English [British] planned a great attack with new forces, supporting the Anzac Corps at the Arıburnu region with 17,500 soldiers from Sedd-el-Bahr [Cape Helles] on 4–5 August. They began a huge attack at Arıburnu on 6 August. Then they started to land troops on the shores of Suvla Bay at night and which continued on 7 and 8 August. The British Corps was of four divisions, some 43,000 soldiers. In the following days, this number reached 80,000. Their aim was to capture V Beach [Teke Bay] and Kocaçimen Hill and thus, after the capture of Chunuk Bair, control the Bosphorus.

Görgülü attributed the defence of Chunuk Bair entirely to the military genius of Kemal:

> The fourth time [was] 10 August. [Kemal] became the commander of the Anafarta Detachment on the 8th, achieved the 'First Anafarta Victory' on 9 August, and concluded that the enemy would attack Chunuk Bair with their overwhelming numbers both to take revenge for the previous day's defeat and to reach a certain result by 10 August. [Kemal] decided to attack from Chunuk Bair in order to disrupt the enemy's offensive. He came to Chunuk Bair at night. What matters here is that the forces at the Bair were too weak to prevent an enemy assault the following morning, but he had made a decision and it would not be possible to take reinforcements from any other point during the night. He thought to attack the enemy with the forces that were too weak to defend their area. That was his military prodigy: heroism combined with his wisdom.

Emphasising his prowess, his heroism, and his insight during the Second Anafarta Battle, Görgülü wrote:

> The enemy started an assault with their six divisions (about 70,000 strong) on Anafarta Plain on 21 August. There were two Turkish divisions (about 18,000 troops) facing them. It was not possible to stop this great attack under the heavy fire of the Allies' navy with so few Turkish soldiers. One Turkish division was in the reserve line and it was impossible for them to move up before the enemy overran the front line. The conditions were so critical that time was needed to get this division to the front. Herein he showed his military prodigy once more. There was only one formation available, and the commander of the Anafarta Detachment, Mustafa Kemal, ordered his men to vault over the defending

> line of troops and counter attack the charging enemy. The time needed for the reinforcements was thus obtained.[7]

This form of hagiography of Kemal was persistent for decades, but has been challenged.

The second explanatory discourse is the 'modernist-institutionalist' one which puts emphasis on the 'military effectiveness' of the Ottoman 5th Army in the Gallipoli at the tactical (that is, battalion and below) and operational (that is, regiments/brigades and above) levels. Edward J. Erickson, as an ardent advocate of this argument, begins with the initial assumption that many of the 'myths' that persist in the Anglocentric orthodoxy are simply due to lack of accurate information available from Turkish archives, most of which remain closed to foreign scholars. He then argues that, during the war, while the Ottoman Empire itself might have been declining, its army was still strong and increasingly adept at the tactical and operational level. What it could not overcome were weaknesses in political decision-making and strategic planning. According to Erickson, for instance, the Ottoman 5th Army's reporting system was, in comparison to the Allies' at Gallipoli, much more effective because of its standardised formations and 'bottom-up' requirements. The 5th Army commanders' cadres, particularly the junior officers at the tactical and lower echelons of the senior officers (that is, regimental and divisional commanders) at the operational levels, were consistently in possession of accurate and timely information that enabled them to make rapid and effective decisions. This also created a superior 'situational awareness', that is, local intelligence, amongst the division commanders, which enabled them to calculate risks and use their initiative in a timely fashion.

For Erickson, cumulatively these factors led to the capability to mass the available forces in an effective and efficient manner. Four operations illustrate this point: Lt Colonel Şefik (The 27th Regiment Commander) and Mustafa Kemal's coordinated attack on 25 April; Kemal's subsequent massed night attacks between 25 April and 16 May; Mahmut Sabri's (3rd Battalion Commander of the 26th Regiment) defence of the Cape Helles; and Nicolai's massing at Kumkale for 32.5 hours on 25–6 April.[8] In each case, the Turks brought their forces to the right place in time to thwart the Allied offensives.[9]

Erickson nevertheless emphasises that, at the strategic level, the Gallipoli Campaign was a 'badly administered success story', as the higher echelons of

---

7 İsmet Görgülü, *The Place where the Saviour Was Born* (Turkish to English) trans. Şafak Horzum (TBB Press, Ankara, 2014), pp. 39–41.

8 Mahmut Sabri and his soldiers (around 1,100 personnel) are famous for their resistance lasting 32.5 hours against 12,000 Allied soldiers. This resistance enabled the counter-attack of the Turkish soldiers to repel the Allied forces trying to settle on the beach.

9 Edward J. Erickson, *Gallipoli: The Ottoman Campaign* (Pen&Sword, London, 2010), pp. 90–91.

the Ottoman General Staff made many mistakes. The most significant mistake made by the Ottoman General Staff, for instance, was the tardy deployment of 13 additional Ottoman Army infantry divisions to the Gallipoli front to reinforce the 5th Army's original six divisions. For Erickson, had the Ottoman General Staff sent six to eight divisions immediately from the massive force pool then held in Thrace in the late spring of 1915, these could have had a dramatic effect on the Ottoman counter-attacks early in the campaign – possibly leading to the destruction of the ANZAC and Cape Helles bridge heads. This was a significant strategic error that immobilised critical military assets when they were most needed. Erickson then asserts that there were two reasons for this: General Ismail Enver Effendi, 'Enver Pasha', then the leading light in the ruling Committee of Union and Progress (CUP), thought that the Russian army was about to launch a corresponding amphibious invasion on the Bosphorus Strait, and, moreover, he worried about a Greco-Bulgarian alliance attacking western Thrace. The fact that he thought these things were possible highlights the generalised weaknesses in strategic thinking and planning which affected the Ottoman high command throughout the war. As the British managed to squander their own strategic advantages, so the Ottomans managed to discard the possibility of a campaign of annihilation.[10]

Erickson asserts that, with a single decisive attack, the Ottoman soldiers could have defeated the Allies on the Gallipoli front. To prove his argument of military effectiveness at the tactical and operational level, Erickson points out the profile of the leading Turkish officers in the highest echelons of the Turkish General Staff during the Turkish War of Independence between 1919 and 1922. He shows that a great majority of these cadres which produced the military effectiveness on the Gallipoli fronts also led the Turkish soldiers to success in their War of Independence.[11]

While Erickson is undoubtedly correct in his reading of the importance of tactical and operational leadership, his conclusion about a decisive engagement can be challenged. Time and again throughout the First World War, the combination of the weight and high rates of fire, defensive structures, obstacles, terrain, and communication systems favoured the defence. Relatively small numbers of infantry, dug in, and with well-directed fire support, could cut down larger numbers of assaulting troops on foot. Several large-scale Ottoman counter-attacks were defeated and it is debatable whether such offensives, on a grand scale, could have achieved any better results.

The third approach to the campaign takes the form of a 'modernist-structuralist' discourse since it seeks to emphasise dynamics hidden below the surface of the war. These include the extensive reform packages in the Ottoman armed forces, the modernisation of Ottoman military education, and the interaction with the Western militaries, both allies and adversaries, in the war. Mesut Uyar, for

10 Ibid., p. 91.

11 Ibid., pp. 228–9.

instance, focuses on how the education of the Ottoman officer corps affected the outcome of the Gallipoli Campaign.[12] For him, the Turkish officer corps benefited from two centuries of Ottoman military reforms. When they came to the Gallipoli front, these officers had had a firm practical and theoretical background in this type of defensive operation. The practical experience they gained on the Gallipoli front made them even more effective. They had learned the tactics and techniques of modern warfare thoroughly, and, as professionalised leaders, they were able to defeat the less experienced Allied forces.[13]

The fourth explanatory approach might be summarised as 'the German influence', as it stresses the importance of German military expertise in the modernisation of the Ottoman armed forces. Ahmet Esenkaya, for example, argues that the German officers were successful in training the Ottoman army and in organising and strengthening the defence system of Gallipoli.[14] For Esenkaya, in accordance with the treaty signed in August 1914, the German military mission began to wield 'effective influence' over the military operations of the Ottoman armies. German generals and staff officers served as advisors and military commanders for the Ottoman forces throughout the war. Just a month before the Gallipoli Campaign, the Ottoman General Staff appointed Otto Liman von Sanders as the commander of the 5th Army. German generals were also put in command of certain corps and divisions. During the Gallipoli Campaign, Esenkaya emphasises that it was German officers, as commanders, advisors and experts, who oversaw the placing of sea mines in the Dardanelles Strait, the organisation of coastal defences, logistics, and medical support for the army, all of which represented a great contribution that paved the way for victory. While drawing attention to the negative view of the German involvement on the Gallipoli front that still prevails in the orthodox Turkish accounts, Esenkaya notes that 'if this ignorance (or betrayal) of the Germans had been the case, the Ottoman General Staff would have surely intervened in Gallipoli and taken the necessary step of keeping the Germans away from the front to avoid any unwanted incidents in this war of survival'.[15]

With a culturalist twist, the fifth type of interpretation concentrates on the identities and collective sentiments which strengthened the morale and motivation of Ottoman soldiers who fought at Gallipoli, and their civilian supporters. It is known that the Allies applied propaganda strategies in a sustained fashion during the Gallipoli Campaign to induce Ottoman soldiers to surrender, desert or rebel, hoping that these individual acts might spread and weaken the defences of the

---

12 'Brothers in Arms: Turkish Officers in The Çanakkale (Dardanelles) Campaign', Paper presented to the Conference 'Gallipoli in Retrospect 90 Years on', Onsekiz Mart University International Conference, Çanakkale, 21–3 April 2005.

13 Ibid.

14 Ahmet Esenkaya, 'Turkish–German Co-Operation in The Gallipoli Campaign (Turkish)', *Çanakkale Araştırmaları Türk Yıllığı*, (Spring 2008, pp. 15–42).

15 Ibid.

Ottoman Army. There were two facts, however, that suggest that these influencing strategies did not work. First, unlike the Sinai and Caucasus fronts, there was no record of unit replacement in the Gallipoli front.[16] In this campaign that lasted almost a year, although there were isolated acts of surrender and desertion on the Ottoman fronts, these stayed at the individual level. Second, the Official History of the Turkish Army suggests that, in total, 2,850,000 soldiers were mobilised in the four-year duration of the war, and there were just 202,152 Ottoman prisoners of war (PoWs) on all fronts, constituting 7 per cent of the total.[17] According to the official war record of the Ottoman General Staff, which was prepared in light of the official war records of the 128 different units which fought on the Gallipoli front, the results are quite different. Of the 315,500 soldiers who fought at Gallipoli, only 10,022 soldiers surrendered and became PoWs, constituting 3.1 per cent of the total. In terms of total captured personnel, with around 85,000 PoWs, the Sinai–Palestine front came first and, with 60,000 PoWs, the Caucasus front came second.[18] Although there is no consensus among Turkish scholars with regard to the exact numbers and percentages of the Ottoman PoWs, one thing is agreed: it is clear that the percentage of the Ottoman PoWs in the Gallipoli was relatively low when compared to the percentages of other fronts. If we accept these figures, we might reasonably conclude that the Ottoman soldiers, for a variety of reasons, fought with more commitment at Gallipoli than on any other front.

The well-known Turkish historian Cemal Kutay defines the Gallipoli Peninsula as a place where 'modern techniques and material superiority was brought to its knees by heroic action deeply rooted in fighting spirit', and thus alleges 'this is the spirit that led to victory'.[19] In the existing literature there are three ways in which this fighting spirit is defined and explained: first is the purely Islamic one which emphasises the religious sentiment as the primary driver; second, nationalists emphasise the distinct characteristics of the Turkish national culture and Turkish history; and third, there is a blending of the two in a more recent Turko-Islamic discourse. Ramazan Hurç, for example, suggests the Islamic sentiment was the prime source of fighting spirit, and he recounts the famous story of Corporal Seyit, an Ottoman artilleryman who allegedly 'sunk' the warship *Ocean* with a single shot:

> [A comrade noted] 'Our friends have joined the choir invisible. We have 14 martyrs and 24 wounded. There is only you and me still standing.'

---

16 ATASE Archive; K. 4174, D. 61, F. 2–5.

17 Official History of the Turkish Military, Vol. 5, 3rd Book (Turkish General Staff Printing House, 2012), p. 463.

18 Cemil KUTLU, *I. Dünya Savaşı'nda Rusya'daki Türk Savaş Esirleri ve Bunların Yurda Döndürülmeleri Faaliyetleri* (Turkish) (Erzurum: Atatürk İlkeleri ve İnkılap Tarihi Enstitüsü, 1997) (Unpublished PhD Dissertation).

19 Cemal Kutay, Turkiye Hurriyet ve Istiklal Mucadeleleri Tarihi, Vol.18, 1962, p. 10315.

Seyit rose on his feet and stared at the sea: the enemy ships edged in closer to the shore, fuming fire and smoke from their turrets. In the bastion, all the guns except the third one had been buried under the earth. Seyit the Great turned his palms to the sky and started praying in the manner he had learned from his mother: '*La hawle wala kuvvete illa billahi'l-aliyyi'l-azim*' [There is no other power and force other than Allah, the supreme and almighty] and, 'Ye, the One who has no deficiency and surplus! Ye, the Lord of all the worlds! May you bestow me such a power to my body that let no other subject of Yours be more powerful than me!'

Tears were flowing down the cheeks of Seyit the Great. His beautiful lips were cracked in lines for the love and passion of his Lord. 'My Lord! My Allah! May you not spare your strength from me . . . . ' Having said these words, he gazed first at the ships, then the gun, and then the shell of about 276 kilos [215 okkas] lying on the ground. With his own words, the shell was whispering to him, 'feed me into the chamber!'

He turned to his friend: 'Come Ali, help me to shoulder this shell.'

Ali first looked at the tilted davit (the loading crane) and then to his friend's face with his surprised eyes.

'You can't lift it, Seyit.'

'Let us just try.'

The greased shell at first slipped through his hands. He covered his hands with earth, and lifted it. Seyit the Great lifted the shell upon his back. He walked towards the gun with stumbling steps, and placed his foot on the ladder. They just managed to feed the shell into the chamber and shut the breech. However, they were both poor at targeting and direction-finding as they were mere crewmen. Seyit turned the barrel towards the ships and adjusted the distance as much as he knew. He recited *bismillah* and fired the first shell. The first shot was too far away. He brought another one and fired it again. This time, it fell short. Yet the third shell hit the British ship, *Ocean*, and exploded on the quarter deck and hull top. The foe's navy panicked as *Ocean* went down. The ships around scattered away.

While Seyit was going to fetch the fourth shell, the commander of the battery, Hilmi Bey, left his shelter as the fighting calmed down and arrived at Seyit's battery with two German officers. It was impossible for Captain Hilmi Bey to believe that Seyit the Great had fired the last shell. He was astounded.

He asked, 'Was it you, Seyit, who hit the ship?'

The fourth shell went to waste. There was only one shell left. Seyit brought that too; the Germans were watching with amazement as he carried the huge shell on his back and loaded the gun.

Later, Commander Cevat Pasha wanted Seyit to lift the shell in his presence, just as he had done during the battle. Seyit the Great tried to lift the shell with his full strength: his face went bloody red; his eyes bulged, but he could not move it at all. He covered his hands with earth and tried it again, but it could not be done. Corporal Seyit the Great replied thus:

> 'When I was lifting these shells, my heart was filled with Allah's power. I felt a difference in myself. It was not some thing to be done with science, virtue, or worship. Yet, the secret of that strength was a gift bestowed on me by Allah there and then. If I was raised to a position to be able to lift that shell, it was thanks to my prayers and His consent. Pasha, if there is an enemy before me again, I can lift it again. Yet, it is impossible now for me to pick it up.' Cevat Pasha told him, 'Well done, son', and patted him on the back.[20]

The difficulties with such stories are obvious. HMS *Ocean* was sunk not by artillery fire, but crippled by a mine. Nevertheless, what the story tries to do is capture the sense of fighting spirit when one's instincts might induce flight. It is well documented that, in these supreme moments of personal crisis, strongly held beliefs or courageous acts in defence of immediate comrades are common.

In summing up this historiography, the best explanation of the outcome of Gallipoli might be situated at the intersection of all these explanatory approaches. The victory of the Ottomans can be attributed to the morale and motivation of the troops, German military techniques and expertise, and the contribution of Mustafa Kemal (who was undoubtedly brilliant, but was not alone amongst educated and highly experienced young officers), and Ottoman Army reforms that had begun long before the war but which were accelerated in the aftermath of the disastrous Balkan Wars of 1911–13.

This volume may be defined not as an adjunct to any particular interpretation, but as a study in the history of war, the goal of which is to focus on the Ottoman war experience, a topic often neglected in the Anglophone historiography. At the same time, by presenting insights from the fields of history, sociology and political theory, it seeks to follow an interdisciplinary path instead of solely concentrating on military studies. We hope this volume can provide insights from a range of explanatory approaches that played a significant role in the outcome at Gallipoli.

This volume has another objective. That is to present a perspective about this campaign's influence on the collective memory and construction of national identity in contemporary Turkey. To achieve these objectives, while the first half of the book reflects on the Dardanelles and Gallipoli Campaign by presenting its causes, conduct and consequences, the second half, with a socio-political angle, carries the debate on the Gallipoli Campaign to contemporary Turkey. The first half therefore scrutinises the Gallipoli Campaign to elucidate the causal mechanism leading to the Ottoman victory. The second half illustrates the political and socio-cultural consequences of the Gallipoli Campaign, and seeks to shed light upon its mobilisation as an instrument in the construction of the collective memory and national identity in Turkey. This dualist approach offers a better understanding of Gallipoli and its context.

---

20 Ramazan Hurç 'Çanakkale Savaşlarının Manevi Yönü (Turkish)' *İlahiyet Fakültesi Dergisi*, Vol. 4, 1999. pp. 61–96.

One may suggest that, in Turkey, what is conventionally defined as 'modern Turkish cultural history and literature' includes both the late Ottoman period in the nineteenth and twentieth centuries and the early Republican period. Nevertheless, the First World War, which brought about the fall of the Ottoman Empire and the consequent creation of the Republic of Turkey, has generally been neglected by Turkish academics, particularly from a socio-political point of view, with the notable exception of the life of Kemal Atatürk. According to the dominant teleological approach, modern Turkish identity was shaped within the context of the post-1923 nation-state after some vague experimentation in the late Ottoman period. This Orthodoxy simply assumes that multi-ethnic late Ottoman cultural life, and its last breath in this war, are only nuances in the search for Turkish national identity. As we hope to show in this volume, this is not the case. To get a better appreciation of the antecedents of Turkish 'modernity', we must refer back to the Gallipoli Campaign in 1915.

Two facts should be mentioned to better understand the scale and depth of the Gallipoli Campaign's strategic impact on the Turkish quest for independence. First is that the Gallipoli experience undoubtedly had a direct cognitive and emotional effect on most of the Turkish high-ranking officers who went on to participate in the Turkish National Independence War. Some 35 of the 67 (52 per cent of the total) high-ranking commanders in the Turkish Independence War were Gallipoli veterans.[21] Second is that, when founding the Turkish Republic, 17 of the founding fathers were the Gallipoli veterans who had benefited from the reputation, fame and prestige they gained on the Gallipoli fronts.[22] Metin Heper, a reputable scholar in the field of contemporary Turkish political history, notes that: 'Those cadres, who looked below at the sharp edges of the Gallipoli cliffs and saw the possibility of a total collapse, founded the Republic of Turkey'.[23] It is thus impossible to understand the national identity and collective memory debates in contemporary Turkey without recognising the strategic narratives mobilised by the Turkish elites when building the new nation-state.

The volume begins with five military analyses. Rob Johnson, Director of the Changing Character of War Programme at Oxford University, analyses the campaign as it is portrayed in Anglophone sources, showing that certain myths have obscured the strategic, operational and tactical obstacles of the campaign and

21 İsmet Görgülü, 'The Impact of the Gallipoli Campaign on the Commanding Cadres of the Turkish National Struggle (Turkish)', *The Yearbook of Canakkale Researches* (95th Anniversary of the Gallipoli Campaign Special Edition, 2010), pp. 13–32.

22 The prominent figures among these founding fathers are as follows: Mustafa Kemal Atatürk, Fevzi Çakmak, İsmet İnönü Kazım Karabekir, Nuri Conker, Yakup Şevki Subaşı, Ali Fuat Cebesoy, Cafer Tayyar Eğilmez, Nazif Kayacık, Fahrettin Altay, Kazim İnanç, İzzettin Çalışlar, Nafiz Gürman.

23 From the class discussion in the PhD course titled 'Turkish Political History' taught by Metin Heper at Bilkent University, 2012.

resulted in a reductionist narrative of failures in leadership. He concludes that the character of war in 1915 favoured the defence rather than the offence.

Ferhat Çalışkan, from the Turkish Staff College, presents a critique on the conduct of operations and analyses the defence plan approved by Liman von Sanders, contrasting these with the defence plan of Turkish Commanders in Gallipoli. As a result of this analysis, Çalışkan concludes that the revision made by Liman von Sanders changed the deployment of the regiments and their sub units, and, by doing so, increased the casualty rate.

Hilmi Kendircioğlu, an artillery officer from the Turkish Staff College, shows that, after past gruelling defeats, respectively in the 1877–8 Ottoman–Russian War, Tripoli War, and Balkan Wars, the Allies expected almost no Ottoman naval resistance in the Aegean Sea. At the beginning of the war, a naval attack to break through the Çanakkale Straits, would, it was assumed, force the Ottoman government to surrender, deliver military aid to Russia, pass through the Marmara Sea and reach the İstanbul straits. For Kendircioğlu, victory was supposed to be relatively easy for this unprecedentedly formidable Allied armada. He argues that, because of their over-confidence, Allied admirals had never thought seriously about a failure of naval operations. He then presents the effective use of Ottoman artillery in the campaign as a 'force multiplying' factor that contributed to the Ottoman victory. For this, Kendircioğlu examines how supposedly 'weak' Ottoman field artillery managed to repel Allied naval forces, arguing that this determined the destiny of the Russian Empire and thus changed the course of the war.

In his chapter, Hasan Tahsin Vanlı from the Turkish Staff College emphasises the significance of initiative at the tactical level and its impact on the course of the operations at Gallipoli. Taking into consideration the size of the battlefield, the number of units involved in the campaign, the proximity of the Allies' landing beaches, nature of the terrain, and lack of necessary means of transportation in the Ottoman Army, Vanlı suggests that taking the initiative, by the commanders in the lower echelon both in the Allies' forces and the Ottoman Army, proved to be more decisive than the remote decisions of the high command. For Vanlı, the tactical-level commanders of small units had to compensate for their own commanders' mistaken decisions by acting on their own initiative. He then explains how these commanders took decisions in the Gallipoli Campaign by giving specific examples from both sides, how decisive they were, and the reasons behind them.

Hülya Toker from the Archives of the General Staff Military History and Strategic Studies Department (ATASE), in her chapter, presents a perspective on naval warfare relying on the Turkish official records in the archive of the Turkish General Staff.

Metin Gürcan, a major from the Turkish General Staff, carrying the debate from the physical to the emotional and cognitive domains, seeks to shed light on influencing strategies used by both the Allies and the Ottoman General Staff on the Ottoman soldiers during the Gallipoli Campaign. He suggests two points. First, among the campaigns the Ottoman military fought in the war, the Gallipoli Campaign is the first one in which both the Allies' propaganda and the

Ottoman General Staff's counter-propaganda strategies were used in a coherent fashion. Second, to better understand the influencing of the Turkish forces and to understand the war of ideas in the context of Gallipoli, and subsequent Turkish nation-building, particularly the 'strategic narratives', there is a need to widen and deepen the traditional conceptualisation of propaganda. In his chapter, Gürcan provides his findings about the 62 original propaganda leaflets and 22 prisoner of war letters produced by the Allied forces during the campaign under thematic classifications. He then presents a follow-up analysis of the content and style of these texts.

In her chapter, Alev Karaduman from Hacettepe University asserts that, besides its political, diplomatic and military consequences, the Gallipoli Campaign also brought different national and cultural identities into confrontation. In other words, for her, as can be clearly seen from memoirs, diaries and letters of the Turkish/Ottoman and Allied soldiers, each side 'othered' the enemy, and with rooted prejudice, antagonism, and cultural solipsism, failed to recognise each other's real identity. Karaduman then suggests that the British and ANZAC soldiers depicted the Turkish identity in their writings in the traditional antagonistic manner, while some oriental colouring was added to this representation of the Turks. However, in time, she argues, as a result of the cultural experiences shared on the battlefield, this prejudice was turned into not only mutual respect for each other but also a respect for Turkey itself. So, the purpose of her article is to demonstrate, on the basis of memoirs, diaries and letters as primary material, how the campaign at Gallipoli was also metaphorically a war of identities, especially between the Turkish and ANZAC soldiers.

The chapter written by Mehmet Akif Okur from Gazi University focuses on the place and power of living memory related to the Dardanelles Campaign in the public imagination and political life of Turkey by using the 'tour guides' debates of the mid-2000s as a case study. To understand the functions of competing narratives on Gallipoli, Mehmet Akif Okur asserts that we need to look to the ideological cleavages still affecting the perceptions of Turkish society through a conceptual framework that shows the ways that power struggles over national symbols, like Gallipoli, are played out. So, for Okur, a perspective which brings studies on national symbolisation processes together with Gallipoli controversies in the Turkish media and national parliament could open a wider window for a more profound interpretation of the Dardanelles Campaign's actual legacy as 'A War on the "True" Meaning of the Nation and of Gallipoli'.

In his chapter, Kahraman Şakul from Şehir University outlines the phases of the evolution of the place of Gallipoli in Turkish politics, society and culture through the analysis of the literary outputs, popular history magazines, and intellectual debates. He contends that disputes over the meaning of the 'spirit of Çanakkale' are emblematic of the general trends in the identity politics of Turkey. Disputes about the sovereignty rights over the Gallipoli Peninsula in the early Republican era gave way to conflicting views, all stemming from larger domestic political issues. The severe political polarisation of the 1970s and the militarisation that followed were the background against which the Kemalists, Islamists, and leftists disputed the nature of the human sacrifice and victory in the Dardanelles. He then argues that each phase of expansion of political participation has been a new occasion to redefine the meaning of the Gallipoli saga, which is one of the building blocks of Turkish political and national identity.

In his chapter, Şafak Horzum from Hacettepe University provides a comparative perspective on the reflections of the battle in both Turkish and British literature especially during the war and subsequently. The repercussions observed in the war poetry of both sides share the similar thematic patterns as well as the verisimilitude and characteristics of the theatre performances that appealed to people on both sides. Horzum asserts that poetry as an art of deep and sincere feelings, and a theatrical stage – which mimics what happens in reality in multiple directions and with myriad interpretations – can be seen in the examples written during and after the fighting at Gallipoli. Therefore, the aim of his chapter is to emphasise the effect of poetic and theatrical works on Turkish, British and 'ANZAC' societies sharing the same grief by providing, in a comparative manner, a detailed presentation of themes exemplified by both sides.

In essence, the Gallipoli Campaign has been the subject of intense interest in a variety of contexts. British, Australian, New Zealand, French, Indian and Turkish commentators have often drawn different deductions and meanings from the events of 1915–16. Historians schooled in empirical approaches through the study of archival sources will find some chapters jar with the traditional interpretations and prioritisation. However, the book also contains much that is new, and the authors of this volume have sought to recover a distinctively Turkish perspective. What is striking is how contested the Turkish view of the campaign still is, the consequence of the early politicisation of its memory. Critics may reflect that in Australia, New Zealand and India, a similar contestation has taken place, and in Britain debates about the decision-making that led to the campaign are still live. In the 100th anniversary year, when this volume was written, the liveliness of the debate is to be welcomed, for it is by means of such discussion that interest, fascination and some awe in the actions of our ancestors will surely continue.

Chapter 2

Contested historiography

Allied perspectives on the Gallipoli Campaign

Robert Johnson

In the Anglophone historiography, Gallipoli is synonymous with defeat, futility and incompetence. Indeed, alongside the battles of the Somme (1916) and Passchendaele (1917), it has come to symbolise the very worst aspects of the First World War. The execution of the Gallipoli Campaign, and the milestones towards the humiliating Allied evacuation, are often held up as the epitome of disaster through bad planning, poor judgement and hubristic over-confidence. One historian, in a recent narrative of the operations, opens his work with the trenchant remark: 'It was a lunacy that could never have succeeded, an idiocy generated by muddled thinking.'[1]

The litany of criticism is so unrelenting it seems almost impossible to give the sort of reasonable analysis that would be offered to any other historical episode. Nevertheless, there are some grounds for doubting the Anglophone orthodoxy. First, it seems unlikely that every single individual in the command and decision-making process was suffering from 'lunacy' or 'idiocy'. Indeed, there is considerable evidence to the contrary. Plans may have been ambitious, even over-optimistic, but this characterises many campaigns and conflicts. What is striking is that individuals are held responsible for the high casualties and mission failures, part of a general approach towards the study of the First World War. This is in spite of the overwhelming evidence that changes in the character of war, not least the increased defensive power of new technologies, had a far greater effect on operational outcomes than individual command decisions. Moreover, at the strategic level, the power of mass, logistics and *materiel* was very influential and far more so than single battles or short campaigns. It is striking that the Ottoman Empire lost the First World War, despite its victory at Gallipoli, because it could produce no solution to its lack of industrial capacity or its infrastructural weaknesses.

The second compelling reason to doubt the standard Anglophone orthodoxy of Gallipoli is the limited number of available Ottoman sources against which a balanced assessment of the Allies' performance can be made. There has been considerable reliance on the Turkish General Staff History and some translated works in the Rayfield papers of the Imperial War Museum in London. Edward Erickson has done a great service to the profession of history by bringing into the English-speaking canon a number of Turkish materials. Nevertheless, Robin

1 Peter Hart, *Gallipoli* (London: Profile Books, 2013), p. vii.

Prior, who has himself written an outstanding operational history, noted recently: 'it is still the case that there is no depth to sources in Turkish, or more accurately, Ottoman. We just do not have the war diaries, after action reports and operations orders on the Turkish side to place against those on the Allied side.'[2] This edited volume, we hope, will go some way to rectifying the problem. The purpose of this chapter is to give an overview of the Anglophone historiography and some explanation of the intentions, decisions and actions of the Allies.

The contemporary British accounts of the Gallipoli Campaign have been subjected to significant criticism. The Report of the Dardanelles Commission (1917) which formed the basis of Brigadier General Cecil Aspinall-Oglander's British official history was soon followed by General Sir Ian Hamilton's own account as commander, *Gallipoli Diary* (1920). The commission correspondence reveals that commanders colluded in their accounts and Hamilton had strong reasons to convey a favourable perspective on his own decision-making. Winston Churchill, the subject of intense criticism in his role as First Sea Lord and 'architect' of the Gallipoli Campaign, had taken the view in the 1930s that the 'Fates' were to blame.[3] Drawing on the atmosphere of some Hellenic tragedy, the operation was described in epic terms. A. Marder, in his series *War at Sea* (1961–70) nevertheless blamed Churchill's 'impetuosity' for trying to 'rush through' the Dardanelles Straits.[4]

For Australia and New Zealand, the Gallipoli Campaign and its leadership have a deeper significance. Alongside bitter criticism of the British senior commanders, there is an almost religious canonisation of the men of the Australian and New Zealand Army Corps (ANZAC) who took part. The iconography of bronzed heroes fighting against the odds for their closest 'mates', often rescuing the wounded, and enduring all manner of hardships, is, in part, representative of events, but it has become sanitised and exaggerated to the point where the Gallipoli Campaign is the 'foundational myth' of the two nations.[5] Large numbers of Australians and New Zealanders visit the sites of the battles of Gallipoli annually, and each pauses to reflect on the sacrifice made by their ancestors. However, the use of the campaign to reinforce a particularly modern identity is problematic. Most of the Australian troops were not hardy men from the outback, but urban dwellers trained rather hastily and barely prepared for the tough fighting on the peninsula. Moreover, the majority were recent migrants to the antipodes who had volunteered to fight

---

2 Robin Prior, *Gallipoli: The End of the Myth* (New Haven and London: Yale, 2010), p. xv.

3 Winston S. Churchill, *The Great War* (London, 1934), III, p.1599, cited in Strachan, *The First World War* (London: Simon and Schuster, 2003).

4 A. Marder, *The War at Sea*, 5 vols (Oxford: Oxford University Press, 1961–70), especially vols IV and V.

5 Charles Bean, *Australian Official History with the AIF at Gallipoli*; see Jay Winter and Antoine Prost *Great War in History* (Cambridge: Cambridge University Press, 2005).

for the 'old country'. They saw no contradiction in calling themselves British, or Australian-Britons.

It is curious that the ANZACs have become associated with the campaign so exclusively. Not only were the ANZACs dwarfed in number by British personnel on the peninsula, but there were also fewer of them than the French, who deployed 18,000. Australians and New Zealanders who are familiar with their own myths are sometimes surprised by these statistics, by the relatively low number of casualties that were sustained, and by the fact that Indian troops also fought at Gallipoli.[6] There is another reason, perhaps, why Gallipoli suits a national myth. By not being a Western European battlefield, where Australians fought in larger numbers, and by dint of being a campaign fought by Caucasian men, it offers a narrative that fits a nation that has struggled to define itself in light of sustained immigration from Asia and by a desire to assert its own, non-British identity. The emphasis on reconciliation, reciprocated by the Turks, combines neatly the celebrated values of Australian courage, solidarity and ruggedness with the ability to form bonds with, integrate and assimilate others. Christian traditions of peace and redemption are weaved alongside a poignant sense of loss, while speculation of what 'might have been' the outcome, not only of the campaign, but also of the fortunes of the young soldiers had they survived the fighting, is prominent.

In the 1950s and 1960s, Anzac Day was not very well observed and the desire to forget the Vietnam War further supressed pride in military achievements. Yet a new generation of young Australians regard Gallipoli as a site of pilgrimage. There are now over 4,000 memorials to the war dead in Australia itself including Remembrance Drive with its markers of Victoria Cross winners which form an avenue to the National War Memorial. The Gallipoli Campaign, with its evident sacrifice, has provided an iconic focus to national heroism in a way that the country's early colonisation could not. The myth of British leadership 'folly' creates a convenient distinction from the enduring, suffering Diggers. Bill Gammage's *The Broken Years* (1974), which chronicled the campaign through veterans' testimonies, deepened the popular sense of poignancy and loss, while Peter Weir's highly impressionistic film *Gallipoli* (1981) simultaneously reinforced the idea of British 'betrayal' and futile destruction of innocence.

Focusing on a sense of loss or the errors of decision-makers allows Western commentators and audiences, while not actually denying an Ottoman-Turkish victory, to reduce its significance by obscuring it in another context. Yet, as this volume indicates, the outcome at Gallipoli had great historical significance for the Turks. The Ottoman army that fought the campaign was overwhelmingly ethnically Turkish, sacrificed large numbers to defend its home territory, and,

---

6 The Australians lost 8,709; the New Zealanders 2,721. Proportionally, some units lost very significant numbers. See Gordon Gorrigan, 'The Gurkhas at Gallipoli' in Rob Johnson, (ed.), *The British Indian Army: Virtue and Necessity* (Cambridge: Cambridge Scholars Publishing, 2014).

in a rare achievement, drove off the Western Allied forces. Mustafa Kemal Atatürk, often the only commander recognised in Western accounts, benefited from organising counter-attacks at the moments of crisis to establish his political reputation as 'Atatürk', the Father of the Nation. Moreover, the Allied withdrawal in January 1916 released Ottoman-Turkish units for other fronts, and an equally stubborn defence was mounted in Palestine, the Caucasus and Mesopotamia. Nevertheless, in Turkish work there is often no mention of the Allied reoccupation of Gallipoli in November 1918, while the eagerness to narrate Turkey's rejuvenation in 1922–23 tends to obscure the deterioration of conditions on all fronts in 1918 and the Ottoman Empire's eventual defeat that year.

Strategy

It is striking that strategic analysis of the campaign is downplayed in favour of the condemnation of the tactical and operational failures of the Allies and the individual heroism of the participants. Yet such a selective approach renders contemporaries' decisions devoid of context. Without acknowledgement of the pressures on the decision-makers and calculations of commanders, the phases of operations appear to be no more than purposeless and hopeless efforts. This is as true of the various tactical assaults on Krithia as it is of the strategic decision to make landings at Gallipoli in the spring of 1915.

The impetus for the Allied invasion was not, as is so often asserted, due to the ambitions of British politicians and commanders: it was provoked by the weaknesses of Russia. Initial Ottoman success in the Sarıkamış campaign prompted a Russian appeal for Allied assistance on 1 January 1915. From the outset, the Russian war machine had been exposed as inefficient and incompetent. It had lost the opening battles of 1914 against Germany. Despite its fearsome reputation as the 'steamroller', it had failed to make headway against the Habsburg armies of Austria–Hungary. It had failed to relieve its Slavic allies in Serbia. Now, in the Caucasus, on its own territory, and despite grandiose ideas of seizing Constantinople to realise its historical destiny, it was being defeated.[7] The British and the French had taken catastrophic losses in the first few months of the war in Western Europe, where there was now stalemate, and their resources were stretched. Any operation to relieve Russia would, therefore, have to be primarily naval in nature, and, if landings were required, they would have to have a disproportionate strategic effect; that is, it would have to achieve significant outcomes at the lowest cost in terms of manpower and munitions commitments. Sir Herbert Horatio Kitchener, the British Secretary of State for War, did not believe that resources could be spared in early

7 Sean McMeekin, *The Russian Origins of the First World War* (Cambridge, MA: Harvard University Press, 2011), p. 115.

1915, but, if an operation was imperative, only a thrust at the Dardanelles would have any strategic value.

There were several advantages to operations through the Dardanelles, and they were articulated as such by the First Sea Lord, Winston Churchill; the Chancellor of the Exchequer, David Lloyd George; and the Secretary of State for War, Kitchener. The strategic reasoning was that an Allied victory could achieve many of the Western allies' 'ends' in the Eastern Mediterranean. It could re-open a merchant shipping route to Russia, equipping this vast imperial army with the *materiel* of industrialised warfare. It could undermine the Central Powers by knocking the Ottomans out of the war. Italy, Bulgaria and Greece might join the Entente if there was a regional campaign, and together the Allies would be able to make a concerted and united effort against the vulnerable fronts of Austria–Hungary. In essence, the Dardanelles offered a chance to 'knock away the props' of Germany. Indeed, victory over the Ottoman Empire held out the possibility of developing a larger alliance against the Central Powers, including all the Balkans states. Operations against the Ottomans would provide a much-needed alternative to the developing stalemate on the Western Front.

From the imperial perspective, the British hoped that a naval blockade and a direct menace to the Ottomans' capital, leading to their surrender, would not only neutralise any sympathy by Muslim subjects of the empire, but also assert British pre-eminence in Ottoman territories, including Syria, which France believed might provide a convenient colony. Crucially, the defeat of the Ottoman Empire would cut off German intrigue which was directed against British interests in the Middle East and India.[8]

Given the need to find alternatives to the Western Front, it was not surprising that there were few voices urging caution or consideration of the consequences of a setback. But this was also an imperial war. The points of strategic vulnerability for the British Empire were twofold: one, its religious composition and the capacity for Islam to be used to mobilise resistance to the Christian or secular authorities; and two, the overwhelmingly non-European ethnic composition of the empire with a corresponding dependence on indigenous sub-imperialists to maintain order, to provide labour and to maintain the flow of trade. The British were dependent on a degree of consent and a great deal of authority, which could be jeopardised by other Europeans' subversion.

The declaration of war by the Ottoman Empire made it easier for the British to justify war in order to persuade their Muslim subjects to participate. Nevertheless, there were some misgivings about asking Muslim troops to fight their co-religionists.[9] The sultan's declaration of Islamic holy war on 14

8 Robert Johnson, *Spying for Empire: The Great Game in Central and South Asia, 1757–1947* (London: Greenhill, 2006), p. 218.

9 'Far from Jihad' Colloquium, Cité nationale de l'histoire de l'immigration, Paris, May 2014.

November 1914 was convenient in making this a defensive war for the British Empire but did not entirely extinguish its concerns. In the war, only a handful of Muslim soldiers deserted or resisted their imperial masters, largely because of the conditions of the war and national, ethnic and linguistic differences, but, amongst the troops of the Indian Army, there was a stronger corporate loyalty to the British than to the Ottoman Caliph.[10]

If the British Empire was vulnerable, the Ottoman Empire was regarded as so weak and dependent that it might fail altogether if pressed hard. In the nineteenth century, Britain's policy had been to offer qualified support to the Ottoman domains, largely as a bulwark against Russia. Rivalry with Russia had continued despite the settling of the 1907 Entente, but propping up the Ottomans had required pressure for financial and governance reform and few believed they would manage any substantial reorganisation. Indeed, the prevailing assessment was that the 'Sick Man of Europe' was in terminal decline. Not that this was welcome to the British either. If the Ottoman Empire broke up, it would have strategic implications. Provinces that lay close to the sea route to India in the Eastern Mediterranean and the Arabian Peninsula might create vulnerabilities for Russia or Germany to exploit.

British assessments of the Ottoman military capabilities were not unreasonable as they were based on recent observations of the Balkan Wars. After a series of setbacks between 1912 and 1913, the Ottoman Army was still considered unready for significant operations as it was undergoing much-needed reform. Germany's assessments were similar. The Kaiser's decision to dispatch General Liman von Sanders as senior advisor, and his instruction to Germanise the Ottoman forces, was as much a recognition of the empire's incapacity as it was a vague attempt to spread German influence in the region. Hew Strachan notes that Ambassador Hans von Wangenheim in Constantinople thought Russia would make a far better partner for German aspirations in the Middle East and that the Ottoman Empire was too 'dependent'.[11] The Ottoman Army made rapid progress in its transformation but it was still untried in 1914: the war came too early even for the Ottoman reformers to be confident about its performance. The army was crippled by shortages in almost every sphere, including artillery, rifles, horses and transport, and Enver believed it would take at least five years to rectify the most acute problems.[12] Consequently, the Ottoman strategic objective in 1913 was to find partners to recover its position in the Balkans and the islands lost to Greece, and it had considered France, Russia and Britain. Germany was the last of the Great Powers to be approached, and an alliance was concluded as late as 22 July 1914.

The British were far more concerned with the growing German threat to the Middle East, and believed, at the outbreak of war, that the Kaiser's ambitions could

10 See, for example, CIGS to GOC Mesopotamia, 7 December 1917, L/Mil/7/18848.
11 Hew Strachan, *The First World War* (London: Simon and Schuster, 2003), p. 101.
12 Strachan, *The First World War*, p. 104.

be checked by an operation against the Ottoman Empire. Once again, there was a strategic threat that Britain could not ignore. Germany owned the Anatolian Railway Company and its much-vaunted purpose was to construct a railway from Berlin to Baghdad. The railway would link central Europe's economies with the resources of the East, circumventing the maritime strength of Britain, France and the United States, a geostrategic concern made more realistic by the assessments of the geographer Halford Mackinder.[13] Moreover, the Kaiser's self-promotion as friend of the Muslims, with rumours of his secret conversion to Islam, while regarded as histrionics, could not be ignored entirely. German designs to raise a holy war against British and French control in Muslim lands were not a *canard*.[14] Once the war had broken out, Ottoman and German missions of subversion were dispatched to Persia, the Gulf and Afghanistan.[15]

From the British perspective, Constantinople was never sincere about its initial 'neutrality'. On 29 July, London impounded two Ottoman dreadnought battleships (the *Sultan Osman* and the *Reshadieh*) which were under construction in Britain, a not unreasonable decision in light of German and Ottoman hostility. The seizure of the vessels was legal under British contractual law, but the popular reaction in Constantinople was angry condemnation. British concerns deepened on 2 August, when the Ottomans signed a treaty with Germany, followed by a similar agreement with Austria–Hungary on 5 August. Here was the smoking gun: these moves effectively ended the Ottoman Empire's claim to neutrality. In the second week of August, two German cruisers, the *Goeben* and the *Breslau*, escaped the British Royal Navy in the Mediterranean by passing through the Dardanelles before reaching Constantinople, where they were transferred into the Ottoman Navy.[16] On 15 August, the façade finally dropped when the Ottoman Navy was, as far as the British believed, transferred to German control. The British thence regarded the Ottoman Empire as a *de facto* belligerent, readying an expeditionary force of the Indian Army to secure the oil in southern Persia with a landing at the head of the Gulf, diplomatic overtures to Greece and a naval blockade. Churchill was a particularly strong advocate of a closer alignment with Romania, Greece and Bulgaria against the Ottomans.[17] As operations unfolded in Europe, on 1 October the Ottomans closed the Dardanelles Straits to all Allied shipping. Russia's export trade, dependent on the waterway, was immediately thrown into crisis.

---

13 H.J. Mackinder, 'The geographical pivot of history', *The Geographical Journal* 23, (1904), pp. 421–37.

14 Peter Hopkirk, *On Secret Service East of Constantinople* (Oxford: Oxford University Press, 1994).

15 Robert Johnson, *Spying for Empire: The Great Game in South and Central Asia, 1757–1947* (London: Greenhill, 2006).

16 Hew Strachan, *The First World War. Volume I: To Arms* (Oxford: Oxford University Press, 2001), pp. 644–51 & 670–73.

17 David French, 'The Dardanelles, Mecca and Kut: Prestige as a Factor in British Eastern Strategy, 1914–1916', *War and Society*, 5(1), 1987, p. 50.

Strategically, the British had lost the Ottoman Empire to the Central Powers, but they had been unable to affect the decision-making process in Constantinople, where operations against the Greek and Serbians were the strategic priority. These Ottoman objectives would have brought the Sultan's empire into collision with Russia and the Entente in due course. As it was, the Ottoman government engineered its entry into the war by pre-emptive naval strikes against Russian Black Sea ports on 29 October 1914.

The Royal Navy shelled the Ottoman fortifications at the mouth of the Dardanelles a few days later, on 3 November 1914. In the 20-minute bombardment, two British battle cruisers and two French battleships damaged the fort at Sedd el-Bahr, killing over 100 Ottoman troops and German advisors. The success of this limited operation raised British expectations, but the Ottomans, realising the vulnerability of the fortifications, redoubled their efforts to prepare for further naval attack. Until then, the focus of their defensive arrangements had been Bulair, on the northern coast of the Gallipoli Peninsula, and the prospects of a Greek naval assault. The possibility of a major attack by the world's largest navy, rather than the limited threat posed by the Greeks, galvanised the Ottoman General Staff.[18] Reinforcements poured in and the new forces rehearsed their anti-invasion drills, anti-ship gunnery, command and communications. Crucially, sea mines were sown in sectors across the straits.

The Royal Navy's initial response to the call for ideas of how to wage war against the Ottoman Empire ranged from multinational operations on several axes to a limited British naval bombardment of Alexandretta. Churchill sought the specific comment of Vice-Admiral Sackville Carden, commander of the East Mediterranean Fleet, who noted that mines were a significant problem but that minesweepers and battleships with 'mine buffers', might, with 'extended operations and a large number of ships' force a passage.[19] Naval gunfire was supposed to silence the shore batteries, allowing smaller vessels to get close inshore and clear the mines. A British 1908 plan concluded that Turkish fortifications were not mutually supporting and 'not strong enough at the crucial point'.[20] In the late nineteenth century, the feasibility of an amphibious operation had been discussed and the former Commander in Chief of the British Army, Sir Garnet Wolseley, had been among those who had considered a *coup de main* at the Dardanelles.[21] In

18 Edward J. Erickson, 'Strength against Weakness: Ottoman Military Effectiveness at Gallipoli, 1915', *Journal of Military History*, 65, 4 (October 2001), p. 991.

19 Tim Travers, *Gallipoli, 1915* (Stroud: Tempus, 2001), p. 21.

20 Naval Intelligence Department, *Turkey Coast Defences, 1908: Part II, Coast Defences*. Admiralty 231/49. The National Archives (hereafter TNA).

21 G.J. Wolseley, 'Secret Memorandum', 2 March 1878, Sir Henry Stafford Northcote, First Earl of Iddesleigh Papers, Add MSS 50022, The British Library; Robert Johnson, ' "Russians at the Gates of India?" Planning the Defence of India, 1885–1900', *Journal of Military History*, 67 (July 2003), p. 731.

common with many strategic plans of the period, it was expected that forcing the straits would compel the Ottomans to sue for peace.[22]

The Russian request for diversionary action in January 1915, coming after a gruelling autumn campaign and a winter stalemate in Europe, prompted the British War Council to consider an alternative, predominantly naval strategy proposed by Churchill. A continental war had given the Royal Navy only rare opportunities to engage in the conflict. Its role was more strategic, confining the Central Powers to Europe and applying a slow stranglehold on the economies of Germany and Austria–Hungary. Therefore, in order to give local commanders the freedom of action they required, the War Council ordered the Royal Navy to 'bombard and take the Gallipoli Peninsula, with Constantinople as its objective'.[23] Opinions were nevertheless divided. Kitchener, mindful of the limited manpower available, hoped the Ottoman garrison on the peninsula would give way without even landing British forces, but there was no evidence to support this assumption.[24] Fisher, the First Sea Lord, mindful perhaps of more recent assessments of mines, torpedoes and shore batteries' effectiveness against ships, thought the naval operation 'hazardous' and later opposed the amphibious scheme.[25] Haldane believed a setback at Gallipoli might actually provoke the Muslim unrest in the empire so many feared.

Yet, in the final analysis, despite all the criticism of the execution of the subsequent campaign, these decision-makers, like all strategists, faced a significant dilemma: how to evaluate risks and costs against the imperative to tackle a threat. The critics have the luxury of hindsight. It is conceivable that *operational* failure at Gallipoli has become conflated with the contemporary strategic assessment. The strategic options for the Allies included sustained land-based campaigns on multiple axes, but in early 1915, the resources were simply not available as priorities lay elsewhere. The Allies had not yet mobilised the manpower and *materiel* that would characterise the operations of 1917–18. Reducing the Ottoman economy through blockade, another option, would take months, if not years, and the Russian war effort might, in the intervening time, be crippled to the point of collapse. Raising local Muslim forces against Ottoman rule, a third option, presupposed Britain could command such loyalty against the lingering authority of the Caliph, which was far from certain. A threat at Gallipoli would have 'strategic effect'. Hew Strachan notes that 'the Germans thought the Gallipoli Campaign the most important in 1915'.[26] Perhaps, then, the strategic failure of 1915 was not that the campaign went ahead, but that the Allies didn't realise the sheer importance of it, and, consequently, it was never properly resourced.

22 French, *Prestige as a Factor in British Policy*, p. 51.

23 Basil Liddell Hart, *A History of the World War, 1914–1918* (London: Faber & Faber, 1938), p. 218.

24 Martin Gilbert, *A History of the Twentieth Century. Volume One: 1900–1933* (London: Harper Collins, 1997), pp. 362–3.

25 Strachan, *The First World War*, p. 113.

26 Strachan, *The First World War*, p. 114, citing General Groener.

Naval operations

The straits presented the Allies with a significant operational problem. With strong currents, abundantly mined and narrow waters overlooked by fortified gun batteries, and no landing forces yet prepared or assembled, the obstacles were considerable. Nevertheless, the British and French had assembled a flotilla consisting of one dreadnought-class battleship, 16 pre-dreadnought battleships, one battle cruiser, 20 destroyers and 35 minesweepers. Details of the Ottoman defences feature elsewhere in this volume so only the briefest outline is required here: The Ottoman 5th Army, under the energetic direction of the General Liman von Sanders, numbered 84,000 men, and was thus more numerous than the initial Allied landing force. As Edward Erickson makes clear, 5th Army was overwhelmingly Turkish in its ethnic composition, giving it a homogeneity exceptional to the Ottoman forces. It consisted of a significant number of men seasoned by the Balkan Wars, practised in the small unit tactics they would need to meet any invasion. They were well rehearsed, spending weeks preparing their trenches, their fighting drills and their communications. The army's five infantry divisions, with a sixth in reserve with a brigade of cavalry, were distributed to cover the most vulnerable points: two divisions on the southern coast of the straits, 9th Division along the western coast of Gallipoli, 19th Division concentrated at Chanak and 7th Division guarding Bulair, the narrow 'neck' of the peninsula.[27]

On 19 February 1915, two British battleships and two destroyers shelled the forts and dummy positions on the tip of the Gallipoli Peninsula. There were subsequent bombardments, but, despite evident damage, Ottoman guns in the narrowest section of the straits remained in action. Silencing the guns was crucial to afford protection to the mine sweepers. To secure the batteries, and augment the effect of naval gunfire, Kitchener and the War Council began to assemble a landing force at Lemnos consisting of the Royal Naval Division and the newly arrived ANZACs. However, initially the Royal Navy enjoyed some success against the outer forts which encouraged the planners to consider extending the operation. One officer aboard HMS *Triumph* was 'surprised at the poor shooting they [the Ottomans] made . . . the next day we closed the range and a close inspection showed the defences had been abandoned'.[28] Parties of marines landed at Seddülbahir and Kumkale and met little resistance. They put out of action several guns. Yet the guns of the inner forts were better protected and field gun batteries were moved between positions, making targeting more difficult. Admiral Sir Sackville Carden, the naval commander of Britain's East Mediterranean Force, was methodical in his approach. He insisted on taking his time, and aimed to protect his ships, especially the *Queen Elizabeth*, his dreadnought, from concealed batteries. Night-time minesweeping was made impossible by Ottoman searchlights while

27 Erickson, 'Strength against Weakness', pp. 998–9.

28 Lt Robert Blackie, cited in Travers, *Gallipoli*, p. 23.

air reconnaissance for the naval guns was made hazardous by small arms fire. Nevertheless, this was interpreted as a 'lack of vigour' in London, and pressure was building for a more comprehensive, all-out attack.

The drive was to have a daylight assault that would 'rush' the Narrows. Commander Worsley Gibson on HMS *Albion* wrote: 'Everyone [believed] it would be madness to try and rush them . . . . Personally, I feel sure that it is pressure from our cursed politicians which is making him [Carden] consider such a thing – A large army of 60 or 70 thousand is collecting for purposes of cooperation, the only way to tackle this job and why not wait for them.'[29]

Carden, compelled to act when faced with a problem beyond the capability of the force at his disposal, fell sick. The second-in-command, Vice-Admiral John de Robeck, who was dismissive of Churchill's pressure to attack, nevertheless proceeded with the plan to push through the Narrows.[30] There were to be three waves in the assault. Six modern British battleships would bombard the forts while four older French ships and six British ships would follow up, anchor close in shore and pulverise the Ottoman guns at close quarters. Once the guns had been silenced, minesweepers would be able to complete their work and the entire fleet would sail on into the Sea of Marmora to regroup.

As the action began, the French commander of the *Bouvet*, who believed he was having some success in his close quarter bombardment, refused to push on up the straits and when finally on the move, hit a floating mine and sank in under a minute, losing over 600 crewmen. HMS *Irresistible* also hit a floating mine, drifted, and was subjected to intense fire from the shore. HMS *Ocean*, in attempting to draw fire from the stricken ship, collided with another mine. Three more vessels were damaged critically by Ottoman guns, many of which simply could not be located from the water. The minesweepers failed to make headway when the shore batteries were intact. Admiral de Robeck called off the operation.

There has been speculation since that, had the attack been resumed, there might have been greater success. This was certainly Churchill's preference. Damage inflicted on Ottoman shore positions was presented as evidence of 'what might have been'. The fact that the shore batteries had run low on ammunition, and the poignant setbacks of the subsequent land campaign, seemed to reinforce the idea that one more determined effort might have provided a breakthrough. However, on 22 March on HMS *Queen Elizabeth,* de Robeck could see for himself that only a combined sea–land operation could have any chance of pushing through to Constantinople.

General Ian Hamilton, veteran of the South African War, was appointed the new commander of the amphibious Mediterranean Expeditionary Force (MEF). He had arrived on 17 March, in time to observe the naval attack, and it was

29 Gibson, Diary, Gibson Papers, Imperial War Museum, 13 March 1915.

30 Trumbull Higgins, *Winston Churchill and the Dardanelles* (London: Heinemann, 1963), p. 118.

evident that only through the ability to control the Narrows from the water, and by dominating the Kilitbahir plateau on the Gallipoli Peninsula itself, could the straits be secured.[31] A second naval assault, without a significant land operation, would clearly have cost a larger number of ships, and even if the Narrows had been passed by some vessels, they would have been harassed by fresh Ottoman artillery and reinforcements from the north and south.

The amphibious operation would require far more men than the contingents of Royal Marines could provide. Only one regular British division, the 29th, was as yet uncommitted to the war, a force grouped together from scattered imperial garrisons. It had been concentrated at Egypt, as had the fresh, if untrained, volunteers from Australia and New Zealand. The latter had been bound for Europe, but this contingent, the Australian 1st Division and the amalgamated New Zealand and Australian Division, collectively known as ANZACs, was re-tasked for Gallipoli. The Royal Naval Division was a third hastily composed force of naval personnel, but they too lacked any experience of tactical land operations, higher formation command or staff work, and they possessed no artillery or land-based logistics. The fourth and final landing force was the French 1st Division of the Corps Expeditionnaire d'Orient, but this had no experience of multi-national cooperation. The entire amphibious force numbered 75,000 men, fewer than the Ottomans, and it faced the prospect of landing on a defended shoreline, without prior rehearsal, topographical intelligence and without the element of surprise.

The Ottoman 9th Division held high ground overlooking all the landing sites, was dug in and well prepared. The period between the naval attack on 18 March and the beach assault of 25 April was crucial for the final adjustments to the Ottoman defensive plans. There was only one significant dilemma: Liman von Sanders, in overall command, sought to reinforce the beaches only when he could be certain of the location of the main Allied attack. He therefore retained an operational reserve at the centre of the peninsula, while concentrating on the most threatened locations at Cape Helles, Bulair and Besika Bay. In contrast, Kemal thought the British would concentrate their attacks only at Helles and at Gaba Tepe, and, as a result, reserves should be placed closer to these points of vulnerability.

Hamilton was aware of the obstacles before him, but there was little time for the preparations that characterised the D-Day operations some 20 years later. To ensure a broad front, reduce congestion and create multiple axes of attack, as well as deceiving the Ottomans as to the direction of the assault, Hamilton selected six simultaneous landings between the headland Arni Burnu (sheltering what was subsequently nicknamed Anzac Cove) and Cape Helles. The southern beaches could be covered by naval gunfire and the Ottoman positions there formed a salient that could be 'pinched out'. To get as many men ashore as fast as possible, he agreed with the suggestion made by Commander E. Unwin to convert the collier *River Clyde* into a landing craft that would be run ashore, disgorging

31 Hart, *Gallipoli*, p. 46.

troops from its sides. Yet the disadvantage of the assault locations was that the hills beyond the beaches, dissected by deep gullies, perfect for small numbers of defenders to hold, would make it far more difficult to break out. The beaches designated for the ANZACs were similarly overlooked by steep and forbidding bluffs. Unless they could secure these high features swiftly, they too risked being hemmed in on the coast. Hamilton's solution was for the ANZACs to make a landing at night, try to secure the high ground at Maltepe as quickly as possible, and then, in the days that followed, make a more deliberate advance across the peninsula. Subsequently, the entire landing force would be able to seize the shore batteries lining the Dardanelles from the rear. As in all amphibious operations, the first 24 hours of progress were vital, but even if a beachhead could be seized, everything depended on the ability to reinforce and supply the troops ashore, to build up reserves rapidly, and maintain the momentum of a breakout.

The landings

On 25 April 1915, from 0500 hours, the leading files of the invasion forces rowed ashore and dashed onto the beaches under intense fire. At Cape Helles, the British and Irish troops leading the attack took heavy casualties as they tried to get through the surf or navigate the barbed wire. Of the first 200 Dublin Fusiliers soldiers who tried to get ashore at V Beach, only 21 survived.[32] The *River Clyde* was run aground into the beach but, as soon as the Munsters and Essex troops emerged from the improvised sally-ports in its side, they were cut down by fire from the bluffs above. When General H.E. Napier arrived with the main body to renew the beach assault at 0830 hours, he was killed along with all his staff. Approximately 40 men from the first wave survived. The soldiers of the Lancashire Fusiliers, who famously won 'six VCs before breakfast', and who faced the same murderous conditions at W Beach, were later given the opportunity to nominate who would receive the gallantry awards in their regiment. Of the nominees, three men were selected who had shown exceptional courage in breaking through the wire, much of it hidden by the waves, showing just how problematic the initial landings had been.[33] Despite a significant naval bombardment, the company of Turkish troops had maintained their defence there and only evacuated once their position became untenable. They had inflicted losses of 533 on the Lancashires, out of an original strength of 950.

By contrast, the landings at Y Beach had been a success. The Royal Marines and Scottish Borderers, having secured the shoreline, moved inland only tentatively,

---

32 Royal Dublin Fusiliers Association, 'Irish Battalions – Major Battles: Helles Landings, Gallipoli, April 1915'.

33 Captain Richard Raymond Willis; Sergeant Alfred Richards; Lance Corporal William Keneally.

even making a reconnaissance as far as Krithia, but they tended to wait for further orders which took hours to arrive.

Despite setting off at 0425 hours, some of the Australian and New Zealand forces, due to strong currents and misinterpretation of orders, landed in batches at the wrong locations, which delayed their advance. Many units clustered in the north of the beachhead, adding to the confusion. Nevertheless, after intense fighting, they struggled up through the gullies above the beach, and from 0600 began to secure the higher ground.[34] Kemal, realising the seriousness of the situation, pushed his reserves into the gaps with great energy, rallying his troops in such an inspirational way that he has become immortalised as the most decisive Ottoman leader that day. The Ottoman soldiers' achievement in this phase of opposing the landings is also rightly praised. It epitomised their dogged courage throughout the campaign which has become so admired in Western writing both at the time and subsequently. It has also provided an explanation for the subsequent failures of the ANZACs, and has overshadowed the fact that large numbers of shocked Australian soldiers demanded to be re-embarked on the ships. Inexperienced, stunned by the effectiveness of the Ottoman fire, and exhausted by the fighting, it is clear that, for some, morale had collapsed. The Royal Navy refused to evacuate them, arguing that the risks and complications were too great, not least because it would take two days to get the wounded off the beaches. Hamilton recommended that the ANZACs dig in, in order to stabilise the situation. Fresh advances further south by the British, he promised, would 'divert pressure' and he urged his subordinates to make 'a personal appeal to your men . . . to make a supreme effort to hold their ground'.[35]

Meanwhile a French attack at Kumkale on the Anatolian coast, which had not got underway until 1000 hours, had also been checked. Gunfire from across the straits had added to the casualty toll on this force. At Liman von Sanders' headquarters the arrival of reinforcements, which had stopped several Allied attacks, was a cause of some satisfaction, but it had been a near-run thing. Within days, Allied troops were exhausted, short of water and depleted by significant casualties. On 28 April, a major attempt to break out from Cape Helles, the first large-scale assault on Krithia, was checked. A second British attack on 6 May against the village, which overlooked much of the surrounding landscape, failed. The third attempt on 4 June fared no better. There was no breakout in this crucial first phase.

There were therefore two strategic options: the first was to overwhelm the defences with 'mass'. The Allies would have to use greater numbers and heavier fire from their confined beachheads if they were to secure the plateau. By July,

34 Edward Erickson, *Ordered to Die: A History of the Ottoman Army in the First World War* (London: Praeger, 2000), p. 83.

35 Cited in John Laffin, *Damn the Dardanelles* (Gloucester: Allen Sutton, 1989), p. 55.

while the Allies increased the number of divisions in the theatre of operations to 12, the Turks had amassed 15.[36] The only other option was to open new fronts with fresh landings elsewhere on the peninsula, in order to envelop the Ottoman defences.[37] Neither of these options proved successful while the need for mutual support between formations constrained the options for landings elsewhere

Despite the enduring tendency to criticise the plans and the commanders, the landings had revealed the fundamental character of the First World War and the reason why success while on the offensive was so elusive. The rate of fire, accuracy and range of new weaponry meant that it was far more difficult to cross open ground than in the past. The machine gun, magazine-fed breech-loading rifle, and field artillery could lay down such a weight of fire, that survival, unless dug-in, was precarious. A Maxim machine gun and a company of riflemen, firing steadily for quarter of an hour – the minimum time taken to disembark and cross a beach – could together fire over 16,000 rounds. Modern field obstacles, especially lightweight barbed wire, could channel and impede troops, delaying them in designated zones of fire. Field telephones enabled a defender to alert reserves to the direction of any attack, so even the loss of forward positions could be sealed off, and, if necessary, counter-attacked before fresh waves of attackers could secure any location. To make matters worse, in 1915 no means had yet been developed for crossing ground other than infantry and cavalry. In the broken terrain of Gallipoli, toiling foot soldiers could rarely advance very far or at speed, further adding to the advantages of the defenders. Communications were dependent on quite vulnerable and slow systems, and ship-to-shore messaging was always difficult. There were frequent episodes of indecision because orders took so long to formulate and arrive. Accusing commanders of idiocy, and criticising their operational plans, is to ignore the fundamental character of war in this period. Had the invasion of Gallipoli been conducted either 20 years before or 20 years later, its character would have been quite different. The outcome of this campaign can only really be understood in the context of its time.

Stalemate

The situation by early May was one of strategic stalemate: the Allies could sustain themselves on the shore and Ottoman forces, despite determined efforts, could not drive them out. The Ottomans had contained the landings, but this did not yet constitute a victory. Having established their lodgement on the coast, the Allies attempted to build up their resources for further breakouts, the aim being to envelop the Kilitbahir plateau from the beaches in the north and south. The

36 Bernard Montgomery, *A History of Warfare* (London: George Rainbird, 1968), p. 487.

37 Erickson, *Ordered to Die*, p. 84.

52nd Territorial Army Division arrived in May but the Ottomans also reinforced their defences. In June, the Ottoman 2nd Division deployed against the beachhead trenches, so the stalemate was reinforced.

The Allies were at a particular disadvantage in having to convey all their logistical support from Egypt via Mudros on Lemnos. However, the nearest suitable port was at Alexandria, some 1,046km (650 miles) away. All the stores, ammunition, guns and reinforcements had to be brought up, and painstakingly disembarked on beaches or improvised piers and jetties which were subjected to desultory and constant Ottoman shelling. The lack of fresh water was a significant and at times acute problem. Wounded personnel also had to be conveyed along the long and hazardous lines of communication, and they suffered from the heat, flies and inevitable delays in their treatment. The losses of the first few days overwhelmed the arrangements that had been prepared. Hamilton was especially frustrated by the lack of lighters to serve the larger transport ships and bring the wounded out and supplies ashore. He wrote in July: 'Ships arrive carrying things urgently required, and then, before they can be unloaded, sail away again.' In one case, ships containing engineering equipment arrived and were forced to depart no less than five times.[38]

In comparison with the Western Front, and despite initial arguments in its favour, Gallipoli was not a strategic priority for the Allies. Joffre, the commander of the French Army, was desperate for more men to mount offensives in France. Britain too could ill afford to release men for the Dardanelles. Yet it was in munitions that the situation became most acute. The scandalous shell shortage in Britain, which made such high profile news in 1915 in the European theatre, affected the troops on Gallipoli just as badly. Field guns found themselves with only three rounds to fire each day, and, on some occasions, with only one. There were too few 60-pdr heavy guns, barely a handful on the whole peninsula, and a shortage of grenades considered essential for trench fighting. Troops took to improvising explosive devices from jam tins, attached periscopes to sniper rifles and dreamt up their own deception plans.

The second attack on Krithia on 8 May suffered from this evident lack of fire support. Despite the heroic efforts of each of the formations involved, infantry assaulting uphill into well-prepared positions could only prevail with the heaviest of casualties. The 2nd Australian Brigade, led by Brigadier General William McKay, went in with 2,900 men and lost 1,056 in their efforts to take 1,000 lateral yards of Ottoman defences. That evening, Hamilton informed Kitchener that: 'The result of the operation has been a failure . . . the fortifications and their machine guns were . . . too strongly held to be rushed . . . Our troops have done all that flesh and blood can do against semi-permanent works and they are not able to carry them. More and more munitions will be needed to do so.' Shortages in Britain

38 Letter from General Sir Ian Hamilton to Lord Kitchener, 15 July 1915, King's College London, Liddell Hart Centre for Military Archives, Papers of General Sir Ian Hamilton, 7/1/6.

meant that only 25,000 shells could be sent, a quarter of the amount that had been expended in a single action at Festubert in France.

To make matters worse, a small German U-boat squadron sent to the Dardanelles torpedoed and sank two British battleships, HMS *Triumph* and HMS *Majestic*. The submarine attacks transformed the strategic situation, since, as the capital ships were withdrawn, it deprived the troops ashore of crucial naval fire support. Subsequently, a British transport ship was sunk, causing further consternation about the precarious supply line.

Much of the fighting across the beachheads through the summer was inconclusive, if bloody. Hamilton believed that Russian intervention against the Ottoman Empire might draw their attention away sufficiently to allow him to seize the heights at Achi Baba and secure the coast. His troops were making some limited progress, trenches and dugouts made the Allies' fortifications stronger and raiding was bringing in valuable intelligence. At Gully Ravine, Cape Helles, continuous fighting between 28 June and 5 July inched the Allied line deeper into Ottoman territory. The Ottoman standing procedure of counter-attacking immediately after each Allied attack cost them significant losses. On the ANZACs' front, small features such as Quinn's Post, Steele's Post and Courtney's Post became the scene of intense struggles. Sniper fire in the congested lines was feared by both sides for its lethal effectiveness, and those sharpshooters who were captured were sometimes executed. Trenches and outposts in certain places were separated by just a few yards of ground, close enough to hear each other. The Allies noted that the Ottomans at Gallipoli invoked their god and together shouted 'Allah u'Akbar' as they fought, but assumed the British and Australians worshipped a deity called 'Bastards' because of the frequency with which the Allied soldiers used this term.

Troops began to suffer from the stultifying conditions as the summer wore on, and there were more casualties from the environment than from combat: 'The trenches were like ovens; the grass had long since withered and vanished, and the hot wind stirred up the dust, . . . loathsome green flies [were] feasting on the corpses in No Man's Land, swarming hideously in the latrines, filling every trench and dug-out and covering the food . . . . '[39] There was an epidemic of dysentery and enteric fever. British casualties from sicknesses are estimated to have been 145,000; more than two-thirds of the casualties of the campaign. The only relief in such conditions was the opportunity in rare armistices to bury the dead, or, if close to the sea, to have the opportunity to swim and cool off, although safety from shelling was never guaranteed.

Hamilton resolved to make a fresh landing with new reinforcements at Suvla, five miles (8km) to the north of Anzac Cove, as part of a concerted assault on the Sari Bair ridge. The War Office in London encouraged Hamilton's plan to seize the summit at Chunuk Bair, although to take such a position would require the forming of a vulnerable salient, and risk taking fire from the flanks, if they were strongly

39 Robert Rhodes James, *Gallipoli* (London: B.T. Batsford Ltd, 1965), p. 221.

held.[40] The new offensive was to be carried out by three 'New Army' Divisions (10th, 11th, and 13th), made up of enthusiastic if barely trained volunteers, under the command of Lieutenant-General Sir Frederick Stopford, who, like Hamilton, was a veteran of the South African War. While the landings were made to outflank the Turkish defences to the north, the ANZACs and the British 13th Division were to break out from Anzac Cove and envelop the Sari Bair ridge. However, the Ottoman 5th Army had also been reinforced and was 16 divisions strong.[41]

Once again, the lack of experience of the Allied troops was a serious handicap. The 10th and 11th Divisions had never seen action before and were pitched straight into the battle from training. Stopford was blamed for his dilatory performance immediately after the landings, but he had little faith that his untried troops could move other than in a methodical manner.[42] Moreover, there is some evidence to suggest that Hamilton had regarded the Suvla landings as a supplementary arm of the more significant assault on Sari Bair by the ANZACs and existing British units, and that he only insisted the Suvla landings were the main effort once the Sari Bair attack had miscarried. That said, Stopford was less than energetic in his pursuit of his objectives and he was fortunate in being able to argue, after the campaign, that his instructions were vague. Despite the controversy, the Suvla operations were an attempt to reassert a strategic solution to the operational stalemate.

On 6 August, the offensive began with attacks at Cape Helles and Anzac Cove prior to the landings at Suvla Bay. At Helles, three battalions belonging to the British 29th and 42nd Divisions, intending to divert the Ottomans to the southern sectors, gradually required the support of the brigades. The fighting intensified and drew in four Ottoman divisions. Counter-attacks over three days and nights prevented any substantial Allied gains until the assaults subsided on 13 August with heavy losses. The second axis of Hamilton's offensive was made by the Australian 1st Infantry Brigade at Lone Pine ridge. They succeeded in carrying the Ottoman trenches and, thanks to the configuration of the ground, they defeated every counter-attack. Nevertheless, their advance was also contained and Ottoman reinforcements were free to switch their effort towards Suvla Bay.

The most poignant episode of the entire campaign was the fate of the Wellington Battalion of the New Zealand Brigade which broke through to the summit of Chunuk Bair ridge on 8 August. Exposed on every side, the defenders clung to its slopes while neighbouring units tried in vain to secure their flanks. Kemal led the counter-attack with three divisions. It took two days of close quarter battle, but, by 10 August, Kemal was able to recover the positions. Some 711 of the 760 men of the Wellington Battalion were casualties. The ANZACs lost a third of the entire

40 Ibid., pp. 236–7.

41 Ibid., pp. 246–7.

42 John Lee, 'Sir Ian Hamilton and the Dardanelles, 1915', in Brian Bond (ed.), *Fallen Stars: Eleven Studies of Twentieth Century Military Disasters* (London: Brassey's, 1991), pp. 45–6.

force in four days. The proportion of British losses was the same: the British 13th Division lost 5,500 men.

At Suvla Bay on the night of 6–7 August 1915, the 10th and 11th British Divisions had made their way ashore. They outnumbered the three Ottoman battalions who contested the assault, but Stopford's troops, unfamiliar with the terrain or even their precise objectives, did not execute the manoeuvres Hamilton later claimed was his intent and which Stopford, with rather more success, subsequently maintained he was unaware of. The two divisions suffered losses of 1,700 on the first day, and matters deteriorated when Ottoman forces, now alerted to the strength and dispositions of the British, launched their counter-attacks. Another thrust was therefore hemmed in on the coast, with the high ground in Ottoman possession. Landing fresh forces on 9–10 August, Stopford pushed the 53rd and 54th Divisions into action, but these formations could not fight their way up onto the high features in the teeth of stiffening resistance. On 15 August, Stopford, much criticised for his failure to act more energetically or to use his initiative, was dismissed. His successor, Major-General Beauvoir de Lisle, made an attempt to cut through to the high ground beyond the beaches a week later, in order to complete the pincer movement originally intended. Once again, his men could not get forward without heavy losses. The attempted breakthrough had failed.

Evacuation

There was no immediate withdrawal from Gallipoli, despite the failure to break out that August. Various options remained open, but evacuation was considered to be too damaging to Britain's imperial prestige. If shown to be defeated by the Ottoman Empire, how, the British imperial governors pondered, might such news be greeted in the various colonies and dominions? The functioning of the British Empire had always been dependent on a small number of British administrators and troops supported by vast number of 'sub-imperialists', locals co-opted, paid and otherwise loyal to Britain's rule. [43] If British military prowess was damaged, the imperial garrisons, already stripped out for the duration of the Great War, might be overwhelmed by agitation and unrest. The fact that the withdrawal from Gallipoli did not spark a general collapse of British imperial rule suggests that their fears were exaggerated.

The British were certainly concerned at the time. The Viceroy of India, Sir Charles Hardinge, feared that: 'defeat, or the necessity of cutting our losses in the Dardanelles, would be absolutely fatal in this country'. He concluded that a setback at the hands of a Muslim power would mean that: 'Pan-Islamism would become

---

43 Ronald Robinson, 'Imperial Theory and the Question of Imperialism After Empire', *Journal of Imperial and Commonwealth History*, 12(2), 1984, p. 44.

a very serious danger'.[44] In India, there was rigorous censorship, and, amid fears of new conspiracies, an increase in surveillance. At least two genuine anti-British plots were uncovered, and two German attempts to reach India, one involving the smuggling of arms, were detected and neutralised.[45] In Egypt, Ottoman units had tried to deliver propaganda material in support of their military campaigns there. The Foreign Secretary, Sir Edward Grey, informed the Cabinet that: 'At present we are practically bankrupt of prestige in the East, and our position could hardly be worse.'[46] Efforts were made to drive forward in Mesopotamia in order to capture Baghdad and thus strike a blow at Ottoman prestige.[47] The small force available reached Ctesiphon before being besieged at Kut al Amara. Attempts to relieve the beleaguered garrison cost the lives of 23,000 men, but the relief force faced the same problems that beset the assaulting troops in Gallipoli and on the Western Front. The weight and lethality of fire was too great for men or horses to overwhelm without taking severe losses.

On the Gallipoli Peninsula, desultory fighting continued from August into the winter. Bad weather worsened the plight of the troops. A three-day rainstorm in late November flooded trenches, turning gullies into torrents, taking the living and the dead with them down into the sea. By December, snow, freezing winds and the cold led to hypothermia and frostbite.

Evacuation had been considered even before the Suvla landings, but the failure to make progress now reinforced the idea more firmly. In October 1915 Kitchener asked Hamilton to consider what the cost of withdrawal might be. When Hamilton was dismissed soon after, General Sir Charles Monro, his replacement, was confronted with the same question. On arrival, Monro carried out a thorough three-day survey of the situation, visiting the key sites and consulting the various commanders at each point. On 31 October, he passed Kitchener a memorandum advising evacuation, but warned the casualties of such an operation might total one-third of the entire expeditionary force.[48] He wrote: 'The position occupied by our troops presented a military situation unique in history. The mere fringe of the coast line had been secured. The beaches and piers upon which they depended for all requirements in personnel and material were exposed to registered and observed artillery fire. Our entrenchments were dominated almost throughout by the Turks . . . . The position was without depth, the communications were insecure and dependent on the weather.' Despite the potential losses, Monro believed that evacuation was preferable because a forward movement was impossible and the logistical chain could not support an advance. Kitchener left London to come and

44 Cited in French, 'Dardanelles, Mecca and Kut: Prestige as a Factor in British Eastern Strategy, 1914–1916', *War and Society* 5(1), p. 54.

45 Johnson, *Spying for Empire*, pp. 225–7.

46 Cited in French, 'Dardanelles, Mecca and Kut', p. 54.

47 Telegram from Sir Austen Chamberlain to the Viceroy of India, 21 October 1915, CUL, Hardinge papers, vol. 94.

48 Ibid.

form his own verdict. At first, Kitchener considered anther naval operation to open the straits, but Monro disabused him of that, and once Kitchener had toured the beachhead front line for himself, he too concluded that a renewed offensive would not succeed.

At a conference at Mudros for the commanders-in-chief in Egypt, Gallipoli, and the new deployment in Salonika in November 1915, the conclusion was that operations from Egypt and in Mesopotamia would have to be stepped up. Kitchener thought that only the forces at Suvla Bay and Anzac Cove needed to be pulled out, while Cape Helles might be held, but the War Committee in London would consider only a complete withdrawal. At the Joint Staff Conference in France on 8 December 1915, the decision was taken to evacuate Gallipoli in order to strengthen the forces at Salonika. Suvla Bay and Anzac Cove were thus evacuated successfully on the night of 19–20 December 1915 and the Allies left Cape Helles on 8 January 1916. In the historiography, these evacuations are praised as model efforts in deception and organisation, as there were none of the losses anticipated by Monro. However, Hew Strachan notes that it was hardly in the interests of the Ottomans to contest the Allied withdrawal and incur unnecessary losses which would not change the outcome of the campaign.

Conclusions

Strategically, the Allies had failed to align their ends, ways and means, and their operational setbacks stemmed from their inability to co-ordinate naval and land operations. That said, the British naval attacks on Ottoman shipping in the region were so comprehensive that by 1918 overland routes were the only reliable ones left. More importantly, the tactical disadvantages the Allies suffered prevented operational plans from being realised. The power of defensive technologies overmatched the ability of infantry to cross open ground. Broken terrain added to the advantages of defence. The determination of the Ottoman defenders must also be taken into account, although no army monopolised courage and resolution.

Churchill concluded that the Gallipoli landings had failed because they were never fully resourced. It is true that the Western Front was always the priority and that Gallipoli was a sideshow.[49] Typically, like every imperial operation, commanders had been forced to improvise and find their own solutions for operations outside of Europe. Moreover the parlous state of artillery ammunition and absence of heavy guns was a major problem, although naval gunnery offset this to some extent. Churchill was also correct in his estimation that withdrawal from Gallipoli reinvigorated Ottoman resistance. He argued that, as a result, the subsequent campaigns in Salonika, Palestine, and Mesopotamia were far more difficult for the Allies. The conclusion of the Gallipoli Campaign certainly enabled

49 Churchill, *The World Crisis*, p. 541.

the Ottoman Army to redeploy reserves to other theatres. Yet Churchill was wrong in his belief that another naval attack might have forced the Narrows, after 18 March, if sufficient resolve had been shown. He had not, unlike Kitchener, been able to visit the key sites, and it is noticeable that all the senior officers who did so reached the same conclusion.

The Turkish national confidence, rather than a profoundly Ottoman imperial one, was boosted by the campaign. Edward Erickson noted that victory had been achieved because 'the Turks fielded a very well-trained, well-led and highly-motivated army'.[50] The infrastructure of Gallipoli gave them a strategic central position on the peninsula from which to deploy their reserves and thus meet each threat as it emerged. Nevertheless, it was a campaign victory that came at an enormous cost. It is estimated that there were 230,000 Allied casualties and up to 300,000 Ottoman losses.[51] Some 86,692 Ottoman soldiers died at Gallipoli, and, despite the successful outcome of the campaign, it has to be said that they were no more able to dislodge the Allies than the Allies were able to get off the coast.

Indeed, it was a pyrrhic victory in the classic sense. In November 1918, the British returned to Gallipoli as occupiers. On the 5th of that month, British aircraft landed at the German-built airstrip above the Narrows. On the 9th, British soldiers came ashore, marching past the scrubby and increasingly overgrown battlefield of 1915 to establish themselves on the peninsula. Having passed through the straits, the Royal Navy anchored off Constantinople on the 13th, determined to impose the conditions of the armistice. It was striking, and of course deliberate, that leading the flotilla was HMS *Agamemnon* which had taken part in the naval operations in the area three years before. The Royal Navy could also claim, with some justification, that the Allied naval blockade had taken its toll on the Ottoman-Turkish war economy. Yet the most significant developments had been on land. The British had demonstrated that, even while engaged in a demanding European war, they had been able to mobilise the resources of their empire, recover from the setbacks at Gallipoli, Kut al Amara and Palestine, and mount larger offensives each year. Maude's drive up the Tigris and Euphrates in 1917 captured Baghdad in March. After the Third Battle of Gaza, the Allies began to assert their superiority over Ottoman forces in Palestine too. Jerusalem capitulated in November and at the Battle of Megiddo in 1918 the British drove back Ottoman forces to such an extent that resistance on that front began to collapse long before the Allies took Damascus. A brief Ottoman counter-offensive in the Caucasus in 1918 against disorganised Russian revolutionaries could do nothing to alter Britain's domination of the Middle East.

---

50 Edward Erickson, *Gallipoli: The Ottoman Campaign* (Barnsley: Pen & Sword, 2010) pp. xiv–xv.

51 Ulrich Trumpener, 'The Turkish War, 1914–18', in John Horne (ed.), *A Companion Volume to World War I* (Oxford: Wiley-Blackwell, 2010), pp. 102–3.

Gallipoli is thus a paradox in the Anglophone historiography. While being held up as an example of folly, waste and incompetent execution, it made no material difference to the outcome of the war, which was an Allied victory. The perspective in Turkey is no less paradoxical: Turkish writers ignore the strategic defeat of their nation, and regard the campaign only as an operational triumph. Moreover, while praising the dedication and sacrifice of Muslim soldiers in the defence of an Islamic state, the most significant development was the political apotheosis of Kemal Atatürk, the architect of a modern, secular Turkish nation. The contradictions of the campaign are, perhaps, appropriate. The Gallipoli battlefields, still preserved today, are haunting and disturbing; they bear mute testimony to a bitter struggle of such intensity that almost defies meaning. Every visitor is left with uncomfortable questions about the causes and the consequences of this grim theatre of war.

Chapter 3
A critique of the defence plans in the Gallipoli battles
Liman von Sanders, Turkish commanders and the conduct of operations

Ferhat Çalışkan

The Gallipoli Campaign affected deeply the course of the First World War and prolonged the conflict. It also had a significant impact on the doctrine of amphibious assaults and the defensive tactics against them. The effects of the Gallipoli landings can be found in the revised edition of the British Manual of Amphibious Operations, dated 1938, and in the British perceptions of the landings during the Second World War.[1] Most studies of Gallipoli have argued that the causes of Allied failure were the mistakes made by the British and French high command, while Turkish success was due to the concept of defence designed by Liman von Sanders. Yet, for all the credit he has received, his 'new' plan was much the same as that of the Turkish staff and the contribution of General Liman von Sanders was, in fact, minimal. Nevertheless, despite their similarity, there were also certain differences that drastically affected the conduct and outcome of operations.

Liman von Sanders' defence plan and its principles

The Turkish forces assigned to the defence of Gallipoli were subordinated to General Liman von Sanders, the commander of the 5th Army. This force consisted of III and XV Corps, and the Çanakkale Fortified Area Command. Two further formations, 5th Infantry Division and 1st Cavalry Brigade, also came under the command of the 5th Army. (See Figure 3.1 below.)

1 David MacGregor, 'The Use, Misuse, and Non-Use of History: The Royal Navy and the Operational Lessons of the First World War', *The Journal of Military History*, Vol. 56, No. 4 (Oct., 1992), pp. 607–8.

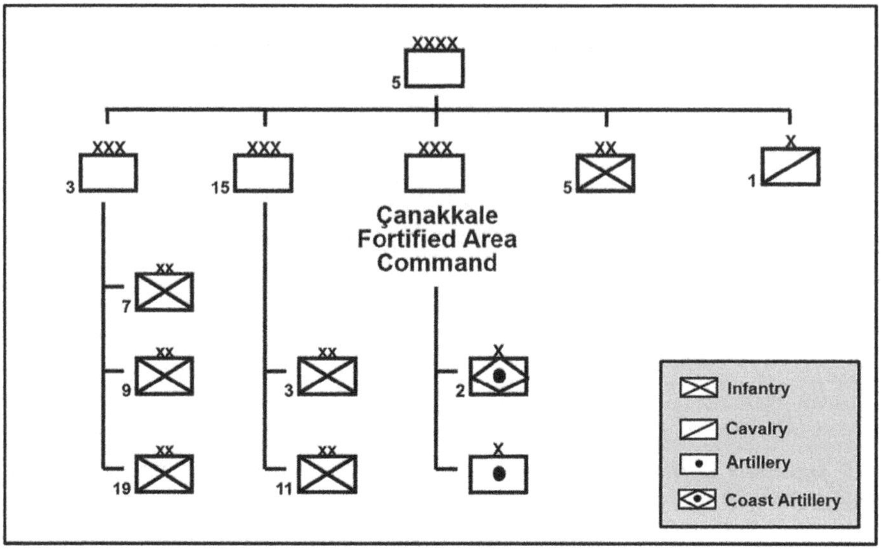

Figure 3.1 5th Army organisational chart[2]

The army's six divisions were assigned to three areas in three groupings. The 3rd and 11th Divisions were deployed on the Anatolian shore, the 5th and 7th Divisions were on the isthmus region (Bolayır, Saros), while the 9th and 19th Divisions were assigned to the defence of the southern part of the Gallipoli Peninsula. Although 19th Division was depicted under the command of III Corps, in fact, with 5th Division, it constituted the reserve of the 5th Army.[3] Çanakkale Fortified Area Command was tasked with the defence of the strait itself and 1st Cavalry Brigade had the responsibility of providing northern flank security.[4] (Figures 3.2, 3.3, 3.4)

When the deployments of the forces in the three regions are analysed together, it is obvious that the priority was given to the isthmus region and Anatolian shore. Two divisions were assigned to each of these two regions. Although on the Gallipoli Peninsula two divisions were assigned to the defence, in fact, as already mentioned, 19th Division was the reserve of 5th Army and it was tasked with the reinforcement of all three regions. That is why it was situated at Bigalı

---

2 The chart was prepared by the author based on the source titled *Birinci Dünya Harbinde Türk Harbi* (Turkish) (Genelkurmay ATASE Bşk.lığı, Cilt V, Çanakkale Cephesi Harekâtı,1'inci Kitap, Gnkur. ATASE Bşk.lığı Yay., Ankara), p. 12, 13.

3 Gnkur. ATASE Bşk.lığı, Birinci Dünya Harbinde Türk Harbi, Cilt V, Çanakkale Cephesi Harekâtı, 2'nci Kitap, Gnkur. ATASE Bşk.lığı Yay., Ankara, p. 9.

4 Çetiner, Selahattin, Çanakkale Savaşı Üzerine Bir İnceleme, Harp Akademileri Basımevi, İstanbul, 1999, p. 70 EK-20.

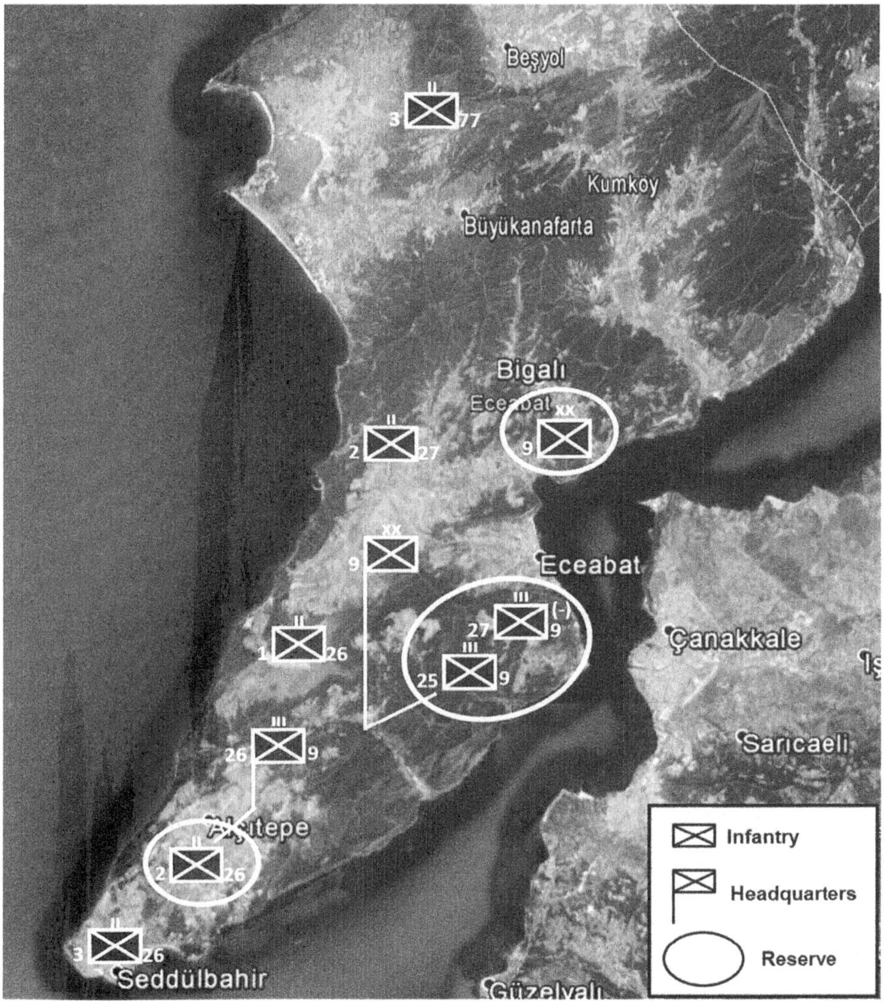

Figure 3.2 Southern part of the Gallipoli Peninsula (25 April)[5]

near Eceabat, a valuable point because of the maritime transportation it provided between the isthmus and the Anatolian shore.[6]

5 This figure was prepared by the author based on the sources below:

1 – *Birinci Dünya Harbinde Türk Harbi* (Turkish) (Genelkurmay ATASE Bşk.lığı, Cilt V, Çanakkale Cephesi Harekâtı,1'inci Kitap, Gnkur. ATASE Bşk.lığı Yay., Ankara), Kroki-27.

2 – Google Earth 7.1.1.1888, 2013, Seddülbahir, 40°07'28"N 26°20'06"E, Eye alt. 51km, http://www.google.com/earth/index.html, (Accessed 11.11.2013).

6 İbrahim Artuç, 1915 Çanakkale Savaşı, Kastaş Yayınları, İstanbul, 1992, p. 130.

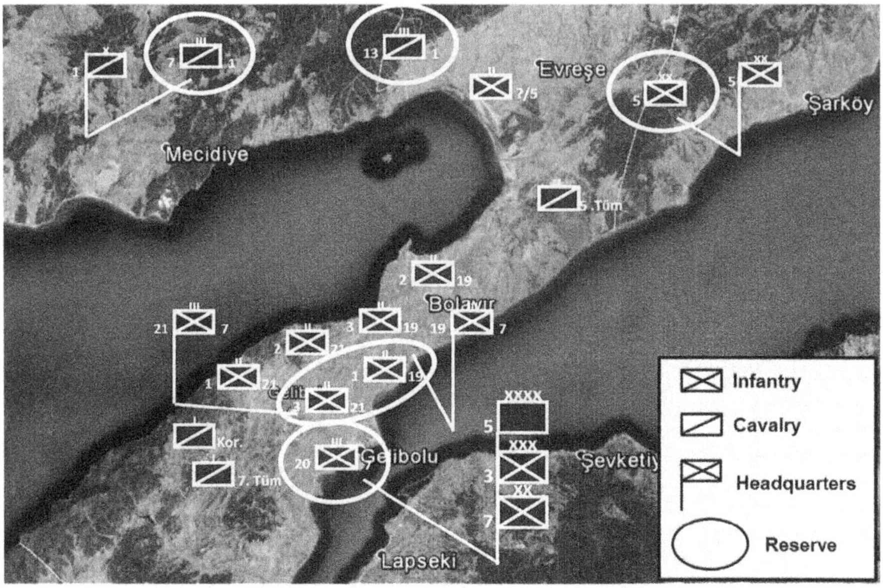

Figure 3.3 Isthmus region[7]

According to the evaluation of Liman von Sanders, the isthmus region (Bolayır, Saros) was the most probable landing site. After the isthmus region, he believed that Kaba Tepe was the next most probable landing area. The third and least likely landing zone was Seddülbahir. On the other hand, on the Anatolian shore, Beşiğe and Kumkale were two areas against which amphibious assaults were expected. The main consideration in Liman von Sanders' assessment of landing sites was his supposition that the Allies would launch an assault from an area that would ensure rapid access to the rear of Turkish artillery batteries in the straits.[8] Furthermore, he assumed that these artillery batteries were primarily for use against ships in the Dardanelles, which left these guns exposed to a rearward attack. For this reason

---

7 This figure was prepared by the author based on the sources below:

1 – *Birinci Dünya Harbinde Türk Harbi* (Turkish) (Genelkurmay ATASE Bşk.lığı, Cilt V, Çanakkale Cephesi Harekâtı,1'inci Kitap, Gnkur. ATASE Bşk.lığı Yay., Ankara), Kroki-1b.

2 – *Birinci Dünya Harbinde Türk Harbi* (Turkish) (Genelkurmay ATASE Bşk.lığı, Cilt V, Çanakkale Cephesi Harekâtı,1'inci Kitap, Gnkur. ATASE Bşk.lığı Yay., Ankara), Kroki-15.

3 – Google Earth 7.1.1.1888, 2013, Gelibolu, 40°24'58"N 26°40'46"E, Eye alt. 84km, http://www.google.com/earth/index.html, (Accessed 11.11.2013).

8 Tim Travers, 'Liman von Sanders, the Capture of Lieutenant Palmer, and Ottoman Anticipation of the Allied Landings at Gallipoli on 25 April 1915', *The Journal of Military History*, Vol. 65, No. 4 (Oct., 2001), p. 972–3.

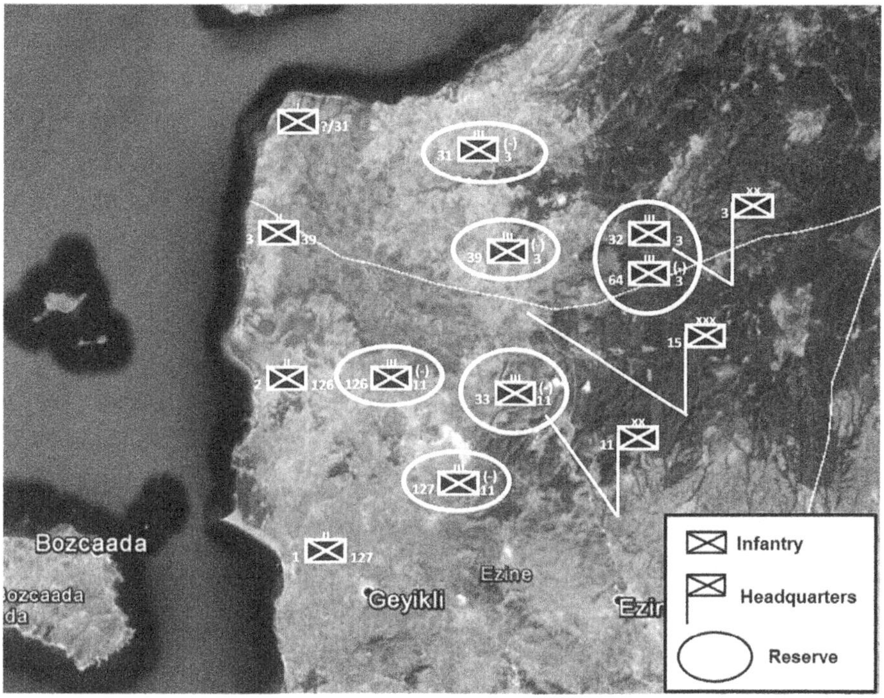

Figure 3.4 Anatolian shore[9]

he considered that any landing on the Anatolian shore would be particularly dangerous.[10]

Taking these divisional deployments into account, Liman von Sanders made little impact, especially on the Gallipoli Peninsula. He made only minor adjustments to the location of 19th Division, moving it some 5km north from Eceabat to

9 This figure was prepared by the author based on the sources below:

1 – *Birinci Dünya Harbinde Türk Harbi* (Turkish) (Genelkurmay ATASE Bşk.lığı, Cilt V, Çanakkale Cephesi Harekâtı,1'inci Kitap, Gnkur. ATASE Bşk.lığı Yay., Ankara), Kroki-4.

2 – *Birinci Dünya Harbinde Türk Harbi* (Turkish) (Genelkurmay ATASE Bşk.lığı, Cilt V, Çanakkale Cephesi Harekâtı,1'inci Kitap, Gnkur. ATASE Bşk.lığı Yay., Ankara), Kroki-1b.

3 – *Birinci Dünya Harbinde Türk Harbiiop* (Turkish) (Genelkurmay ATASE Bşk. lığı, Cilt V, Çanakkale Cephesi Harekâtı,1'inci Kitap, Gnkur. ATASE Bşk.lığı Yay., Ankara), Kroki-15.

4 – Google Earth 7.1.1.1888, 2011, Kumkale, 39°52'07"N 26°20'50"E, Eye alt. 53,35km, http://www.google.com/earth/index.html, (Accessed 11.11.2013).

10 Liman Von Sanders, Türkiye'de Beş Yıl, Cilt-1, Yeni Gün Haber Ajansı Basın ve Yayıncılık A.Ş., 1999, p. 82.

Bigalı.[11] But one principle, which deeply affected the deployments of the units at the regimental level and below, underscored the distinctiveness of the defence plan conceived by the German general. This principle was based on the assumption that the landing sites of the Allies could not be determined entirely. His plan was simply to hold the shores with fewer troops: small security and observation units were assigned to defend the shore while the rest of the defending force was held, concentrated, inland.[12] This new arrangement meant that the Allies would be allowed to make landings and hold the beachhead, before a significant counter-offensive was launched. The southern shoreline of Gallipoli was especially weak. In this area, just four battalions were assigned to the defence of a 58.4km-long coast. The number of battalions assigned per kilometre was 0.07. (Table 3.1)[13]

In the Kaba Tepe region, which was under the responsibility of the 2nd Battalion of 27th Regiment, 10.3km of shoreline was to be defended by only six platoons. This means that approximately half of a platoon was deployed per

Table 3.1 Number of troops assigned to the southern part of the Gallipoli Peninsula (25 April)

Criteria	26th Regiment		27th Regiment	77th Regiment	Total
Shore responsibility (km)	24.9		10.3	23.2	58.4
Number of battalions (bn) assigned	2		1	1	4
Number of battalions assigned per kilometre	0.08		0.1	0.04	0.07
Distance of reserve battalions to the first defence line battalions (km)	**1st Bn**	**3rd Bn**	**2nd Bn**	**3rd Bn**	**Average**
	9.3	5.3	7.3	12.7	8.7
Time taken for reserve battalions to reach the first defence line battalions (hours)[14 15 16]	2.3	1.3	1.8	3.2	2.2

11 Edward J. Erickson, *I. Dünya Savaşı'nda Osmanlı Ordusu: Çanakkale, Kutü'l-Amare ve Filistin Cephesi* (Kerim Bağrıaçık, Çeviri), İstanbul: İş Bankası Yayınları, 2009, p. 35.

12 Liman von Sanders, Türkiye'de Beş Yıl, Cilt-1, Yeni Gün Haber Ajansı Basın ve Yayıncılık A.Ş., 1999, p. 83.

13 Gnkur. ATASE Bşk.lığı, Birinci Dünya Harbinde Türk Harbi, Cilt V, Çanakkale Cephesi Harekâtı, 1'inci Kitap, Gnkur. ATASE Bşk.lığı Yay., Ankara, Kroki-15.

14 In this table and the other tables, the march speed is assumed to be 4km/hour. This speed is calculated based on the parameters of 57th Regiment's march from Bigalı to Kocaçimen Hill on 25 April. İn this march, 57th Regiment marched 5.8 km in 1.5 hours.

15 Gnkur. ATASE Bşk.lığı, Birinci Dünya Harbinde Türk Harbi, Cilt V, Çanakkale Cephesi Harekâtı, 2'nci Kitap, Gnkur. ATASE Bşk.lığı Yay., Ankara, Kroki-17.

16 İbrahim Artuç, 1915 Çanakkale Savaşı, Kastaş Yayınları, İstanbul, 1992, p. 200.

kilometre. Regional reserves, which were tasked with supporting this small unit, and their distances to the units on the coast are presented in Table 3.2.[17]

In the Seddülbahir area, which was under the responsibility of 3rd Battalion of 26th Regiment, 6.6km of shoreline was to be held by five platoons. Here, a force approximately between the strength of two squads and a platoon was deployed per kilometre. Regional reserves, which were tasked with supporting this small unit, and their distances to the units on the shoreline are presented in Table 3.3.[18]

When the distances and the travel times between regional reserves and the coastal units are analysed, considering the transportation means of 1915, when there were no motor vehicles and when units were dispatched on foot,[19] they reveal that resistance against any landings was primarily directed, not during the first phase of the enemy's landing operations, but against their beachheads once they were ashore.

Table 3.2 27th Regimental reserves and travel times

Reserve unit	Distance and time to the sector of 2nd Bn 6th Coy		Distance and time to the sector of 2nd Bn 7th Coy		Distance and time to the sector of 2nd Bn 8th Coy	
	Km	Hour	Km	Hour	Km	Hour
Reserve platoon of 6th, 7th and 8th Coy	1	0.25	0.7	0.2	1.4	0.35
5th Coy	3.6	0.9	1.6	0.4	4.4	1.1
27th Regiment	7.3	1.8	6.8	1.7	8.4	2.1
25th Regiment	6.5	1.6	8.3	2.1	11.2	2.8

Table 3.3 26th Regiment reserves and travel times

Reserve unit	Distance and time to the sector of 3rd Bn 9th Coy		Distance and time to the sector of 3rd Bn 10th Coy		Distance and time to the sector of 3rd Bn 12th Coy	
	Km	Hour	Km	Hour	Km	Hour
Reserve platoon of 10th and 12th Coy	No reserve platoon		0.6	0.15	0.5	0.13
11th and 9th Coy	1	0.25	1.1	0.3	1.3	0.33
2nd Battalion	4.7	1.2	6.1	1.5	6.3	1.6
25th Regiment	15.5	3.9	17.1	4.3	17.2	4.3

17 Gnkur. ATASE Bşk.lığı, Birinci Dünya Harbinde Türk Harbi, Cilt V, Çanakkale Cephesi Harekâtı, 2'nci Kitap, Gnkur. ATASE Bşk.lığı Yay., Ankara, Kroki-13, Kroki-14.

18 Gnkur. ATASE Bşk.lığı, Birinci Dünya Harbinde Türk Harbi, Cilt V, Çanakkale Cephesi Harekâtı, 2'nci Kitap, Gnkur. ATASE Bşk.lığı Yay., Ankara, Kroki-30 a, Kroki-28.

19 Gnkur. ATASE Bşk.lığı, Birinci Dünya Harbinde Türk Harbi, Cilt V, Çanakkale Cephesi Harekâtı, 1'inci Kitap, Gnkur. ATASE Bşk.lığı Yay., Ankara, p. 29.

The Turkish commanders' defence plan and its principles

The foundations of the defence of the Gallipoli Peninsula were laid in the 1880s which made it one of the most fortified regions of the Ottoman Empire. Sea mines and coastal defence artillery were the basis of the defence system. However, after the First Balkan War, between 1912 and 1913, the Gallipoli defence plan was reviewed. Before Liman von Sanders assumed the command of 5th Army in 1915, the Turkish commanders' own defence plan was based on the design adopted during the Balkan Wars.[20] The disposition of the Ottoman Army on the peninsula and on the Anatolian coast in 1912 is presented in Figure 3.5.[21]

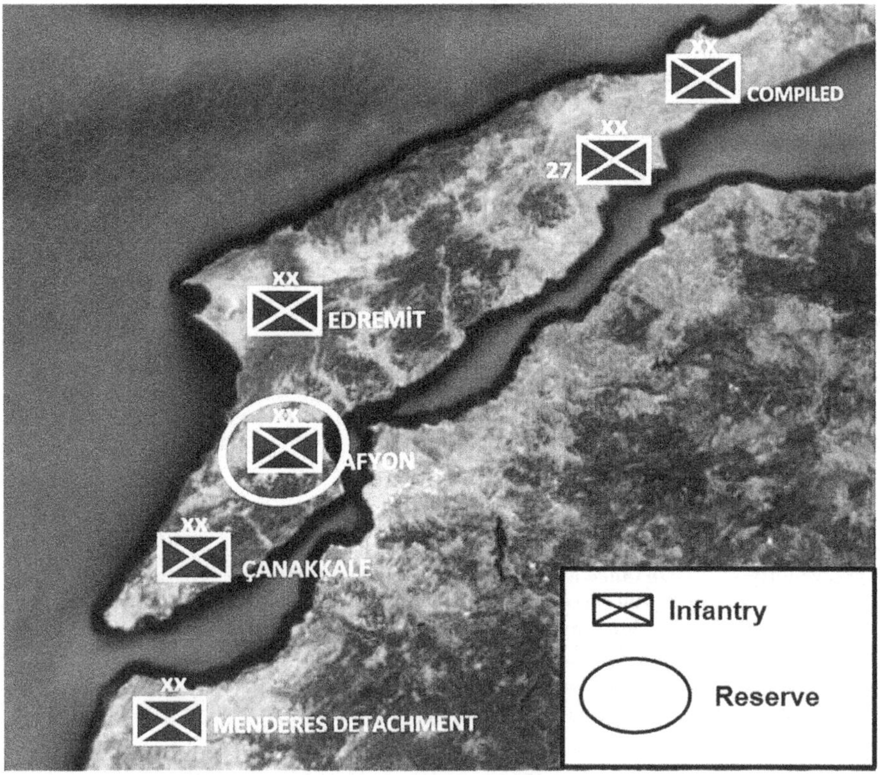

Figure 3.5 Gallipoli defence plan of the Ottoman Army in the Balkan Wars[22]

20 Erickson, Edward J., *I. Dünya Savaşı'nda Osmanlı Ordusu: Çanakkale, Kutü'l-Amare ve Filistin Cephesi* (Kerim Bağrıaçık, Çeviri), İstanbul: İş Bankası Yayınları, 2009, pp. 28–9.

21 Edward J. Erickson, *Gelibolu, Osmanlı Harekâtı* (Orhan Düz, Çeviri), İstanbul: İş Bankası Yayınları, 2012, pp. 14–15.

22 Google Earth 7.1.1.1888, 2013, Gelibolu,40°13'01"N 26°21'24"E, Göz hizası 130km, http://www.google.com/earth/index.html, (Accessed 11.11.2013).

The Edremit Reserve Division was deployed in the Arıburnu and Suvla areas, and the Çanakkale Reserve Division was in the Seddülbahir area, while the 27th Infantry Division and Composite Division were assigned to the defence of the Bolayır sector. This defence arrangement was based on the idea of battalion resistance points located on vantage points. Furthermore, all landing sites were under the cover of guns firing on 'open sights', that is, near horizontal trajectories. In support, the Afyonkarahisar Reserve Division constituted a mobile reserve in the Eceabat area. Comparatively weaker forces were deployed in defence of the Anatolian shores, and the Menderes Detachment was given the responsibility of this sector at a divisional level.[23] When this defence plan is analysed, it can be clearly seen that it was designed to resist the landing forces on the shoreline before the enemy succeeded in gaining a beachhead. This is particularly the case where special attention was given to determining points where battalion-sized resistance would be focused and where rifle companies could direct their fire without the need to change positions. Moreover, when the general deployment of the units is assessed, it is evident that the Seddülbahir, Arıburnu-Kabatepe and Kumkale areas were assumed to be the most probable landing points. That the reserve division was deployed on the Gallipoli Peninsula reveals the common thinking in the minds of Turkish commanders, namely that Gallipoli was the priority as a landing zone, rather than the Anatolian shores. The exact location of the reserve division in the peninsula also suggests that they anticipated landings in the Arıburnu-Kabatepe and Seddülbahir areas.

When General Liman von Sanders changed the defence plan, Turkish commanders at all levels, including 19th Division Commander Lieutenant Colonel Mustafa Kemal and 9th Division Commander Colonel Halil Sami, expressed their objection to the new plan. In his report dated 6 April 1915, Colonel Halil Sami criticised the German plan and proposed to adopt the old concept of defence. The arguments in this critique are important in that they give details of the thinking of the Turkish commanders of the period. The main points from this report were fivefold:

> One, naval gun fire will not be effective against well-fortified positions. Furthermore, at this point, the Allied forces' willingness to avoid any fratricide among themselves will also reduce this effect. The weakest period of the Allies' operation will be at the moment of landing and this must be exploited.
>
> Two, there are limited numbers of probable landing sites, which can be strongly defended.
>
> Three, reinforcement of the reserves waiting *en masse* in the rear will be subjected to heavy bombardment.

23 Edward J. Erickson, *I. Dünya Savaşı'nda Osmanlı Ordusu: Çanakkale, Kutü'l-Amare ve Filistin Cephesi* (Kerim Bağrıaçık, Çeviri), İstanbul: İş Bankası Yayınları, 2009, p. 31.

Four, while we wait to determine the main landing site, the flanks of our troops may be exposed to the risk of encirclement.

Five, the Gallipoli Peninsula should be divided into two areas of responsibility and two divisions should be assigned to these two areas. Furthermore, each division should set aside at least one regiment as a reserve.[24]

As a response to the telegram dated 13 March 1915, which explained General Liman von Sanders' considerations about the defence of the area, the Ottoman Supreme Command sent a telegram on 22 March 1915 including its own thoughts about the defence plan. The Ottoman Supreme Command also put its emphasis on confronting the landing forces on the shoreline before the enemy succeeded in gaining a beachhead. Nevertheless, in the end, the Ottoman Supreme Command left the final decision to Liman von Sanders.[25]

In 1921, at the end of the Turkish translation of Liman von Sanders' book, *Five Years in Turkey*, the Turkish Chief of Staff added a chapter in order to give answers to the allegations put forward in the book. These answers clearly explain the considerations of the Turkish Chief of Staff about the defence plan. According to this official line, until General Liman von Sanders assumed command of 5th Army on 26 March 1915, the Ottoman command staff planned to attrit the mass of the landing forces while they were still at sea. Thus, the defence concept included deployment of strong surveillance and screening units and positioning of reserves near probable landing sites in order to counter-attack immediately. They considered that, once the Allies held the beachhead, it would be very difficult to throw them back into the sea. Furthermore, in contrast to Liman von Sanders' evaluation, Turkish commanders claimed that, by analysing the topography, they could predict the landing sites and establish strong fortifications there. The Kilitbahir Plateau was seen as the key terrain in any attempt to force a sea route to İstanbul and as early as the 1890s it was thought that Kaba Tepe and Seddülbahir were the most probable landing sites.[26] The Isthmus and Anatolian areas were considered as the secondary landing sites and they were to be defended with fewer troops. In addition, 19th Division would constitute a reserve further to the south.

In 1915, all three regiments of 9th Division were given an area of responsibility and their reserves were positioned near the shoreline in their sector. In total, three battalions were set aside as reserves and these battalions would be used on the initiative of the regimental commanders. There was no reserve at the regimental level. (Figure 3.6)

24 İsmet Görgülü, Çanakkale İlk Günde Biterdi, Bilgi Yayınevi, Ankara, 2008, pp. 311–14.

25 İsmet Görgülü, Çanakkale İlk Günde Biterdi, Bilgi Yayınevi, Ankara, 2008, pp. 321–2.

26 Sermet Atacanlı, *Atatürk ve Çanakkale'nin Komutanları*, MB Yayınevi, İstanbul, 2007, pp. 195–6.

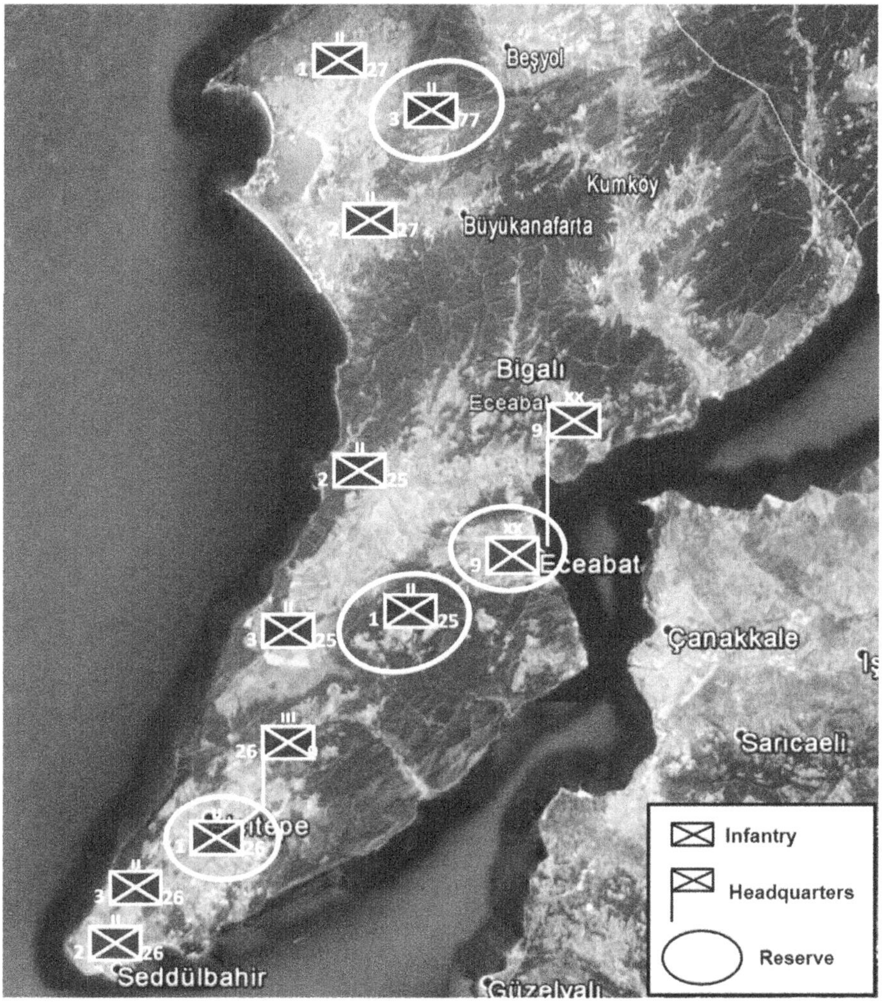

Figure 3.6 Southern part of the Gallipoli Peninsula (31 March)[27]

In the plan, the shoreline in the southern part of the peninsula was defended strongly. In this area six battalions were assigned to the defence of a 51.6km shoreline. The number of battalions assigned per kilometre was 0.12. (Table 3.4)[28]

---

27 This figure was prepared by the author based on the sources below:

1 – *Birinci Dünya Harbinde Türk Harbi* (Turkish) (Genelkurmay ATASE Bşk.lığı, Cilt V, Çanakkale Cephesi Harekâtı,1'inci Kitap, Gnkur. ATASE Bşk.lığı Yay., Ankara), Kroki-14.

2 – Google Earth 7.1.1.1888, 2013, Seddülbahir, 40°07'28"N 26°20'06"E, Eye alt. 51km, http://www.google.com/earth/index.html, (Accessed 11.11.2013).

28 Gnkur. ATASE Bşk.lığı, Birinci Dünya Harbinde Türk Harbi, Cilt V, Çanakkale Cephesi Harekâtı, 1'inci Kitap, Gnkur. ATASE Bşk.lığı Yay., Ankara, Kroki-15.

Table 3.4 Number of troops assigned to the southern part of the Gallipoli Peninsula (31 March)

Criteria	26th Regiment		25th Regiment		27th Regiment		Total
Shore responsibility (km)	16		15.8		19.8		51.6
Number of battalions assigned	2		2		2		6
Number of battalions assigned per kilometre	0.13		0.13		0.1		0.12
	2nd Bn	3rd Bn	2nd Bn	3rd Bn	1st Bn	2nd Bn	Average
Distance of reserve bns to the first defence line bns (km)	4.1	2.9	7.5	6.7	7.5	6.2	5.8
Travel time of reserve bns to the first defence line bns (hours)	1	0.73	1.9	1.7	1.9	1.6	1.45

Comparison of the two plans and analysis

In order to understand what General Liman von Sanders changed from the earlier plan, we should look at the new deployment of the units at the level of regiment and below. Figure 3.2 shows that Liman von Sanders gave the responsibility of the shores to battalions and kept the reserves at regiment level further inland. In contrast, as seen in Figure 3.6, the older plan gave the responsibility of the shores to regiments while their reserve battalions were kept nearer to the coast. Table 3.5 shows the differences between the two plans.

According to the plan drawn up by Liman von Sanders, the concept of defence was based on counter-attacks by reserves held in depth. But this design needs sufficient depth to stop and drive back the enemy. In the southern part of the peninsula distances between the shores are 2.2km in Morto Cove, 5.7km in the Alçı Tepe sector, 9.8km in the Kilitbahir area and 6.9km in the Eceabat sector. When Table 3.2 and Table 3.3 are analysed, it can be seen that, from a geographical perspective, the peninsula is not a suitable battlefield for defence in depth.

When the landings started on 25 April 1915, Turkish commanders were proven right in their predictions about the landing sites. Thinking the landings in Seddülbahir and Kaba Tepe might be deception plans or demonstrations, Liman von Sanders maintained a monitoring view of the situation in Bolayır and he was therefore too late to send reinforcements to the southern part of the peninsula. A day after the landings got underway, on 26 April, 7th Division was sent to the south. In his book Liman von Sanders claims that, on that day, he understood that the landing in the Saros area was a deception and he immediately ordered the dispatch of 5th Division to the southern part of the

Table 3.5 Comparison of plans

Criteria		Liman von Sanders' plan	Turkish commanders' plan
Probable landing sites		Bolayır, Kumkale–Beşiğe	Kaba Tepe, Seddülbahir
Position where the landing would be countered		After beachhead held and inland	Before beachhead held and at the shore
Use of 19th Division		At Bigalı in order to be used in Bolayır, Kumkale or Kaba Tepe	At Eceabat in order to be used primarily in Seddülbahir or Kaba Tepe
Troop assigned to the southern part of Gallipoli Peninsula	**Shore responsibility (km)**	58.4	51.6
	Number of battalions assigned	4	6
	Number of battalions assigned per kilometre	0.07	0.12
	Average distance of reserve battalions to the first defence line battalions (km)	8.7	5.8
	Travel time of reserve battalions to the first defence line battalions (hours)	2.2	1.45
	Number of reserve bns at regiment level	1.7	0
	Relative combat power (Ottoman/Allies)	1/11	1/6

peninsula.[29] But, in fact, it was Enver Pasha who had to step in and order 5th Division to the south. Upon this order, some three days after the landings had begun, that is, on 28 April, Liman von Sanders sent 5th Division to reinforce the southern sectors.[30]

29 Liman von Sanders, Türkiye'de Beş Yıl, Cilt-1, Yeni Gün Haber Ajansı Basın ve Yayıncılık A.Ş., 1999, pp. 89–90.

30 Tim Travers, 'Liman von Sanders, the Capture of Lieutenant Palmer, and Ottoman Anticipation of the Allied Landings at Gallipoli on 25 April 1915', *The Journal of Military History*, Vol. 65, No. 4 (Oct., 2001), p. 979.

The size of the force that the Allies would use in the landings was known very accurately by Turkish intelligence. In an intelligence report dated 22 March 1915, the Military Attaché in Rome stated it had estimated that the number of Allied troops for the assault would be about 80,000.[31] On 25 April, in the Arıburnu area, the ANZACs succeeded in getting its two divisions ashore as planned.[32] In addition, by 28 April, at Seddülbahir, 86th, 87th and 88th Brigades, the Marine Division, and one French Brigade managed to get ashore, while the rest of the French Division made its landing later.[33] Therefore, by the evening of 28 April, more than 70 per cent of the landing force, numbering 75,000, close to the predicted 80,000, was engaged to the extent that they could not be used in any other area other than these two landing sites. Although the situation was thus clear, Liman von Sanders waited a whole day to send 7th Division and three days to send 5th Division. His delay cannot be attributed only to the idea that he was still expecting the landing from the isthmus region. It is not a realistic argument that Liman von Sanders could not appreciate the situation while Enver Pasha understood the situation from İstanbul. There is another explanation. Liman von Sanders perhaps designed his defence to prolong the inevitable campaign and keep as many Allied troops engaged on the Gallipoli front as possible.

At the critical moment on 25 April, Lieutenant Colonel Mustafa Kemal assessed the vulnerability of the situation, and, without waiting for orders from General Liman von Sanders, he used his initiative and reinforced the Arıburnu area with the 57th Regiment and one mountain battery at 08:00 hrs, with the 77th Regiment at 13:30 hrs and the 72nd Regiment at 16:30 hrs.[34] The deployment of the reserve is the most important tool for a commander to affect the course of battle. General Liman von Sanders' plan was based on the use of reserves when the suitable moment came. But when this moment arose, he could not communicate with 9th Division. Thus the reserve division of 5th Army was used by Lieutenant Colonel Mustafa Kemal without his knowledge. This far-sighted intervention may be considered as a deviation from the plan although it changed the course of the battle.

When the military technology of 1915 is considered, the vulnerability of the amphibious forces during the landing is evident. In the beach assault, the Allies used rowing boats carrying 36 soldiers. Four of these rowing boats were tied

31 Tim Travers, 'Liman von Sanders, the Capture of Lieutenant Palmer, and Ottoman Anticipation of the Allied Landings at Gallipoli on 25 April 1915', The Journal of Military History, Vol. 65, No. 4 (Oct., 2001), p. 971.

32 Gnkur. ATASE Bşk.lığı, Birinci Dünya Harbinde Türk Harbi, Cilt V, Çanakkale Cephesi Harekâtı, 2'nci Kitap, Gnkur. ATASE Bşk.lığı Yay., Ankara, Kroki-19.

33 Gnkur. ATASE Bşk.lığı, Birinci Dünya Harbinde Türk Harbi, Cilt V, Çanakkale Cephesi Harekâtı, 2'nci Kitap, Gnkur. ATASE Bşk.lığı Yay., Ankara, Kroki-32.

34 Gnkur. ATASE Bşk.lığı, Birinci Dünya Harbinde Türk Harbi, Cilt V, Çanakkale Cephesi Harekâtı, 2'nci Kitap, Gnkur. ATASE Bşk.lığı Yay., Ankara, pp. 109–14.

together one after another and one picquet boat towed them. But since the shores are shallow, picquet boats had to leave the rowing boats some distance from the shore. In short, in front of the Ottoman troops, positioned in trenches, there were slowly moving rowing boats fighting against crosscurrents with their 30 passengers, each of whom was encumbered with at least 30 kilogrammes of arms and equipment.[35] Liman von Sanders' idea of a weaker defence on the shores prevented the Ottoman Army from exploiting this crucial vulnerability of the Allies.

One of the reasons why Liman von Sanders wanted to keep the shore defences weak was that he wanted to protect the troops from Allied naval gun fire. But the effects of the naval guns on those soldiers waiting in their trenches were of little significance. Naval guns used high speed and low trajectory direct firing techniques, so their shells invariably did not fall on the trenches. Much of the ordnance passed overhead. In order to provide indirect fire and to make it more effective against Ottoman trenches, the ships drew further offshore but this reduced their accuracy.[36] There is no doubt that some of the firing was successful and caused casualties, especially in those areas where the slope of the terrain changed abruptly. However, thanks to the perseverance and discipline of Ottoman soldiers in not leaving their trenches, casualties were limited.[37] Liman von Sanders had already anticipated that navy gunfire would not be as effective as others assumed. Three months before the landing, on 19 February 1915, the Allied forces had bombarded Seddülbahir and Kumkale with no significant effect. This was an adequate planning factor for showing the ineffectiveness of navy fire.[38]

General Liman von Sanders foresaw that, in order to render Ottoman artillery ineffective, Allied forces would have to land at the Kumkale and isthmus areas. But, when we look at the sectors where Ottoman guns were concentrated, at the straits, it was mainly between Dardanos and Kilitbahir. In this area, there were 161 of the 230 guns that defended the straits, or, put another way, 70 per cent of the total.[39] In order to have an impact on this area, the Allied forces landing at Kumkale had to go 20km to the north, in the direction of Çanakkale. On the other hand, Allied forces landing at the isthmus zone would have had to go 50km to the south, in the direction of Eceabat. (Figure 3.7[40])

---

35 Peter Hart, *Gallipoli*, London: Profile Books, 2011, p. 142.

36 Sermet Atacanlı, *Atatürk ve Çanakkale'nin Komutanları*, MB Yayınevi, İstanbul, 2007, p. 208.

37 Peter Hart, *Gallipoli*, Profile Books: 2011, London, p. 142.

38 J.G. Hill, The Dardanelles Campaign – Lost Opportunities: An Allied Perspective, Çanakkale Savaşları, Sebep ve Sonuçları Uluslar arası Sempozyumu, XVI. Dizi, Sayı 64, Türk Tarih Kurumu Basımevi, Ankara, 1993, pp. 169–70.

39 Gnkur. ATASE Bşk.lığı, Birinci Dünya Harbinde Türk Harbi, Cilt V, Çanakkale Cephesi Harekâtı, 1'inci Kitap, Gnkur. ATASE Bşk.lığı Yay., Ankara, Kroki-11, Kroki-13.

40 Google Earth 7.1.1.1888, 2013, Gelibolu, 40°24'58"N 26°40'46"E, Göz hizası 124km, http://www.google.com/earth/index.html, (Accessed 11.11.2013).

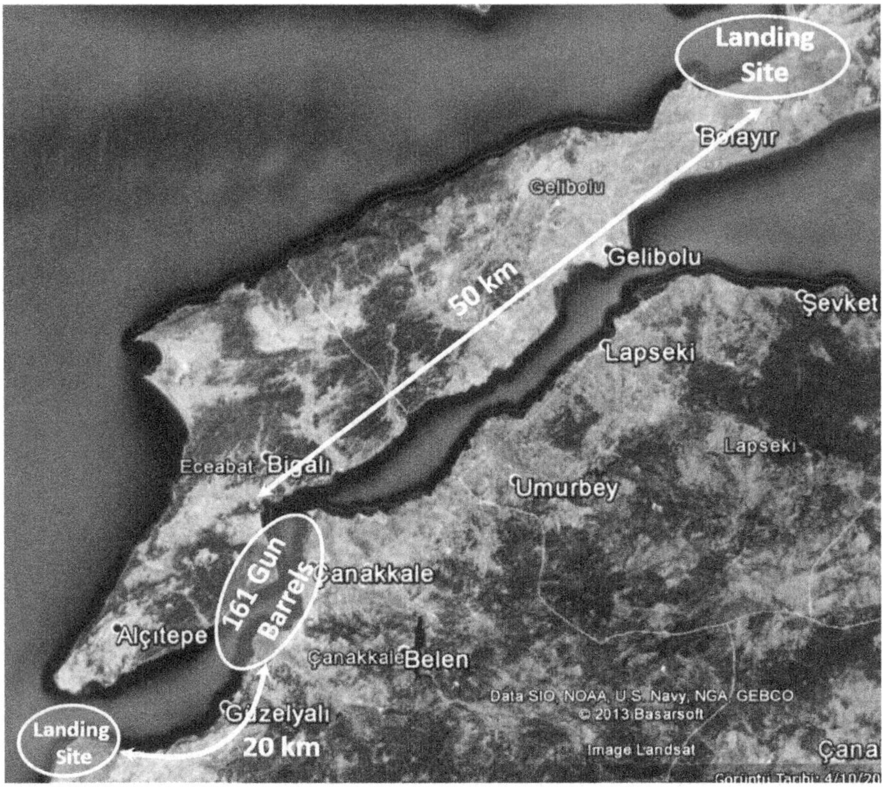

Figure 3.7 Distances to the area where Ottoman artillery was concentrated[41]

By capturing the isthmus region but without pushing to the south it does not seem possible to silence the guns that have the power to stop a naval assault through the strait. On the other hand, the possibility of driving on from the isthmus to the south would have been harder and less promising than a thrust from Seddülbahir and Kaba Tepe. By assaulting over a shorter distance, the Allies could reach the Kilitbahir Plateau where they could attack the artillery from the rear more easily. From this point of view there is no consistency between Liman von Sanders'

41 This figure was prepared by the author based on the sources below:

1 – *Birinci Dünya Harbinde Türk Harbi* (Turkish) (Genelkurmay ATASE Bşk.lığı, Cilt V, Çanakkale Cephesi Harekâtı,1'inci Kitap, Gnkur. ATASE Bşk.lığı Yay., Ankara), Kroki-11, Kroki-13.

2 – Google Earth 7.1.1.1888, 2013, Gelibolu, 40°24'58"N 26°40'46"E, Eye alt. 124km, http://www.google.com/earth/index.html, (Accessed 11.11.2013).

anxiety about Ottoman artillery being attacked from the rear and his prediction of the possible landing sites, especially in the isthmus area.

Liman von Sanders claimed that the artillery positioned on the shoreline of the strait was deployed only to be used against threats from the sea and they would be useless against land manoeuvres from the rear. This claim cannot be true because these guns were capable of directing fire to the opposite shore, and, indeed, inland. Figure 3.8[42] displays the range and the mutual support of the artillery positioned on the shoreline of the strait (Mesudiye battery: 9km; Dardanos battery: 10km; R.Hamidiye bastion, R.Mecidiye bastion, Namazgah bastion: 11km). A possible attack from Kumkale to the north or from Bolayır to the south would expose the flanks of the Allies to the fire from the artillery on the opposite shore. Furthermore, an attack from Kumkale to the north would deprive the Allies of the support of naval fire. In short, Liman von Sanders' predicted landing sites could not be a logical starting point for an attack with the objective of silencing Ottoman artillery from the rear.

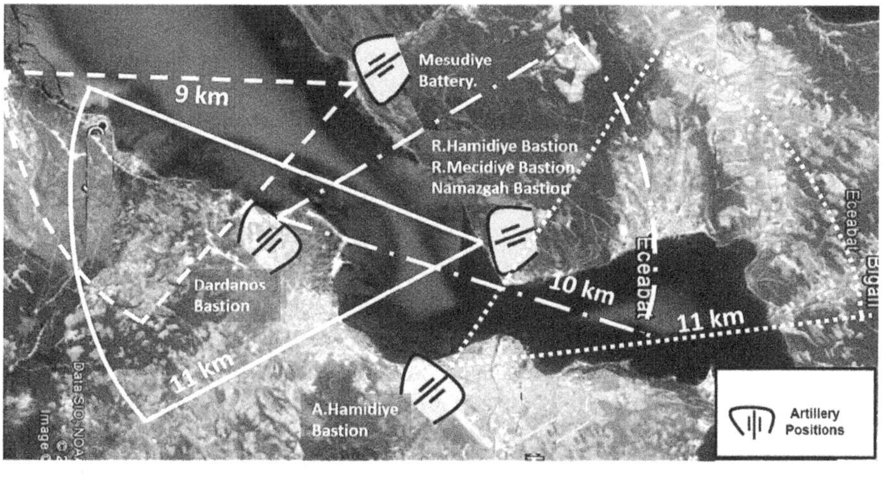

Figure 3.8 Mutual support of the Ottoman artillery positioned on the shoreline of the strait[43]

42 Google Earth 7.1.1.1888, 2013, Gelibolu,40°24'58"N 26°40'46"E, Göz hizası 45km, http://www.google.com/earth/index.html, (Accessed 11.11.2013).

43 This figure was prepared by the author based on the sources below:

1 – *Birinci Dünya Harbinde Türk Harbi* (Turkish) (Genelkurmay ATASE Bşk.lığı, Cilt V, Çanakkale Cephesi Harekâtı,1'inci Kitap, Gnkur. ATASE Bşk.lığı Yay., Ankara), Kroki-11, Kroki-10.

2 – Google Earth 7.1.1.1888, 2013, Gelibolu,40°24'58"N 26°40'46"E, Eye alt. 45km, http://www.google.com/earth/index.html, (Accessed 11.11.2013).

Liman von Sanders' defence plan did not represent a significant difference to the deployment of units at the level of division and above envisaged by the Turkish commanders. However, the deployment of the units at the level of regiment and below was changed to accord with his principle of a weak shore defence in order to confront the enemy in depth. The concept of defence was based on counter-attacking with reserves waiting inland. Yet, from a geographical perspective, the peninsula was not a suitable battlefield for a defence in depth.

At Gallipoli, in the new defence plan, the number of battalions assigned per kilometre was half that of the Turkish commanders' previous plans. Furthermore, in the new defence plan, the distances the reserves would have to cover were on average 2.9km farther than that of the old defence plan. Because of these changes, during the actual operations, counter-attacks could be launched only after the Allies had secured a beachhead rather than while they were getting ashore when they were in the most vulnerable situation. Thus, operations were transformed into a classic trench warfare stalemate, characteristic of the First World War, and this prolonged the campaign and increased casualties. Lengthening the campaign forced the Allies to commit more troops and exert more effort on the Gallipoli front, which relieved the Germans in other fronts.

Liman von Sanders was too late in dispatching troops to the southern part of the peninsula. At this point, Lieutenant Colonel Mustafa Kemal took the initiative and reinforced the Arıburnu region with the 57th Regiment without General Liman von Sanders' knowledge. This represents a diversion from the actual plan, but it was a diversion that, in fact, changed the outcome of the operations. The Ottomans won the Gallipoli Campaign by deviating from General Limon von Sanders' defence plan rather than by implementing it.

One of the key lessons learned from the Gallipoli Campaign is the importance of reflecting the impact of the terrain on operational plans and including subordinate commanders in the decision-making process. The Turkish officers were proven right in their assessment of the Allies' plan and their conduct of operations. At the heart of amphibious operations lies the challenge of shifting from a position of acute disadvantage to a level of coordinated operations. This is the most vulnerable phase of any landing operation. In the end, Liman von Sanders' plan, which was based on a weak shoreline defence, lacked the ways and means to exploit the Allies' greatest vulnerability.

Chapter 4

Taking the initiative at the tactical level in the Gallipoli Campaign and its effects

Hasan Tahsin Vanlı

As the Çanakkale Strait, south of Gallipoli, is the only waterway from the West to the Black Sea, the rivers of the Danube, Dnieper and Dniester, and the ports of Sebastopol, Odessa and İstanbul, together with the Bosphorus and Marmara Sea, it is one of the most important waterways in the world.[1] For the Entente Powers, locked in stalemate on the Western Front, it seemed possible that by knocking the Ottomans out of the war, there was a better chance to support the Russians on the Eastern Front, and, ultimately, change the course of the war. The biggest obstacle to this was the Çanakkale Strait.

In 1807 a British fleet was able to pass through Çanakkale and reach İstanbul despite the existence of local fortifications, and it was able to return from the Marmara Sea to the Aegean, in spite of tougher resistance on its return. But thanks to the developments in artillery weapons, by 1836, such eminent critics as Helmuth von Moltke could argue that no armada in the world could dare enter the Çanakkale Strait, if it was prepared properly for defence with modern artillery.[2] It is clear that the British naval commanders were aware of this situation, but the fact that the Ottoman Army was defeated so easily by the newly founded weak Balkan States, Greece, Bulgaria and Serbia, meant that everyone believed that the Ottoman Empire was not only 'the sick man of Europe' but practically a corpse waiting for post-mortem. Thus they expected little resistance from the Ottoman armed forces. After failing to get through in a purely naval operation in March 1915, the Allies decided to execute a land campaign in order to enable their fleets to pass through the Çanakkale Strait. Yet, because of the failed attempt by the French and British navies, the Allies lost the effect of surprise for their amphibious offensive, and the Ottoman Army had sufficient time for defensive preparations.

The land campaign took place primarily on the Gallipoli Peninsula on the European side with some operations on the Biga Peninsula on the Asiatic side,

---

1 Jonathan Schroden, 'A Strait Comparison: Lessons Learned from the 1915 Dardanelles Campaign in the Context of a Strait of Hormuz Closure Event', Center for Naval Analyses, p. 7.

2 Robert Rhodes James, *Gelibolu Harekâtı*, trans. Haluk V. Saltıkgil (Ankara: Belge Yayınları, 1965), p. 4.

but the decisive struggles were waged on a very narrow strip in the southern part of Gallipoli. The objective of the land campaign was not to occupy any particular place, but merely to enable the fleets to pass through the strait. They wanted to take control of Kilitbahir Plateau, located at the narrowest part of Çanakkale, destroy artillery positions both on the Asian and European sides, and finally prepare favourable conditions for the fleets to reach the Marmara Sea. To achieve their objectives the Allies preferred the shortest route. With the main landings at Helles (Seddülbahir) and Gabatepe (Kabatepe), they wanted to take control of the Kilitbahir Plateau as quickly as possible. The distance to their objective was about 20km from Helles (Seddülbahir), and eight kilometres from Gabatepe. Landing in the Seddülbahir and Gabatepe areas offered several advantages, such as naval fire support from three sides of the peninsula, shorter distances to the objective, the ability to deploy smaller forces and fewer means of transportation, and the proximity of their main logistics base on Limnos Island. On the other hand, the terrain is more suited to defence.[3] Although there are many coves and beaches for landing forces, most of them are very narrow so landing a large force in a single wave was not possible. Moreover, the narrow landing places enabled the Ottomans to defend them with a small number of troops. Even a single platoon could inflict heavy casualties on the Allies during the landings.

Liman von Sanders had calculated that, since there were so many beaches suitable for landing, his forces were not numerically strong enough to defend every beach effectively, and the naval fire support of the Allies was anticipated as sufficiently powerful to neutralise the shoreline defences. Consequently the beaches were to be defended with weak forces, while strong reserves were to be centralised and deployed from depth in order to conduct counter-attacks. Liman von Sanders regarded Saros Bay as the most threatening landing zone, since a successful landing at this point could cut the land lines of communications and isolate the Ottoman forces in the southern sector of the Gallipoli Peninsula. On the other hand, General Ian Hamilton intended to paralyse Liman von Sanders, and prevent the essential movement of the Ottoman reserves at the beginning of the operation, by landing troops on almost all the beaches suitable for landing in the south of the Gallipoli Peninsula, and at Kumkale on the Asiatic side. In addition, an amphibious demonstration was carried out to take Liman von Sanders' attention away from the main landings. At first, Hamilton managed to put Liman von Sanders in dilemma regarding the direction of the main assaults, but, because of strong resistance at Helles (Seddülbahir), Allied operations advanced slower than planned.[4]

The decisive operations at Gallipoli took place in the first 48 hours of the campaign. When faced with strong resistance, the Allies were compelled to dig

3 G.S. Patton, Jr. *The Defense of Gallipoli*, A General Staff Study, p. 10.

4 T.H.E. Travers, 'Command and Leadership Styles in the British Army: The 1915: Gallipoli Model', *Journal of Contemporary History* 29 (1994), p. 411.

trenches to hold the areas they had seized. Thus the campaign became characterised by trench warfare, one of the most significant aspects of the First World War. From this point on, the Allies waged many attacks to breach the Ottoman trenches, while the Ottoman forces carried out many counter-attacks to repel the Allies or drive them into the sea. All these attacks and counter-attacks proved to be futile, and created a casualty toll of almost 500,000 soldiers.

The opportunities and risks which might have changed the course of the operations at the Gallipoli front had emerged in the first two days of the campaign. From this perspective, it can be said that taking the initiative at the tactical level affected decisively the outcome of the operations.[5]

Examples of taking the initiative in the Ottoman Army

Collaboration of three staff officers

The Gallipoli landings started very early on 25 April with amphibious attacks by the Allies on the peninsula and at Kumkale. The Allies deployed forces appropriate for waging an amphibious offensive. With the first reports arriving at the Fifth Army headquarters, Liman von Sanders moved to the Bolayır ridges so as to be able to respond to a landing at Saros Bay. Before leaving headquarters he ordered the 7th Division to be ready to move to Saros. Although no troops landed at Saros Bay until 17:30, Liman von Sanders stayed at Bolayır. The Fifth Army headquarters had been sending hourly reports to the commander to inform him and obtain the necessary orders.[6] But, Liman von Sanders could not appreciate the overall situation, and failed to make crucial decisions, since he was not physically present at the headquarters. While there was no action at Saros Bay, violent clashes were occurring in the Seddülbahir (Helles) and Arıburnu vicinities. Several hours after the first landings in the southern sectors of the Gallipoli Peninsula, another landing was made at Kumkale by the French forces, which posed no, or very little, risk to defending troops at the Asiatic side.

Judging that the situation at Seddülbahir and the Anzac Cove was critical, Colonel Halil Sami Bey, commander of the 9th Division, requested reinforcements from Army headquarters. But Liman von Sanders failed to give clear orders to the commander of the XV Corps to reinforce this sector of III Corps' area. Rather he gave ambiguous orders to the XV Corps to send troops to Gallipoli if there was no serious landing at the Anatolian side, and if the situation was suitable.[7] General

---

5 Edward J. Erickson, 'Strength against Weakness: Ottoman Military Effectiveness at Gallipoli, 1915', *The Journal of Military History*, Cilt 65, Nu. 4 (Ekim., 2001).

6 Fikret Günesen, Çanakkale Savaşları, Kastaş Yayınları, p. 111.

7 T.C. Genelkurmay Harp Tarihi Başkanlığı, *Birinci Dünya Harbinde Türk Harbi, 5'inci Cilt, Çanakkale Cephesi, 2'nci Kitap* (Ankara: Gnkur. Basımevi, 1978), pp. 15–22.

Weber, commanding XV Corps, did not react to Liman von Sanders' orders for a long time.

Three staff officers of III Corps, XV Corps and the Fortified Area Command Headquarters appreciated the worsening situation in southern Gallipoli, and cooperated to convince the Army commander, General Liman von Sanders, to issue the required reinforcement order. Thanks to this cooperation Colonel Fahrettin (Altay), the Chief of Staff of III Corps, repeated his reinforcement requests and Lieutenant Colonel Selahattin Adil, Fortified Area Command Chief of Staff, gave priority to the communication. This ensured the messages were received promptly by Army headquarters. Moreover, Captain Nihat, G3 (Operations & Plans) of the XV Corps, sent reports to the Army headquarters stating that the XV Corps could send reinforcements and were ready to do so.[8]

Although there was no serious threat in the XV Corps' area of responsibility, and the tactical situation was suitable to transfer a divisional-sized force to Gallipoli, the failure of the Army commander to intervene in the situation encouraged these staff officers to seek an alternative solution. Although this cooperation cannot be seen as an example of seizing the initiative in the classic sense, it was thanks to their efforts that the Army commander released the necessary reinforcements. Ultimately a regiment was sent to Gallipoli from XV Corps on the afternoon of 25 April. On this occasion, Captain Nihat informed Army headquarters that XV Corps could reinforce III Corps, without authority, which implies that he appreciated the situation and was motivated purely by the crisis to take the initiative.

Commander of the 19th Division, Lieutenant Colonel Mustafa Kemal

It is well known that one of the most influential commanders in the Gallipoli Campaign, who changed the course of the operations on his own initiative, was the commander of the 19th Division, Lieutenant Colonel Mustafa Kemal. On 25 April, the Australian and New Zealand Army Corps (ANZAC) landed in the Arıburnu area, where the Ottomans had not expected any amphibious offensive. Since the area was defended with only one company, 4th Company of 2nd Battalion of the 27th Regiment of the 9th Division, the first and the second waves of landings were achieved with very little difficulty. Despite the rugged terrain, ANZAC units made rapid progress, and they took control of the first and the second ridge lines which threatened Kocaçimen Hill, one of the most valuable areas for the defending forces.

Receiving reports of the ANZAC landing at Arıburnu, Mustafa Kemal initially monitored the course of the operation in this sector. When the situation worsened, Colonel Halil Sami Bey, commander of the 9th Division, requested a battalion as reinforcement from the 19th Division. Upon receiving the request, Mustafa Kemal thought that a battalion would not be sufficient, and he dispatched the 57th

8 Ibid. pp. 66, 67.

Regiment supported with an artillery battery and a cavalry squadron. Because the ANZACs advanced towards Kocaçimen Hill, Mustafa Kemal regarded this as the main landing force, and employed the 57th Regiment to stop them without receiving an order from the Army commander.[9] When Mustafa Kemal rode in front of the 57th Regiment towards Conkbayırı to clarify the situation, he ran into a platoon withdrawing in disorder, since they were out of ammunition. He ordered the platoon to lie down and fix bayonets, which caused the ANZAC soldiers to stop. Soon afterwards ANZAC forces were repulsed at the first ridge line with the timely counter-attacks of the 57th and the 27th Regiments.[10] The ANZACs could not approach Kocaçimen Hill, the most important feature in the Arıburnu area, as close as they did on the first day of the land operations, until the end of the campaign.

In order to intervene in the situation Mustafa Kemal did not wait to receive an order from the Army commander. Taking into consideration the gravity of the situation, Mustafa Kemal dispatched the 57th Regiment immediately, and managed to re-organise the defence single-handedly. Kemal realised it might not have been possible to retake control of Kocaçimen Hill if it had been lost on the 25th. In his book, *Zabit ve Kumandan ile Hasbihal*, Mustafa Kemal later emphasised that officers should take every necessary measure to achieve the mission. He thought that a military unit cannot be regarded as an effective force unless the officers seize the initiative by themselves.[11]

According to Liman von Sanders' defence plan, it was vital to buy time required for central reserves to come up and launch their counter-attacks. The importance of winning time was due to the necessity of understanding the enemy's intention, the inadequacy of the road system, and the lack of transportation to move reserves. As noted above, Liman von Sanders could not make the crucial decisions to respond to the enemy advance since he was away from the Army headquarters. All in all, if Mustafa Kemal had waited for Liman von Sanders to send reserves, it might have been too late to repulse the ANZAC forces. He undoubtedly changed the outcome of the campaign in the first 48 hours with his foresight, initiative and courage.[12]

X Cove landing and Captain Yusuf Kenan

On 25 April, the area between 'X' and 'S' Coves, which is 3.5km long, had been defended by the 3rd Battalion of the 26th Regiment. At the start of the operation, the most violent collisions took place at Anzac Cove in the north and Seddülbahir in

---

9 Peter Hart, *Gallipoli* (London: Profile Books Ltd., 2011), p. 95.

10 Ibid. p. 98.

11 Mustafa Kemal Atatürk, *Zabit ve Kumandan ile Hasbihal* (Türkiye İş Bankası Yayınları: İstanbul: 2011), p. 18

12 İlker Başbuğ, 20. Yüzyılın En Büyük Lideri Mustafa Kemal (1881'den 1923'e), (İstanbul: Remzi Kitabevi, 2012), p. 83.

the south. Because there were not enough troops in the 3rd Battalion's area, Major Mahmut Sabri, commander of the 3rd Battalion, had to use battalion reserves to stem the enemy advance. Consequently, Mahmut Sabri requested reinforcements from the 26th Regiment. The regiment commander assigned the 7th Company to serve as the 3rd Battalion's reserve. Leaving Kirte about 06:50 hrs, 7th Company marched through Zığındere, since the closest way to Seddülbahir was open to the enemy's observation and naval fire. When the 7th Company approached X Cove, Captain Yusuf Kenan, commander of the 7th Company, saw a battalion-size enemy force advancing towards the rear of the 3rd Battalion. There were no troops to counter this enemy force emerging from X Cove. Although Kenan was ordered to be the reserve of the 3rd Battalion, taking into consideration the threat posed by the enemy to the right flank of the 3rd Battalion, he ordered his company to attack the enemy from the Kızıltoprak Ridges. The fighting lasted until evening, and, except for a small unit, which continued to advance towards Karacaoğlan Hill, 7th Company managed to fix the enemy.[13]

Thanks to Captain Yusuf Kenan's use of initiative, the 3rd Battalion secured its right flank, and continued its defence. If the enemy landing on X Beach had not been contested by the 7th Company, it could have enveloped the 3rd Battalion from its right rear, and the Allies' advance would have picked up momentum sufficient to carry it deep inland much earlier in the day.

Gözcübaba defence and Sergeant Yahya from Ezine

On the afternoon of 25 April, British forces captured Karacaoğlan Hill, and advanced towards Ay Hill with some of the troops they had landed on 'W' and 'X' Beaches. Their objective was to secure their beachhead on 'W' and 'V' landing areas by taking control of this significant high feature. While the Allies were developing their offensive towards Ay Hill, the nearby Gözcübaba Hill was being defended by a platoon made up of five squads. This platoon was being commanded by an NCO, Sergeant Yahya, since their officer had been killed. Sergeant Yahya's platoon blocked the Irish Battalion which was proceeding towards Gözcübaba Hill successfully. Realising the enemy was then approaching towards Ay Hill, Sergeant Yahya decided to intervene against the enemy with two squads while continuing to defend Gözcübaba Hill with the rest of the platoon. But, when he reached Ay Hill, it was too late to defend it. The British forces took control of this key high terrain before Sergeant Yahya arrived. Subsequently, Yahya returned and maintained the defence of Gözcübaba Hill.[14]

Although his mission ended in failure, Sergeant Yahya's decision is an example of NCOs taking the initiative in the Ottoman Army. Even a sergeant trusted himself to intervene in a situation, which was not his responsibility, but which he believed

13 Harp Tarihi Başkanlığı, *Çanakkale Cephesi, 2'nci Kitap*, pp. 243, 244.

14 Harp Tarihi Başkanlığı, *Çanakkale Cephesi, 2'nci Kitap*, p. 261.

was necessary. As mentioned before, landing beaches were defended with weak forces, and central reserves were retained for use against the most significant axes of the enemy advance. But, because central reserves could not respond to rapidly emerging threats at the beginning of the campaign, the commanders of troops defending the landing beaches had to find their own solutions to slow down the enemy assault.

3rd Battalion Commander Major Mahmut Sabri on 26 April 1915

Having failed to acquire their objectives on 25 April, the Allies planned to clear Turkish forces defending the south of Karacaoğlan Hill and Harapkale Hill, and hold the southern tip of the Gallipoli Peninsula, prior to further offensive operations. To achieve this objective, first they planned to seize Gözcübaba Hill and the village of Seddülbahir, and then make a converging attack to Harapkale Hill from the Gözcübaba feature and from Seddülbahir. The British first reinforced troops fixed in Seddülbahir, and managed to take the town after house to house fighting. When the British advanced towards Harapkale Hill, Major Mahmut Sabri sent a report to the 26th Regiment commander stating that the battalion was maintaining its defence but reinforcements were needed. The regimental commander ordered Sabri to withdraw to the second defensive line to prevent the destruction of the battalion. But Major Mahmut Sabri sent his report only requesting reinforcements, as he felt there was no risk of being destroyed by the enemy. Taking into consideration the fact that an early withdrawal would have accelerated the British advance, he did not obey the order immediately and ordered his battalion to continue defending the area. Thanks to Sabri's decision the British operation was delayed for at least six hours. On this occasion Sabri took the initiative to slow the Allies' offensive, and to forgo the opportunity to withdraw the battalion to a more secure position. Major Mahmut Sabri's role in the Gallipoli Battle was therefore very important. In the first 48 hours of the landings, he defended Seddülbahir, along a front of 3.5km, against an enemy who was much stronger than his battalion, and he responded to the threats in a timely manner.

Using initiative in the Allied Forces

According to Hamilton's plan, the most difficult part of the operation was the landing. Once the landings were achieved, he believed that the Turkish resistance would be eliminated relatively easily. Because of this, in the offensive orders given to the troops, there was almost no consideration of other developments. There were a lot of redundant details in the plans, which made them complicated.[15] Critical

15 T.H.E. Travers, ' The 1915: Gallipoli Model', p. 411.

points in the plans were not clarified, and officers in the lower echelon were not encouraged to use their initiative.[16] The British planners were apparently drowned in detail, and, with ironic humour, two British staff officers were caricatured by Orlo Williams while they were preparing landing plans.

> The first staff officer (pensive): . . . then, by approaching one on the left and one on the right, two tugboats, both of which will be towing four boats, will load the First Field Laundry, except one of the platoons, and –
>
> The second staff officer (angry): Yes, but, 29 soldiers, two hot water bottles and a wax candle would be left behind. As I said, two destroyers are necessary . . . .[17]

Although criticised in several respects, Liman von Sanders' defence plan enabled small unit commanders to use their initiative, while Hamilton's plans were very strictly controlled.[18] Since the Ottomans were not in a position to choose the ground on which to wage the decisive battle with the Allies, they preferred a more flexible approach, while the British did not need flexibility, since they felt certain of victory.

'S' Cove (Eskihisarlık Ridge) landing

Eskihisarlık Ridge (above 'S' Cove) is just the eastern part of Morto Cove controlling both the entrance of Çanakkale Strait and the Morto Cove itself. The eastern slopes of the ridge are an appropriate objective for an amphibious attack while the western slopes are more rugged and steep. The mission of the 2nd South Wales Borderers, the landing battalion, was to seize De Tott Battery, which was out of action at the time, and to hold the area until the troops landing on 'W' and 'V' beaches advanced to join them. Afterwards, they were to go on with these troops further inland.

Eskihisarlık Ridge was defended with only one platoon while the British forces attacked with a full battalion whose fire support was provided by the pre-dreadnought *Cornwallis*. However, the lack of landing vessels, and the additional equipment required, particularly ammunition, water and rations, overloaded the available boats and the added effect of the adverse current meant the operation started one and a half hours later than planned.[19]

According to the instructions of Lieutenant Colonel Hugh Casson, the commanding officer of the 2nd South Wales Borderers, two companies were to be landed on the western slopes of Eskihisarlık Ridge, while one company was

16 James, Gelibolu, p. 128.

17 Ibid., p. 128.

18 Ibid. p. 130.

19 Hart, *Gallipoli*, pp. 129–30.

sent to the intersection of Morto Cove and Çanakkale Strait. In the event, the companies landing on the western side were blocked by the effective fire of the Turkish platoon and the terrain, while the other company landed without any resistance and soon threatened the rear of this defending sub-unit.[20] The platoon commander decided to withdraw to prevent heavy casualties.

The 2nd South Wales Borderers had achieved its first objective, which was to seize De Tott Battery. Since no follow-on objective was given to the SWB, they stayed inactive on Eskihisarlık Ridge without being threatened by any Turkish troops. The British planners expected a tougher resistance at 'S' Cove (Eskihisarlık) and had predicted a longer operation.

At 'S' Cove, Colonel Casson missed the opportunity to attack the Turkish 3rd Battalion from its left and rear. If he had taken the initiative and attacked this Turkish unit, the British advance at the very south of Gallipoli might have accelerated, which, in turn, might have ended in the complete collapse of the Turkish resistance in the south.

Together with the 2,000 troops that landed on 'Y' Beach (Sarıtepe Altı), the failure to seize the initiative at 'S' Cove had a direct effect on the outcome of the Çanakkale Campaign. Due to these forces' inertia, the 3rd Battalion of the 26th Regiment was saved from being enveloped, and the Allied offensive had effectively peaked on the second day of the campaign.

'Y' Cove (Sarıtepe Altı) landing

The most threatening Allied landing for the Ottoman Army was at 'Y' Cove. British intelligence found that there were no Ottoman troops defending Sarıtepe, and, according to the offensive plans, the mission of the force was to destroy an Ottoman artillery position in the area, to draw in the Ottoman reserves, and to protect the left flank of the troops landing on 'W' and 'V' Beaches.[21]

The landings in 'Y' Cove were started about 04:45 hrs. Without any intervention, two battalions and a company (totalling 2,000 troops) landed at Sarıtepe. The landings were detected by an Ottoman observation post, made up of just four soldiers, but the British forces managed to kill two of them, and to take the others as prisoners of war.[22] The successful landing was reported to General Hunter-Weston, commander of the 29th Division, and to Hamilton. Hamilton ordered his troops here to start advancing after reinforcements had arrived. But, since there were no extra landing boats available, the naval officers were not able

20 Harp Tarihi Başkanlığı, *Çanakkale Cephesi, 2'nci Kitap*, pp. 243, 244.

21 Anthony Richards, 'Helles: The Landing on 'Y' Beach, 25 April 1915' (http://archive.iwm.org.uk/upload/package/2/gallipoli/pdf_files/YBeach.pdf, accessed 12 December 2013).

22 James, Gelibolu, pp. 173–4.

to modify the landing plan to bring extra troops to 'Y' Cove. Subsequently, this force was rather forgotten. No Ottoman troops had opposed the 'Y' Cove landing for about 11 hours but there was inaction on the Allied side. It is noteworthy that the troops that landed at 'Y' Cove were equal in number to all the Turkish troops at the south of Alçıtepe. If the British troops had attacked the settlement of Kirte, there were no Ottoman troops to oppose them there, except a reserve company of the 26th Regiment.[23] Furthermore, in these 11 hours, the Allies' forces on Sarıtepe did not prepare the area for defence. The 'Y' Beach operation ended in failure with counter-attacks of a battalion of the Ottoman 25th Regiment at about 21:00 hrs.

The landing forces at 'Y' Cove were one battalion and a company of the 29th Division, and a Royal Marine Light İnfantry Battalion. The infantry battalion was led by Lieutenant Colonel Archibald Koe, and the commander of the Royal Marine Light İnfantry Battalion was Lieutenant Colonel Godfrey Matthews. After the troops landed on the beach, the two battalion commanders had a discussion about who would command the operation. Following the landing, Lieutenant Colonel Matthews had gone up to within 500 metres of Kirte with his adjutant, but saw no Turkish troops there. Although the circumstances for an attack to cut the line of communications of the Ottoman troops deployed south of Alçıtepe was more than appropriate, Mathews and Koe failed to take the initiative, and preferred to wait, in accordance with their original orders, for those crucial 11 hours.

The Allied commanders' inability to take the initiative had a decisive effect on the course of the Çanakkale Campaign. Hamilton managed to put Liman von Sanders in a dilemma, and make landings on several unexpected beaches, but the failure to seize the initiative prevented the Allies from achieving their objectives, namely to take control of Kilitbahir Plateau. Until the end of the campaign the British never approached Kirte village as closely as Lieutenant Colonel Matthews had done that day.

Evaluation of the Allied Forces' willingness to take the initiative

The British Army commanders had not consulted any of their subordinates during the planning phases to ensure the secrecy of the operations.[24] However, they had not taken the necessary precautions to maintain the operational security of the campaign either. The letters sent to Egypt were taken there by the ordinary postal service. Daily news and predictions were taking place in the Egyptian press about the arrival of Allied forces.[25] The junior officers were not engaged in the planning process due to intelligence concerns, but that hindered their understanding of what

23 Harp Tarihi Başkanlığı, *Çanakkale Cephesi, 2'nci Kitap*, p. 245.
24 Travers, 'The 1915: Gallipoli Model', p. 420.
25 James, Gelibolu, p. 112.

the main objectives of the operations were. Unnecessary details had made the plans unnecessarily complex. Accordingly, a lack of situational awareness made it difficult for the officers in the junior ranks to use their initiative.

During the operations, one of the main problems encountered in the Allied forces was their unwillingness to use their initiative. That problem made it harder to benefit from the success that was attained.[26] The use of initiative by the junior commanders was restricted by their orders, and therefore the opportunities could not be exploited. Highly detailed orders directed the commanders to make erroneous interpretations of the operation plans.[27] While restricting the initiative of junior officers, the right orders were not issued by senior commanders to the troops when they were needed.

The main reason why the British commanders looked down on the Ottoman Army's fighting capabilities was that it was a force that had started to weaken from the beginning of the seventeenth century, and was thought to have declined irretrievably by the time of the Balkan Wars. However, when evaluating the fighting capabilities of the Ottoman Army, the British commanders had ignored its stubbornness and successes in defence, its 30-year preparation for the defence of the Çanakkale Strait and the construction of defensive works on the Gallipoli Peninsula.[28] That is why they did not make their plans with the required flexibility, and the detailed, strict orders they issued had minimised the troops' initiative.

Results of the initiative used by the Ottoman Commanders

During the Gallipoli Campaign, unlike the Allied commanders, Ottoman officers gave short and clear orders. When considering their orders it is evident that Ottoman officers never hesitated to take the initiative. For example:

> It is thought that the enemy is about to attempt to land troops between Kumkale and Yenişehir. The 39th Regiment commander, Lt Col Nurettin, will take command of all units west of Menderes. A mountain artillery battalion will come under command of 39th Regiment through Kalafatlı. Repel the enemy landing.[29]

And then:

> (0545 hrs, 25 April) 9th Division commander's order to 27th Regiment commander Lt Col Şefik:

26 G.S. Patton, Jr. *The Defense of Gallipoli*, A General Staff Study, p. 7.

27 Patton, *The Defense of Gallipoli*, p. 18.

28 Edward J. Erickson, 'Strength against Weakness: Ottoman Military Effectiveness at Gallipoli, 1915', *The Journal of Military History*, Oct 2001, pp. 65, 985.

29 Harp Tarihi Başkanlığı, *Çanakkale Cephesi, 2'nci Kitap*, p. 56.

> Enemy is landing troops between Arıburnu and Kabatepe. 27th Regiment, by taking the command of the Mountain Battalion in Çamburnu, will promptly go towards Kabatepe to repel the enemy.[30]

Issuing short and clear orders and leaving the 'how' part to the commanders encouraged the leaders in the Ottoman Army to use their initiative.

In the Ottoman Army, operational plans were also rehearsed where necessary.[31] This led to shortened time in decision-making and increased the self-confidence of commanders. Moreover, Ottoman officers managed the operation as close to the front lines as possible. Here they were able to see the threats as they emerged and had the opportunity to take precautions. This was all the more important when insufficient transportation and communication are taken into consideration.

Because of lack of sufficient forces to defend all suitable landing areas and uncertainty as to where to halt the enemy, flexibility was essential in the planning phase. According to the plan, the landing of enemy troops would first be engaged with weak forces, and then counter-attacked with strong reserves in depth. Whereas the Ottoman forces were scattered evenly nearly all over the Gallipoli and Biga peninsulas, and the reserves were not deployed appropriately, commanders in the lower echelons had used their initiative to buy time for the central reserves to intervene. From the outset, several places were neither defended, nor planned for defence, in any alternative plans. British intelligence detected these gaps successfully, and exploited them effectively. To respond to these emerging threats, from NCO to divisional commanders, most leaders in the Ottoman Army were inclined to assume responsibility and took the initiative.

Conclusions

From the platoon level upwards, Turkish commanders did not refrain from taking the initiative and assuming responsibility during the campaign. The most important example of the use of initiative in the Ottoman Army was Lieutenant Colonel Mustafa Kemal's intervention against the ANZAC advance in Arıburnu, without waiting for the Army commander's order. The reasons for this effective seizing of the initiative by the Turkish commanders were that: Liman von Sanders' flexible defence concept necessitated the use of initiative below divisional level; it was an obligation of the commanders of troops defending the beaches to buy time for the reserves to make their counter-attacks; the preparations of the Ottoman Army for defence were of a high standard; commanders and soldiers were well trained, and they possessed self-confidence; and short and clear orders were given to subordinates during the execution of the operations.

30 Ibid. p. 101.

31 Erickson, 'Ottoman Military Effectiveness at Gallipoli', p. 1000.

The Allies had the opportunity to eliminate the Ottoman defences with the forces that landed on 'X', 'Y' and 'S' beaches to the south of Alçıtepe. The British leaders predicted that operations at 'W' and 'V' would develop faster, but they provided little or no freedom of action to subordinate commanders at 'S', 'Y' and 'X' to exploit probable quick successes. The lethargy of forces on these beaches enabled the Turkish forces to hold their positions. The explanation of the lack of initiative in the Allied forces can be summarised thus: extremely detailed and binding orders made it difficult for officers to act on their initiative; probable failures or unexpected achievements were not included in the plans; subordinates were not included in the planning process; and planning and execution were too centralised.

The ability to take the initiative was not the only factor contributing to the outcome of the Gallipoli Campaign. For sure, one can count many reasons which affected the course and outcome of the battles there. Nevertheless, there were opportunities for the Allies to change the course of the fighting in the first 48 hours of the campaign, but the British leaders signally failed to use their initiative after their initial rapid successes.

Chapter 5

Ottoman defences and Allied naval operations in the Çanakkale Straits

Hilmi Kendircioğlu

By reviewing events between August 1914 and 22 March 1915, it is possible to determine why the Allied naval operations against the Çanakkale Straits failed. An analysis can reveal the mistakes made at the strategic and operational level, particularly the misplaced centre of gravity and importance of the enduring principles of war.

The evolution of the idea of the Çanakkale Strait Campaign[1]

On 3 November 1914, British and French fleets patrolling off the Çanakkale bombarded the outer defences of the Strait, namely the Seddülbahir and Kumkale forts, for 20 minutes without receiving any counter-fire from the Turkish side, two days before the formal declaration of war by the British.[2]

The naval bombardment was part of a more general conception of an offensive through the Çanakkale Strait. On 19 August 1914, Greece proposed the idea of conducting a campaign against Çanakkale and invited Great Britain to contribute troops for a combined operation.[3] Winston Churchill, the First Lord of the Admiralty, and Lord Kitchener, Minister of War, discussed the Greek plan on 31 August 1914. The next day, Churchill ordered the Army Staff to study a plan that combined a naval assault with a synchronised amphibious landing. Two days later, General Callwell, Operations Director of the Army Staff, presented a report. In it there was an assumption that the Ottomans had 27,000 soldiers on the peninsula, so at least 60,000 soldiers, including a Russian Corps, would be needed to occupy Gallipoli. General Callwell also stated that such an operation would be a great challenge for the Allied powers.[4] However, this operational plan was abandoned a few days later when Greece announced that they would not send troops to Gallipoli without an Ottoman assault directed against Greece.

---

1 Alan Moorehead, *Çanakkale Geçilmez*, Milliyet Yayınları, Mart 1972, p. 38.

2 Nigel Steel, Peter Hart, *Gelibolu Yenilginin Destanı*, Sabah Kitapları, İstanbul, 1996, p. 5.

3 Ibid., p. 1.

4 Robert Rhodes James, *Gelibolu Harekâtı*, Belge Yayınları, İstanbul, 1965, p. 15.

Five months later, on 2 January 1915, Grand Duke Nicholas, the Commander in Chief of the Russian Army, concerned by the possibility of Ottoman success in Sarıkamış, asked Lord Kitchener whether a demonstration could be conducted to compel the Ottomans to withdraw troops from the Caucasus.[5]

Sir John Fisher, the First Sea Lord of the Royal Navy, offered a detailed campaign plan on 3 January 1915 whereby 75,000 British and Indian troops in Egypt, under the pretext of going on to the Western Front in France, would land at Beşiğe bay.[6] The Greeks would advance on Gallipoli; the Bulgarians would march towards Edirne, while Romanians, Russians and Serbians would assault Austria–Hungary.[7] While army operations were underway, a fleet, consisting of mainly obsolete vessels, would force through Çanakkale.

Because the British Minister of War and French officials firmly opposed withdrawing troops from the Western Front, Fisher's plan had to be shelved. Nevertheless, regardless of the Western Allies' decision, there was no way that Greece, Bulgaria and the other Balkan countries could take part in such a campaign in 1914.[8]

Without deploying any troops on the Gallipoli peninsula, Churchill thought about making a purely naval assault: forcing Çanakkale with old British armoured ships, thereby offering assistance to Russia by compelling the Ottomans to withdraw troops from the Caucasus.[9] At the end of long negotiations, it appeared to be the most viable option. Opponents asserted that passing through Çanakkale only with an armed fleet was no more than a fantasy. They insisted on a synchronised amphibious landing. On 3 January, Churchill sent a message to the commander of the fleet waiting off Çanakkale, under the command of Admiral Carden. He asked whether he thought it possible to force Çanakkale with a fleet consisting of obsolete ships and minesweepers. Due to the importance of the outcome, Churchill admitted such an operation would risk heavy casualties. On 5 January, Carden replied: 'I do not think we can rush through Çanakkale. But, if we deploy enough war ships and bombard all the batteries step by step, it is possible.'[10]

To make a decision about the Çanakkale Campaign, the British War Cabinet gathered on 13 January. Churchill, leading the discussions in the meeting, had great influence over the decision taken. Because no troops would land on Gallipoli, Lord Kitchener agreed to the Çanakkale naval operations without strong opposition. At the end of the meeting it was agreed that 'the Cabinet would support the plan and the navy would pass through the Straits by naval bombardment and occupy a position off İstanbul by February'.[11] The fleet consisting of British and French

---

5 Hanri Benazus, *Çanakkale'den Gelibolu'ya*, Bizim Kitaplar, İstanbul, 2007, p. 74.

6 Nigel Steel, Peter Hart, *Gelibolu Yenilginin Destanı*, 1996, p. 7.

7 Ibid., p. 7.

8 Ibid., p. 7.

9 Ibid., p. 7.

10 Alan Moorehead, *Çanakkale Geçilmez*, 1972, p. 47.

11 Ibid., p. 50.

warships gathered in Limnos.[12] Admiral Carden, who was the commander of the fleet based in Malta, was assigned to command the naval assault on the Çanakkale Strait.

The naval operation to break through the Çanakkale Strait and the Ottoman defences

Before the bombardment on 3 November, the defences of the Çanakkale Strait were weak and neglected.[13] Most of the fortifications and artillery positions along the Çanakkale Strait had been constructed by French and English engineers during the 1877–78 war.[14] After the outbreak of the First World War, two minefields were laid in the waterway of the Çanakkale Strait on 4–5 August 1914.[15] The Ottomans' 9th Division, commanded by Colonel Cevat Bey, including two artillery regiments, deployed on both sides of the strait. The coastal batteries consisted of as many as 100 guns, most of which had limited firing angles, but with a range of 7,500 to 9,600m.[16] Nevertheless, there were only four forts, on both sides of the entrance of the strait, and here only four of 20 guns were active. On 10 August, Cevat Bey was assigned as the commander of the Çanakkale Fortified Zone Command, and charged with its development.

To confirm the intelligence about the straits' fortifications and to test the capabilities of the Allied ships against Turkish forts, Churchill ordered the bombardment of the entrance to the strait, regardless of the warnings of the experienced Mediterranean naval officer Rear-Admiral Arthur Henry Limpus.[17] On 3 November, at 06:45am, six British ships bombarded Seddülbahir and Kumkale.[18] The result of the bombardment was better than they had expected. The weak fortifications were destroyed. An ammunition store exploded when an artillery round scored a direct hit on Seddülbahir. Almost all artillery batteries and forts in the vicinity of the explosion were destroyed. Coastal batteries tried to respond, but due to their short range, all their rounds fell into the sea. There was dense smoke on both sides of the Çanakkale straits when the British turned back without any casualties.[19]

---

12 Ibid., p. 51.

13 Ibid., p. 53.

14 Maurice Larcher, Mehmed Emin Bey, Murat Çulcu, *Çanakkale 1915-Boğaz Harekâtı*, E Yayınları, İstanbul, 2008, p. 48.

15 Ibid., p. 53.

16 Ibid., p. 49.

17 General C.F. Aspinall-Oglander, *Büyük Harbin Tarihi: Çanakkale Gelibolu Askeri Harekâtı I.Cilt*, 2005, p. 67.

18 T.C. Başbakınlık Devlet Arşivleri Genel Müdürlüğü, Osmanlı Belgelerinde Çanakkale Muharebeleri-I, Başbakanlık Basımevi, Ankara, 2005, p. 9.

19 Robert Rhodes James, *Gelibolu Harekâtı*, 1965, p. 19.

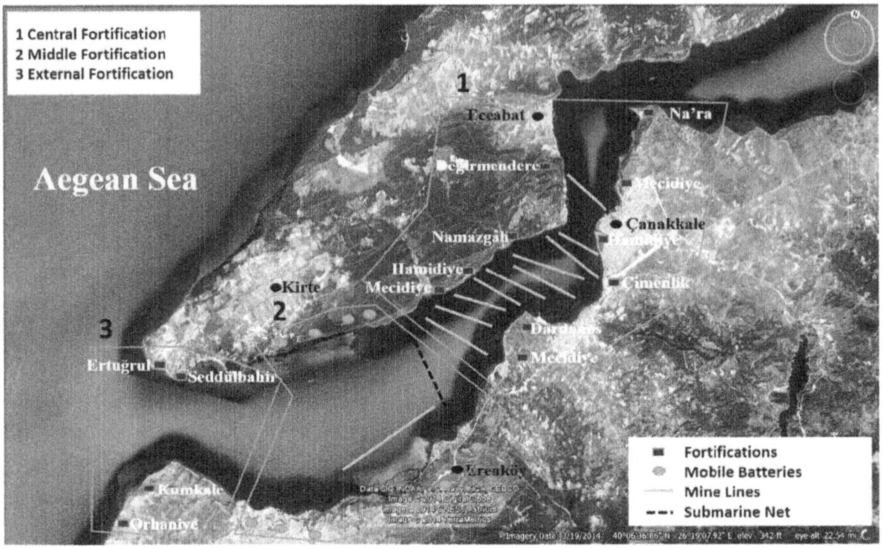

Figure 5.1 Defence composition of the Çanakkale Fortified Zone Command[20]

Six weeks before the first major coordinated naval attack, the bombardment that November revealed the weakness of the Turkish fortifications. Having enough time to restructure their defences, Ottoman and German officials reinforced their fortifications by laying mines and placing new mobile and stationary batteries on the coasts.

By 18 March, the Çanakkale Fortified Zone consisted of three main parts: external, intermediate, and central defences (see Figure 5.1). External defences comprised the Kumkale, Orhaniye, Seddülbahir, and Ertuğrul forts. Intermediate defences, including the 11th mine line, laid parallel along the coast, and mobile

20 This figure was prepared by the author based on the source below:

1 – Şemsettin Bargut, Birinci Dünya Harbi'nde ve Kurtuluş Savaşı'nda Türk Deniz Harekâtı (Turkish), (Deniz Kuvvetleri K.lığı Basımevi, Ankara, 2000) p. 21

2 – Çanakkale Boğaz Komutanlığı, Çanakkale Deniz Savaşları 1915, Kültür Yayınları Tarih Dizisi No:51 (Turkish) (Deniz Basımevi Müdürlüğü, İstanbul, 2004) p. 86

3 – Alan Moorehead, Çanakkale Geçilmez, 1972, p. 97

4 – Google Earth 7.1.1.1888, 2013, Gelibolu,40°06'36"N 26°19'07"E, Eye alt. 22.54km, http://www.google.com/earth/index.html (Accessed 21.07.2014)

5 – Peter Doyle and Matthew R. Bennett, 'Military Geography: The Influence of Terrain in the Outcome of the Gallipoli Campaign, 1915', The Geographical Journal, Vol. 165, No. 1 (Mar., 1999), p. 13, published by: The Royal Geographical Society (with the Institute of British Geographers), http://www.jstor.org/stable/3060508 (Accessed: 25.09.2013).

batteries positioned on both sides, began at the entrance and ended at the Kepez Horn. The inner defences were the main part of the system, including 10 lines of mines and forts, from south to north, at Mesudiye, Dardanos, Çimenlik, Hamidiye, Mecidiye, Nara on Anatolian coasts, and Mecidiye, Hamidiye, Namazgah and Değirmendere on the Gallipoli coasts. Iron nets were laid between the intermediate and inner defences to close the waterway to submarines.

Some 403 mines had been laid down in 11 lines by 18 March 1915.[21] However, according to the diary of the Mine Group Commander, Captain Nazmi Bey, 30 to 35 of those mines had been either washed ashore or collected after having surfaced.[22] Most of the mines in the strait were old and were laid down with wide 80–90-m intervals.[23]

Mobile batteries had been positioned on both sides to complement the fixed batteries but also to protect mines from getting cleared by minesweepers. Searchlights were placed to detect the manoeuvres of enemy ships during darkness. Dummy batteries emitting black fumes were placed on both coasts.[24] Some batteries were located on top of the hills for further deception. By binding tubes to the muzzles of guns, the Ottomans had found a primitive but effective method for misleading Allied warships about the real calibres of the batteries.[25]

Table 5.1 Batteries in external defences/mobile batteries in the intermediate defences[26]

External defence batteries			Mobile batteries		
Battery	**Gun Calibre**	**Quantity**	**Calibre**	**Quantity**	**Type**
Seddülbahir	24/22	2	15cm	24	Howitzer
	26/22	2	12cm	8	Mountain Howitzer
	28/22	2	21cm	10	Mortar
Kumkale	26/22	2			
	28/22	4			
Ertuğrul	24/35	2			
Orhaniye	24/35	2			

21 Şemsettin Bargut, *Birinci Dünya Harbi'nde ve Kurtuluş Savaşı'nda Türk Deniz Harekâtı*, Deniz Kuvvetleri K.lığı Basımevi, Ankara, 2000, p. 21.

22 Çanakkale Boğaz Komutanlığı, *Çanakkale Deniz Savaşları 1915*, Kültür Yayınları Tarih Dizisi No: 51, Deniz Basımevi Müdürlüğü, İstanbul, 2004, p. 86.

23 Alan Moorehead, *Çanakkale Geçilmez*, 1972, p. 97.

24 Nigel Steel, Peter Hart, *Gelibolu Yenilginin Destanı*, 1996, p. 10.

25 Alan Moorehead, *Çanakkale Geçilmez*, 1972, p. 99.

26 Çanakkale Boğaz Komutanlığı, *Çanakkale Deniz Savaşları 1915*, Kültür Yayınları Tarih Dizisi No: 51, Deniz Basımevi Müdürlüğü, İstanbul, 2004, p. 105.

Table 5.2 Batteries of the intermediate fortification[27]

Batteries of the intermediate fortification					
Battery	**Gun Calibre**	**Quantity**	**Battery**	**Gun Calibre**	**Quantity**
Rumeli	24/25	4	Anadolu	24/35	7
Mecidiye	28/25	2	Hamidiye	35.5/35	2
Namazgah	21/22	5	Çimenlik	21/22	1
	24/22	7		24/22	1
	24/35	2		35.5/22	1
	28/22	2		35.5/35	1
Rumeli	35.5/35	2	Anadolu	21/22	1
Hamidiye			Mecidiye	24/22	3
				26/22	3
				28/22	2
Değirmendere	21/22	1	Nara	26/22	1
	24/22	6		24/22	6

The plan and the execution of the Allied naval attack

In order to destroy fortifications and suppress the coastal batteries, the naval attack was to be executed in three phases: a long-range bombardment, followed by a medium-range barrage, and, ultimately, a devastating short-range cannonade. (Figure 5.1) With the help of this heavy fire, minesweepers would clear mines on the entrance of the strait.[28] The Allied navy had 247 heavy and light guns, including eight of the biggest 15-inch howitzers of the *Queen Elizabeth* with a range 21,385m. On the other side, the external defences of the Ottoman system consisted of 19 guns, only four of which were new, and these guns had a range of 5,500–7,400m.[29]

On 19 February 1915, after a heavy bombardment lasting from dawn until 14:00 hrs, Admiral Carden ordered his vessels to get as close as 6,000m to the Turkish shore. There was no fire from the Turkish side. Nevertheless, due to their visible silhouette, his ships could be easily targeted, so Admiral Carden ordered the withdrawal of the fleet at sunset. The results of the day were not satisfactory. Moreover, the weather deteriorated that night, with storms, snowfall and biting cold over the next five days. The storm ceased on 25 February 1915 and a second attack was carried out near the entrance of the strait. However, in the following days, the weather again worsened.

On 2 March 1915, Admiral Carden reported to London in his telegraph that, weather permitting, they would be in İstanbul within 14 days.[30] However, the

27 Ibid., p. 105.

28 Alan Moorehead, *Çanakkale Geçilmez*, 1972, p. 69.

29 General C.F.Aspinall-Oglander, *Büyük Harbin Tarihi: Çanakkale Gelibolu Askeri Harekâtı I.Cilt*, 2005, p. 106.

30 Alan Moorehead, *Çanakkale Geçilmez,* 1972, p. 71.

weather worsened again on 8 March 1915, and minesweeping operations continued intermittently until 13 March. Due to unfavourable weather conditions and the inexperienced civilian crews, the minesweepers couldn't achieve the desired results. The inexperienced civilian crewmen were therefore replaced with volunteer sailors from the warships. Despite continuing bad weather conditions and heavy artillery fire from the shore, many mines were eventually cleared.

The nearest forts were supposed to be destroyed in the days of 17–18 March 1915.[31] In spite of Admiral Carden's commitment to reach İstanbul in 14 days, operations were not proceeding as quickly as planned. In addition to the political pressure from London, the stress of delayed minesweeping operations and adverse meteorological conditions caused Admiral Carden to fall ill. He was perhaps suffering from a nervous condition. Although it would mean ending his military career, Admiral Carden asked for his dismissal from the command of the fleet on 15 March.[32] Just 48 hours before the main assault, a new commander therefore had to be found for the fleet. Admiral Wemyss, the most senior commander in the region, demanded his exemption in favour of Vice-Admiral de Robeck who had been the deputy commander under Admiral Carden from the beginning of operations. On 17 March 1915, Churchill approved de Robeck's appointment and ordered operations to continue without interruption. Admiral de Robeck reported to London that the attack would indeed be carried out on 18 March as planned.[33]

The naval battle of 18 March 1915

Regardless of the artillery batteries and forts emplaced ashore, endeavouring to pass the Çanakkale Strait with only warships was an example of asymmetrical warfare. The whole action would take place on a one-mile (1.6km) wide and a five-mile (8km) long expanse of water.[34] According to the plan, de Robeck would position the fleet in three waves. British warships *Queen Elizabeth, Agamemnon, Lord Nelson* and *Inflexible* in line 'A' would advance in formation side by side; and two ships, *Prince George* and *Triumph,* would accompany them on the flanks of line 'A'. The French warships, *Gaulois, Charlemagne, Bouvet* and *Suffren* in line 'B', would follow one mile (1.6 km) behind 'A'; and two British warships, *Majestic* and *Swiftsure,* would be on the flanks of 'B'. Six warships in the third line, 'C', consisting of minesweepers and destroyers, would be waiting outside of the strait. After emplacements on both sides had been crushed by heavy bombardment, minesweepers would clear the whole strait and the way to İstanbul would be opened for Allied forces.[35]

At 10:30 am, warships on lines 'A' and 'B' entered the strait and around at 11:25 am the bombardment commenced from positions eight miles (12 km) out. *Queen Elizabeth*

31 Ibid., p. 75.
32 Ibid., p. 77.
33 Ibid., p. 78.
34 Ibid., p. 79.
35 Ibid., p. 80.

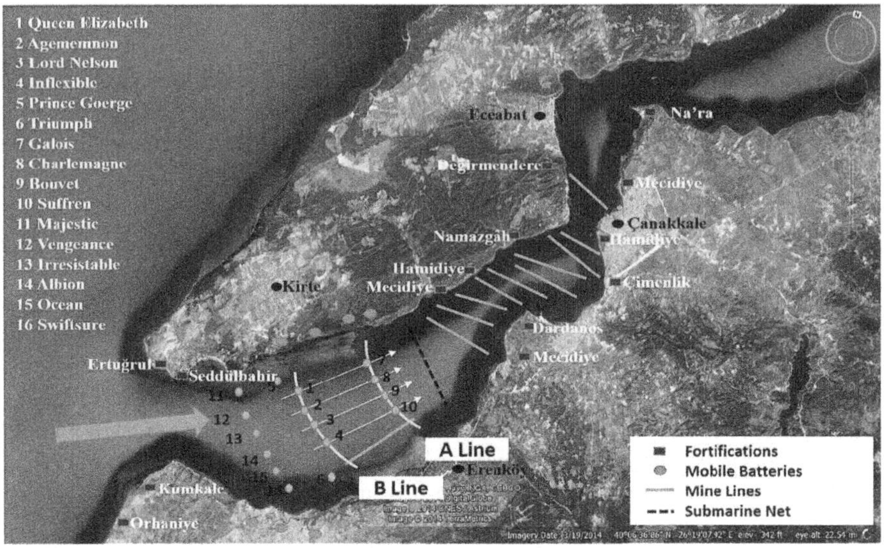

Figure 5.2 The Allied naval assault 18 March[36]

targeted the emplacements on both sides of Çanakkale. *Agamemnon, Lord Nelson* and *Inflexible* started shelling targets on Kilitbahir. Since the Allied fleet was still out of effective range, Turkish coastal artillery stopped firing after a couple of rounds. Exactly at noon, de Robeck ordered the French fleet in line 'B', under the command of Admiral Guepratta, to move half a mile ahead of 'A' line. A terrible exchange of fire then continued for more than 45 minutes. *Gaulois* was hit below sea level; *Inflexible* and *Agamemnon* were hit several times by Ottoman artillery. Nevertheless, casualties in the entire fleet's crew were no more than a dozen.

On the Ottoman side, many batteries were buried, communication lines and fire control networks were destroyed, some of the guns were jammed and morale among the artillerymen began to sink. After two and a half hours of resistance, the fire of the coastal artillery had stopped completely, at around 13:45. Interpreting this to mean that Ottoman emplacements and artillery were now suppressed, de Robeck ordered the withdrawal of the French fleet and other warships on line 'B'. There seemed to be no obstacle to impede the success of the minesweepers.[37]

The French ships *Suffren* and *Bouvet* manoeuvred to withdraw. Following the Erenköy coasts and while passing by the *Queen Elizabeth* in line A, *Bouvet* was suddenly shattered by a great explosion: it immediately burst into flames and tilted

36 This figure was prepared by the author based on the source below:

1 – Alan Moorehead, Çanakkale Geçilmez, 1972, p. 80

2 – Google Earth 7.1.1.1888, 2013, Gelibolu,40°06'36"N 26°19'07"E, Eye alt. 22.54km, http://www.google.com/earth/index.html (Accessed 21.07.2014).

37 Ibid., p. 82.

down. In a few seconds, *Bouvet* sank with 639 crewmen and disappeared. An officer who witnessed this tragedy noted that, 'just like a dish slides and sinks in the water, *Bouvet* sank and disappeared in seconds'.[38]

Heartened by the disappearance of *Bouvet*, Ottoman gunners responded to the Allied bombardment for a further two hours until 16:00. Then all the batteries were effectively silenced again. Admiral de Robeck ordered the minesweepers to fulfil their mission, but there was something of a panic among the inexperienced civilian crew. As soon as they encountered heavy artillery fire, all four minesweepers turned back and rushed out of the strait.[39]

At 16:11 in the same location where *Bouvet* sank, *Inflexible*, keeping her position in line 'A', hit a mine and sank down on her right side. It immediately abandoned its position and headed towards Bozcaada. No sooner had *Inflexible* left line 'A' than *Irresistible*, the nearest ship to the coast on the right side of line 'A', hit another mine and 610 crewmen were evacuated.[40]

At 17:00, three battleships were out of the action: *Bouvet* sank, *Inflexible* was severely damaged and *Irresistible* was abandoned and drifting towards the coast. Realising that nothing more could be done, Admiral de Robeck ordered the withdrawal of the Allied fleet. Except for the attempt by *Ocean* and *Swiftsure*, commanded by Commodore Keyes, to rescue *Irresistible*, the Allied fleet withdrew out of the Çanakkale Strait. Under heavy artillery fire, *Ocean* and *Swiftsure* couldn't manage to rescue *Irresistible*. Commodore Keyes offered to attempt another rescue operation after midnight.

By 17:30 the Rumeli Hamidiye bastion had been hit several times and there were 14 killed and 24 wounded. Sergeant Seyit, one of the greatest heroic characters of the Çanakkale Campaign on the Turkish side, lifted rounds of a 24/35mm gun, which was estimated to weigh between 140 and 215 kilograms.[41] With the help of his friend Ali, Seyit loaded the gun himself and aimed at *Ocean*. *Ocean* was hit and her steering damaged.[42] Unable to manoeuvre, *Ocean* hit a mine at 18:05 and a horrifying explosion shook the sea. In seconds *Ocean* was crippled and was abandoned at 19:30.[43] *Irresistible* and *Ocean* sank a few hours later. Keyes, who would be assigned as commander of British Naval Forces, recalls in his memoirs that: 'In the afternoon at 14:00, I had a firm belief that the enemy was defeated. At 16:00, I believed that I was defeated, and at midnight I had a firm belief that I *was* defeated.'[44]

38 Ibid., p. 83.

39 Çanakkale Boğaz Komutanlığı, *Çanakkale Deniz Savaşları 1915*, Kültür Yayınları Tarih Dizisi No: 51, Deniz Basımevi Müdürlüğü, İstanbul, 2004, p. 99.

40 Hanri Benazus, *Çanakkale'den Gelibolu'ya*, 2007, p. 129.

41 Gürsel Göncü, Şahin Aldoğan, *Çanakkale Muharebe Alanları Gezi Rehberi, MB Yayınevi*, İstanbul, 2006, p. 155.

42 Fikret Günesen, *Çanakkale Savaşları*, Kastaş Yayınları, İstanbul, 1986, p. 80.

43 Çanakkale Boğaz Komutanlığı, *Çanakkale Deniz Savaşları 1915*, Kültür Yayınları Tarih Dizisi No: 51, Deniz Basımevi Müdürlüğü, İstanbul, 2004, p. 131.

44 Alan Moorehead, *Çanakkale Geçilmez*, 1972, p. 89.

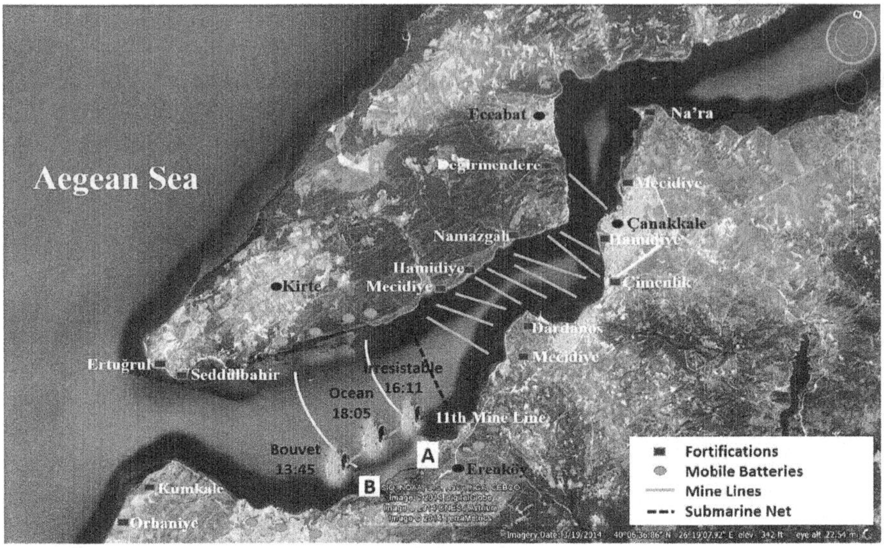

Figure 5.3 Allied armoured ships hitting the 11th mine line[45]

At night, on 18 March 1915, de Robeck and Keyes decided to re-organise the fleet and embark on a new attack. The fleet was harboured in Bozcaada. The weather was bad and the wind was getting stronger. It was determined that civilian crewmen on the minesweepers would be sent home and new crew would be selected among volunteers. On the morning of 19 March, the British Admiralty insisted on sustaining the attacks and informed the fleet that lost ships would be compensated by British ships *Queen*, *Implacable*, *London*, *Prince of Wales*, and the French ship *Henri IV*.[46]

General Ian Hamilton, Commander of the Mediterranean Expeditionary Force, arrived at Limnos in the evening of 17 March 1915. Five days later, Admiral de Robeck met General Hamilton. Before the meeting, Admiral de Robeck was determined to launch another naval attack, but, after the meeting, his ideas

---

45 This figure was prepared by the author based on the source below:

1 – Alan Moorehead, *Çanakkale Geçilmez*, 1972, p. 82

2 – Çanakkale Boğaz Komutanlığı, *Çanakkale Deniz Savaşları 1915*, Kültür Yayınları Tarih Dizisi No: 51, Deniz Basımevi Müdürlüğü, İstanbul, 2004, p. 99

3 – Hanri Benazus, *Çanakkale'den Gelibolu'ya*, 2007, p. 129

4 – Çanakkale Boğaz Komutanlığı, *Çanakkale Deniz Savaşları 1915*, Kültür Yayınları Tarih Dizisi No: 51, Deniz Basımevi Müdürlüğü, İstanbul, 2004, p. 131

5 – Google Earth 7.1.1.1888, 2013, Gelibolu,40°06'36"N 26°19'07"E, Eye alt. 22.54km, http://www.google.com/earth/index.html (Accessed 10.12.2013).

46 Ibid., p. 110.

Table 5.3 Casualties of Allied fleet on the night of 18 March 1915

Flotilla 1	Flotilla 2	Flotilla 3	Additional
Queen Elizabeth	*Vengeance*	*Suffren* (crippled)	*Lord Nelson*
Agamemnon (crippled)	*Albion*	*Gaulois* (crippled)	*Swiftsure*
Inflexible (crippled)	*Cornwallis*	*Charlemagne*	*Majestic*
Ocean (sunk)	*Irresistible* (sunk)	*Bouvet* (sunk)	
	Triumph		

completely changed. De Robeck was no longer sure that he would pass through the strait with his fleet.[47] General Hamilton stated in his memoirs that; 'As soon as the meeting started, de Robeck expressed that it wouldn't be easy to pass through the strait without a synchronised army landing. In fact, before boarding the ship, I, Birdwood and Braithwaite had decided not to interfere with the ideas of the Admirals. Then the navy asked for help and it was [thus] out of duty from now on [for us to act] . . . . '[48] After this meeting, the naval offensive did not resume.

Why did Allied forces lose the naval battle?

Ignorance of the historical facts

In 1807, Admiral Duckworth of the Royal Navy had passed through the Çanakkale Strait with his fleet in the teeth of resistance but had barely managed to make the return passage. In 1836 General Moltke stated that: 'If the artillery batteries and their fortifications were properly arranged, no fleet in the world would dare to traverse the straits.'[49] Admiral Sir Geoffrey Phipps Hornby, Commander of the British Fleet charged with preventing Russian attacks against İstanbul and the Bosphorus in the Russo-Ottoman War (1877–78), noted that Çanakkale could be passed without much effort, but he also asserted that, if both sides of the channel were held by an enemy, no fleet in the world could keep the straits open for unarmed commercial ships.[50]

Lord Fisher, who had rigorously objected to the naval assault through the Çanakkale Straits in 1914–15, had served in the same fleet as Admiral Hornby

47 Ibid., p. 112.

48 Ibid., p. 113.

49 Robert Rhodes James, Tercüme eden: Haluk V. Saltıkgil, *Gelibolu Harekâtı*, 1965, p. 4.

50 General C.F. Aspinall-Oglander, *Büyük Harbin Tarihi: Çanakkale Gelibolu Askeri Harekâtı I.Cilt*, 2005, p. 47.

in the 1877–78 naval campaign. As First Sea Lord and Commander of the Mediterranean Expeditionary Fleet in 1904, Fisher had examined the question of passing through the straits when opposed and decided it was 'too risky'. In 1906, he reiterated his observations in the most detailed study ever made about the Çanakkale Straits. In the report it was noted that: 'even if the oldest and least expensive ships of His Majesty's Navy are to be used in this operation, Britain should avoid such an endeavour.'[51]

In spite of these historical reports and warnings, Churchill, in his comments during the War Council meeting of 25 November 1914, stated that: 'we all know that Ottoman Empire is weak, and this was proved in the Balkan Wars. Our Navy can capture the Dardanelles in the first strike. When our ships show up off the Topkapı Palace, this "Sick Man" will immediately surrender.'[52]

Mistakes made in the study of the operating environment: terrain

The Çanakkale Strait is approximately 85km in length. The width of the entrance of the strait is 3,657m. It broadens considerably in the Erenköy region, then suddenly narrows after Erenköy, and reaches the narrowest point between the Kilitbahir and Çanakkale region at which it is just 1,463m wide.[53] The first 21km of the strait from the entrance requires the most attention for a military operation. Both coasts of the strait are steep-sided.[54]

The water in the strait flows towards the Marmara at the bottom but flows strongly towards the Aegean at 9.2km per hour in the upper part. Geographic features of the strait therefore favour the defender and make it harder for the maritime attacker.[55] With intelligence about the characteristic features of the strait, the Allies employed trawlers as minesweepers through the narrow waterway. However, these trawlers had engines of insufficient power to overcome the strong water flow which greatly slowed the speed at which they could sweep mines. Civilian crewmen couldn't endure the artillery fire coming from the upper parts of both sides of the narrows, and therefore panicked and quickly headed out of the strait.

Weather

The naval bombardment started on 19 February 1915, and, in order to get the best results, it should have been continued without interruption. But for the next

51 Robert Rhodes James, *Gelibolu Harekâtı*, 1965, p. 5.

52 Hanri Benazus, *Çanakkale'den Gelibolu'ya*, 2007, p. 70.

53 Robert Rhodes James, *Gelibolu Harekâtı*, 1965, p. 1.

54 Kur.Alb.İ.Özbay, Dr.Öğr.Alb.Z.Türkmen, Hv.Öğ.Yzb.F.R.Ünalp, Uzm.A.Çalışkan, *Harp Tarihi Gezileri-II (Gelibolu-Çanakkale)*, Genelkurmay Askeri Tarih ve Stratejik Etüd Başkanlığı, Ankara Genelkurmay Basımevi, 2010, p. 4.

55 Robert Rhodes James, *Gelibolu Harekâtı*, 1965, p. 2.

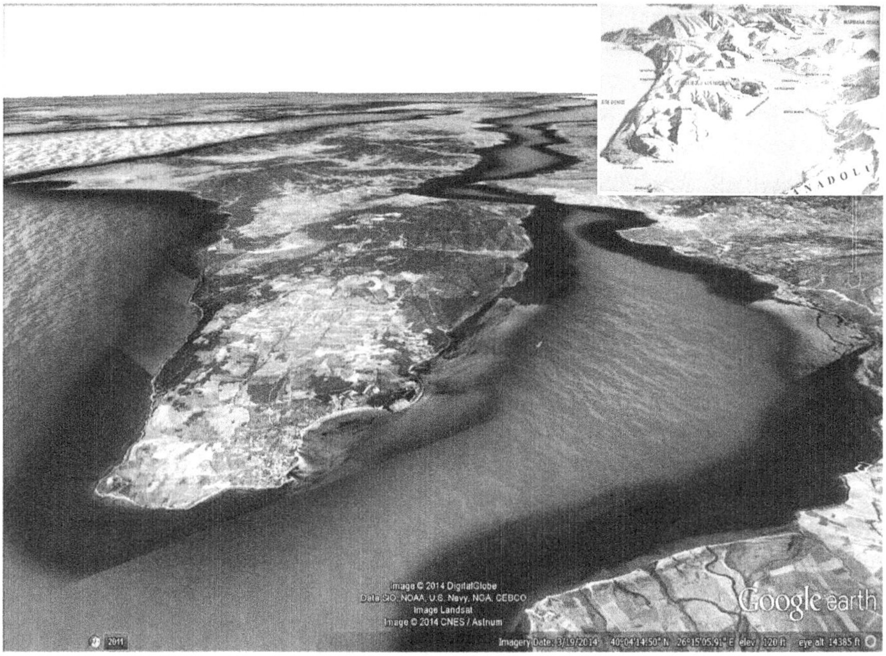

Figure 5.4 Geographic features of the Çanakkale Straits

Source: Prepared by the author based on Google Earth 7.1.1.1888, 2013, Gelibolu, 40°04'14"N 26°15'05"E, Eye alt. 14385 ft, http://www.google.com/earth/index.html (Accessed 21.07.2014).

five days stormy weather prevented the movements of the fleet. The second naval assault, made on 25 February 1915, was delayed due to the bad weather until 4 March. No planes could make their reconnaissance missions over Ottoman positions at this time. Over the next three days the weather was good and the bombardment continued, but, on 8 March, the weather was bad again. Admiral Carden, responding to a telegram received from Churchill on 2 March, stated that he needed at least 15 days of good weather, which he did not get.[56] These forced interruptions gave the Ottomans enough time to repair and fortify their trenches, forts and positions.[57]

Strategic level mistakes: discord in the British political decision-making system

It was clearly understood that Greece and Russia would not contribute to an operation against the Çanakkale Strait. Lord Kitchener absolutely refused to withdraw any

56 Ibid., p. 110.

57 General C.F. Aspinall-Oglander, *Büyük Harbin Tarihi: Çanakkale Gelibolu Askeri Harekâtı I.Cilt*, 2005, p. 106.

troops from the Western Front in France. Admiral Jellicoe, the commander of the Grand Fleet, had to focus on confronting the German 'Hochseeflotte' and had great reservations about losing superiority against Germans in the North Sea. Consequently, he would release only older ships and conceded just one of the most powerful and modern vessels of the fleet, the *Queen Elizabeth*, to be sent to Çanakkale.[58]

Churchill, in a Cabinet meeting back in 1911, had stated that the days of traversing the Çanakkale Strait purely with ships had passed, and no country would risk a modern fleet for such an operation.[59] Yet, in September 1914, Churchill was the most enthusiastic supporter of the idea of passing through the straits without an amphibious landing.[60] In his book *The World Crisis* he answered the most prominent criticism about his actions and argued: 'this war brought about lots of surprises. We have seen that many forts and fortifications regarded as insurmountable were surrendered in a few days even without a regular siege.'[61]

Churchill regarded the most powerful ship of the fleet, *Queen Elizabeth*, as 'the new fact' in purely naval operations.[62] It was obviously proved in Belgium in 1914 that modern guns with increased ranges could easily destroy old fortifications. Aircrafts, another new innovation, were also soon used for reconnaissance over modern battlefields.[63] Moreover, Churchill thought that relatively old ships such as the *Majestic* and *Canopus* class were not powerful enough to counter the German fleet, but they could easily be used to destroy old and weak Ottoman fortifications and emplacements in Çanakkale.[64] Churchill claimed that, when all these technological improvements were taken into account, many of the objections stated in the 1906 Çanakkale Report could be overcome with new technologies.[65] In his memoirs General Callwell concluded: 'Churchill was very enthusiastic about the naval assault against the straits from the first day, and he was also really keen to arrive in İstanbul whatever happened.'[66]

After the war, a commission was formed to investigate the execution of the Çanakkale Naval Campaign (Dardanelles Committee), the results of which were not published and kept as a secret for many years. It was stated in the report that:

---

58 Jürgen Rohwer, 'The Fight for The Turkish Narrows', *Çanakkale Savaşları Sebep ve Sonuçları Uluslararası Sempozyumu Çanakkale, 14–17 Mart 1990*, Türk Tarih Kurumu Basımevi, 1993, p. 155.

59 Robert Rhodes James, *Gelibolu Harekâtı*, 1965, p. 5.

60 Ibid., p. 17.

61 Ibid., p. 16.

62 J.G.Hill, 'The Fight for The Turkish Narrows', *Çanakkale Savaşları Sebep ve Sonuçları Uluslararası Sempozyumu Çanakkale, 14–17 Mart 1990*, Türk Tarih Kurumu Basımevi, 1993, p. 166.

63 General C.F. Aspinall-Oglander, *Büyük Harbin Tarihi: Çanakkale Gelibolu Askeri Harekâtı I.Cilt*, 2005, p. 50.

64 Alan Moorehead, *Çanakkale Geçilmez*, 1972, p. 46.

65 General C.F. Aspinall-Oglander, *Büyük Harbin Tarihi: Çanakkale Gelibolu Askeri Harekâtı I.Cilt*, 2005, p. 51.

66 Ibid., p. 17.

'In order to get the desired end states with such an operation, the army, navy and air force had to be involved in the planning and execution phases.'[67]

Charles Bean, the official historian,[68] argued that 'Churchill's rather imaginative nature, lack of experience about artillery, and his great competence to convince older brains, begot the Gallipoli tragedy.'[69] Contemporaries though drew different conclusions. Keyes argued as late as 1934: 'In the light of our experiences today, can anyone doubt that breaking through the Çanakkale Strait would have ended the war in two years, and could really have saved millions of innocent lives?'[70]

A Royal Commission authorised to investigate the conduct of the Gallipoli Campaign published two severely censured reports in 1917 and 1918. According to these reports, the only thing which deserved the appreciation in the Çanakkale Campaign, which cost the lives of thousands of men, was the courage of the soldiers who fought there.[71]

Lack of intelligence

After Admiral Limpus, the British military advisor who had been tasked with restructuring and training the Ottoman Navy, left the country on 9 September 1914. As a result, Britain failed to obtain enough intelligence about Ottoman mobilisation and the subsequent preparation of the straits for defence. The bombardment of 3 November 1914 raised an excessive self-confidence. Britain's operational plan had two major flaws. The first one was that stationary batteries and forts on both sides were regarded as the main threats for the navy and the operational plan was designed accordingly. However, as a result of reinforcement of the fortifications, after the bombardment in November, the Çanakkale Strait was laced with mines while mobile field artillery was deployed to protect these new mined lanes. It was the mines which inflicted the most significant damage to the Allied fleet.

The second error was to place too much reliance on the power of the guns on their battleships.[72] Designed for naval warfare, the shells of the ships fired on a flat trajectory, and their armour-piercing rounds had little shrapnel effect. Unless the fortification and batteries were hit directly, rounds would not cause significant damage.[73] In order to silence coastal artillery, the ships had to execute accurate long-range fire. However, increased distances reduced the hit rate of the high-velocity

---

67 Robert Rhodes James, *Gelibolu Harekâtı*, 1965, p. 510.

68 Charles Edwin Woodrow Bean, Australian historian and writer, charged to keep historical records and report on the campaign in the Dardanelles.

69 Robert Rhodes James, *Gelibolu Harekâtı*, 1965, p. 512.

70 Ibid., p. 51.

71 Ibid., p. 510.

72 Nigel Steel, Peter Hart, *Gelibolu Yenilginin Destanı*, 1996, p. 8.

73 J.G. Hill, 'The Çanakkale Campaign – Lost Opportunities: an Allied Perspective' Çanakkale Savaşları Sebep ve Sonuçları Uluslararası Sempozyumu Çanakkale, 14–17 Mart 1990, Türk Tarih Kurumu Basımevi, 1993, p. 168.

munitions. The probability of *Queen Elizabeth* hitting coastal forts precisely from 12,000 yards (10,972 m) was 2.25 per cent.[74] Moving ships struggled to estimate the distances and detect targets accurately. Excessive amounts of ammunition were consumed in order to destroy Ottoman artillery positions. Misconceptions about the expected effects of the naval guns were revealed on 1 March 1915, when it was detected that only one out of nine guns of the 6th Battery in Kumkale was out of action and seven of them were almost undamaged.[75]

Ottoman coastal observers realised that the Allied fleet generally used Erenköy Bay for their withdrawal manoeuvres. Contrary to the usual deployment of mines in perpendicular lines, the last mine line was laid parallel to the direction of movement in Erenköy Bay.[76] The mission to lay these mines was given to *Nusrat* mine ship.[77] On the morning of 8 March, *Nusrat* departed from Nara Cove, in a light fog and rain, and reached the shores of Erenköy at 7 o'clock. It laid 26 mines some 4.5m in depth, at 100-m intervals, parallel to the coast.[78] On the way back, Captain Hakki Bey, who had a heart condition, had a cardiac arrest and died. He therefore did not see the results of his last mission, the best mine laying operation in military history, and one which changed the fate of the campaign.[79]

Although the last mine line was laid on 8 March, it was not detected until 18 March. The day before, a seaplane flew over this area and reported that there were no mines in the waterway. Because it was known that planes could detect mines some 5.5m deep in clear water, there was no reason not to rely on this report.[80] However, atmospheric conditions might have obscured the detection of the mines.[81]

The failure to ascertain the centre of gravity at the operational level

Allied forces failed in their analysis of the centre of gravity of the Ottoman defence.[82] British military experts, resorting to intelligence gathered on 3 November, had interpreted that, in order to pass the strait, fortified emplacements and artillery

74 Ibid., p. 170.

75 Nigel Steel, Peter Hart, *Gelibolu Yenilginin Destanı*, 1996, p. 13.

76 Çanakkale Boğaz Komutanlığı, *Çanakkale Deniz Savaşları 1915*, Kültür Yayınları Tarih Dizisi No: 51, Deniz Basımevi Müdürlüğü, İstanbul, 2004, p. 97.

77 Built in 1910 in Germany, *Nusrat* was 40m long, 7.5m wide, and 360 tons with a coal boilered engine. *Nusrat* could carry 40 mines on its deck and make 24km per hour. Yusuf İzzettin Barış, *Çanakkale Savaşları*, Matsa Basımevi, Ankara, 2000, p. 29.

78 Çanakkale Boğaz Komutanlığı, *Çanakkale Deniz Savaşları 1915*, Kültür Yayınları Tarih Dizisi No: 51, Deniz Basımevi Müdürlüğü, İstanbul, 2004, p. 97.

79 İnönü Üniversitesi, Webpanel, *Çanakkale Geçilmez*, p. 11.

80 Alan Moorehead, *Çanakkale Geçilmez*, 1972, p. 85.

81 İnönü Üniversitesi, Webpanel, *Çanakkale Geçilmez*, p. 12. http://iys.inonu.edu.tr/webpanel/dosyalar/910/file/canakkalegecilmez.pdf, erişim tarihi, 10 Aralık 2013.

82 Clausewitz, *On War*: 'Center of Gravity' is 'the source of power that provides moral or physical strength, freedom of action, or will to act'.

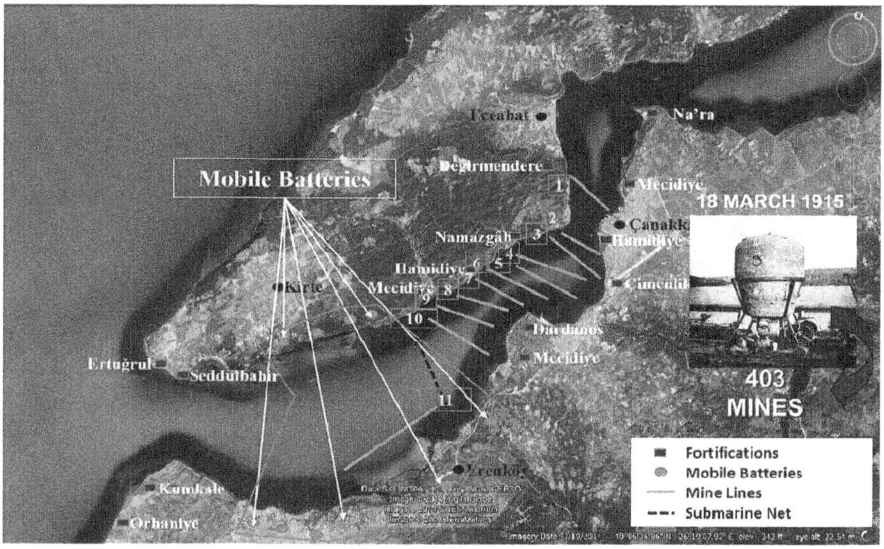

Figure 5.5 Centre of gravity and mobile batteries of the Çanakkale Fortified Zone Command[83]

batteries on both sides had to be neutralised. Their main effort was therefore allocated to the destruction of the forts and stationary batteries on both coasts.

On the other hand, the Ottomans changed the defence arrangements at the Çanakkale Strait after the bombardment of November 1914. The Ottoman Fortified Zone Command's defence plan depended on no less than 11 mine lines. The Ottomans' centre of gravity, its mines, was thus lying in the midst of the sea. In order to deny enemy efforts to clear the mines, mobile artillery batteries in addition to stationary forts and emplacements were positioned on the covered hills on both sides. Colonel Cevat Bey, Commander of the Fortified Zone Command, noted that: 'The main principle of the defence was "enabling

83 This figure was prepared by the author based on the sources below:

1 – Şemsettin Bargut, *Birinci Dünya Harbi'nde ve Kurtuluş Savaşı'nda Türk Deniz Harekâtı* (Turkish), Deniz Kuvvetleri K.lığı Basımevi, Ankara, 2000, p. 21

2 – Çanakkale Boğaz Komutanlığı, *Çanakkale Deniz Savaşları 1915*, Kültür Yayınları Tarih Dizisi No: 51, Deniz Basımevi Müdürlüğü, İstanbul, 2004, p. 86

3 – Alan Moorehead, *Çanakkale Geçilmez*, 1972, p. 97

4 – Google Earth 7.1.1.1888, 2013, Gelibolu,40°06'36"N 26°19'07"E, Eye alt. 22.54km, http://www.google.com/earth/index.html (Accessed 21.07.2014)

5 – Peter Doyle and Matthew R. Bennett, 'Military Geography: The Influence of Terrain in the Outcome of the Gallipoli Campaign, 1915', The Geographical Journal, Vol. 165, No. 1 (Mar., 1999), pp. 13, published by: The Royal Geographical Society (with the Institute of British Geographers), http://www.jstor.org/stable/3060508 (Accessed: 25.09.2013).

Table 5.4 Principles of war[84]

Principles of war	
• **Objective**	• **Offensive**
• **Mass**	• **Security**
• **Economy of force**	• **Surprise**
• **Manoeuvre**	• **Simplicity**
• **Unity of command**	

batteries to engage with enemy battleships by establishing fire barrages before they reach and eliminate the mines".'[85]

On the other hand, the British Navy, as a result of erroneous analysis of the Ottomans' centre of gravity, brought extraordinarily powerful battleships to destroy the stationary batteries, forts and positions, but they used rather feeble fishing trawlers to clear Turkish mines.

Analysis of the mistakes made in light of principles of war

In this part of the study, mistakes made during the Dardanelles naval campaign can be examined in light of the principles of war.

The Objective

The British hoped that İstanbul would surrender immediately when the Allied fleet passed the straits and there would be no further resistance to the British occupation. All kinds of material would be easily transferred through the open straits to Russia, while Russian wheat would be sent to the Western Front. However, when the desired end states and the effort allocated for this operation are compared, there was a significant imbalance between the expected outcome and invested resources.

However, there was no agreement between Britain, France and Russia about the possession of the Turkish Straits. Napoleon had expressed the dilemma succinctly: 'Who is to have Constantinople? That is always the crux of the problem.'[86] Because of the great disagreement about this fact, they could never take advantage of the troops offered by Greece, nor resolve the problems of cooperation and coordination.

84 Department of Army, FM 3–0 Operations, Washington D.C.2011, p. A-1.

85 Robert Rhodes James, *Gelibolu Harekâtı*, 1965, p. 21.

86 Alan Moorehead, *Çanakkale Geçilmez*, 1972, p. 11.

Mass

In order to achieve the desired outcomes, the main point stressed in most of the previous reports was that a detailed joint planning and a synchronised amphibious landing on the Gallipoli Peninsula was indispensable. If commercial ships were to use this waterway, all the fortifications on both sides of the strait had to be captured and the enemy forces defeated. Because the Allies gave priority to the Western Front, insufficient resources, especially manpower, were allocated. It was not until 16 February 1915 that the Allied governments agreed upon the allocation of troops for the Çanakkale Campaign. General Ian Hamilton decided that, without a synchronised amphibious landing, it was impossible to accomplish the objectives. The principle of mass requires employing the bulk of the forces harmoniously at the decisive point. Because the surprise effect had already been lost for a synchronised landing, it would also be hard for such a relatively small army to secure the peninsula from that time on.[87]

Economy of force

The best thing about the operational plan for the decision-makers in Britain and France was that it didn't require any significant transfer of troops from the Western Front. The Allied powers decided to deploy old battleships and civilian trawlers as minesweepers. This was a proper application of the economy of force principle, but, because they underestimated Ottoman defence capabilities, it didn't work in Çanakkale. The idiom 'inadequate precaution is not a precaution' was proved correct at Gallipoli.

Unity of command

Admiral Carden, assigned as the commander of the Allied fleet waiting off the Çanakkale Strait, was at odds with the findings of Rear-Admiral Limpus who had served as the advisor to the Ottoman Navy for two years. With considerably more experience and information about the Ottoman Navy, the straits, and Turkish people, he was, however, the best candidate to command the Allied fleet.[88]

Security

British and French officials concentrated their efforts on the Western Front and they deployed most of the troops and munitions there. Security of the Western

87 General C.F. Aspinall-Oglander, *Büyük Harbin Tarihi: Çanakkale Gelibolu Askeri Harekâtı I.Cilt*, 2005, p. 93.

88 Ibid., p. 4.

Front was regarded as the first priority. On the other hand, insufficient resources sent to Çanakkale undermined the security of the Gallipoli Campaign. Concerns about personal security sometimes outstripped the security of operations. During minesweeping operations, civilian crewmen aboard the minesweepers should have accomplished their mission at the expense of their lives, but they risked neither their lives nor their vessels. In order to exploit the security obtained by the surprise effect, the tempo of the operation should be maintained: significant risks are inevitable. Inexperienced civilian crewmen did not maintain the tempo of the operation and this led to an unsecure environment for the Allied fleet.

The idea, which was common through all navies, that the 'ship is more valuable than the men' was another reason for Allied failure. A general characteristic of Admiral de Robeck's generation was that, however old the ships may be, all measures had to be taken to save big battleships. In the evening of 18 March, Admiral de Robeck lost three of his biggest battleships. This shock might have made him change his idea about another naval attack on 22 March before his meeting with General Hamilton.[89]

Surprise

It is evident from the Turkish documents that the strait wasn't prepared for a military operation in the summer of 1914. Reports indicate that 'guns and fortification in the Çanakkale Strait were quite inadequate during the mobilisation. In addition to the limited ammunition, most of the guns had low rates of fire, and short ranges.'[90]

General Weber of the German Army was assigned as Assistant to Çanakkale Fortified Zone Command, and managed to carry out a series of precautions for the defence of the strait. German officials' attempts to strengthen the strait were nevertheless sometimes hindered by Turkish unwillingness to cooperate.[91] However, the bombardment on 3 November, six weeks before the first coordinated attack, aroused concerns about the composition of the defensive forces and the state of the fortifications of the Çanakkale Strait, leading the Ottomans and Germans to take the necessary measures. Fortifications on both sides of the strait were strengthened. Colonel Cevat Bey, Commander of the Fortified Zone Command, stated in his memoirs: 'The bombardment on 3 November warned me, and I understood that I should spend all my time, and resort to all options, to reinforce the defence of the strait.'[92]

Enver Pasha, who believed that Allied forces would not be able to pass the straits, stated that it was nonsense to embark on such an endeavour. In his memoirs, he wrote: 'If the British could have enough courage to gather a lot more battleships

89 Alan Moorehead, *Çanakkale Geçilmez*, 1972, p. 115.

90 Ibid., p. 54.

91 Ibid., p. 56.

92 Ibid., p. 56.

to attack the strait once more; they could have arrived in İstanbul. But the six week delay of their naval assault gave us enough time to strengthen fortification of the peninsula and straits. In the meantime we positioned more than 200 German Skoda[93] guns into the area.'[94]

Underestimation of Ottoman units

On 18 March, Ottoman casualties amounted to 118 killed and there was a significant reduction in available ammunition after the Allies' seven-hour naval bombardment. Indeed, half of the ammunition was used and only 30 armour-piercing rounds of ammunition remained.[95] Ottoman soldiers' behaviour was nevertheless admirable. Soldiers maintained their high morale. They were eager to die for their cause. Imams in the trenches encouraged soldiers against the enemy. Each man encountered the exploding bombs and shrapnel with great courage. While the Allies had nothing at stake, the Ottoman soldier believed he was about to lose his country and his dignity.[96] Indeed, Ottoman soldiers' fire discipline was unbelievable. Unless the enemy ships came within range, they would not fire. To deceive the enemy ships, the Ottomans used smoke. By placing field artillery on high hills, they exploited cover and visual deception.[97] In the event of a position being detected, the troops were always ready to quickly change their location.

Conclusion

History is replete with interpretations. The Allies hoped to obtain an extraordinary outcome from the naval attack on the Çanakkale Strait. The main motive which encouraged Britain to embark on such an operation was the desperate pre-war state of the Ottoman Empire, which was defined as the 'sick man' of Europe. Technological developments and excessive self-confidence, as well as ignorance of historical facts or lessons about previous naval operations conducted in Çanakkale, led to failure.

The chain of mistakes at the strategic, operational and tactical level resulted in an inevitable failure. Surprise is a crucial principle for a successful assault. Not being a part of a coordinated and well-planned offensive, the initial Allied bombardment on 3 November, six weeks before the first coordinated naval attack, resulted in loss of surprise. Ottoman forces had more than four months to strengthen

93 Mountain cannon (75mm) used by Austria–Hungary between 1911 and 1914 in WWI.

94 The Coast Artillery Journal, Vol. 58, No.6, Whole No. 202, June 1923, p. 497.

95 Alan Moorehead, *Çanakkale Geçilmez*, 1972, p. 97.

96 Ibid., p. 98.

97 Ibid., p. 99.

the defences along the Çanakkale Strait. On the other hand, the effectiveness of this bombardment increased the self-confidence of the British and Allied navy and contributed to the reckless decision to try to force the Çanakkale Strait by naval attack. Moreover, intelligence gathered in this bombardment about the Ottoman defences misled the Allies' operational plans.

The 3 November bombardment raised concerns amongst Ottoman and German officials about the ability to defend the straits. With the help of mines and guns transferred to Çanakkale and Gallipoli, the defence of the strait changed completely. Allied forces failed to determine correctly the centre of gravity of the Ottoman defences. Clausewitz called this the hub of all power and movement, on which everything depends. Correctly identifying the enemy's centre of gravity is the most important task of an operational or higher-level headquarters. The British determined that Ottoman defences relied upon the stationary artillery batteries and forts on both sides of the Straits, when, in fact, it was dependent on the mine lines. Ottoman artillery had nevertheless played a vital role by denying enemy efforts to clear the mines.

One of the other main Allied errors was the idea that passing through the strait with just naval forces would force the Ottoman government to surrender. They expected to end the First World War in a substantially shorter time by capturing the Turkish straits and reaching Russia. But the common idiom 'deficient precaution is not a precaution' proved to be true once more. As stated in the reports published by the British investigation commissions, the best way to achieve the success of an operation directed against the straits was to execute a synchronised joint land and sea campaign.

The Turkish soldiers' – Mehmetçiks' – heroism and sacrifice in Çanakkale was admired and recognised by the entire world. A few years after the campaign, when Atatürk was roaming Gallipoli, one of the journalists asked him 'why there were no monuments of the Turkish soldiers'. He replied: 'The best monument ever is Mehmetçik – the Turkish soldier – himself.'

Chapter 6

The Çanakkale naval battles in Turkish official records[1]

Hülya Toker

The Ottoman Empire had limited time to carry out the necessary reforms in the aftermath of the conflicts in Tripolitania and the Balkans, before war came again in 1914. During this time, the Ottoman state was trying to restructure its army and negotiate diplomatically in order not to stand alone in a possible world war, which seemed imminent. However, the Ottoman regime could not find the support it was looking for in these negotiations. While Britain said it could not form new political relationships at that time,[2] the answer the Ottomans got from France was that an alliance would not be possible unless Russia would agree to it.[3] There were alliance offers directed at Bulgaria, Greece, Romania and Russia as well but these too were rejected. In the end, the Ottoman state entered the war alongside Germany, a decision still regarded as controversial today. As a result, the Ottoman state fought alongside the Central Powers throughout the four years of war. Even though it was labelled the 'sick man' of Europe, the Ottoman Empire fought on four fronts, and, while occasionally defeated, there were also successes. Among these battles, the Çanakkale naval actions constitute an important part of Ottoman and Turkish national history.

The naval battles of Çanakkale, in which the Allied fleet exerted immense pressure to break through the highly important Çanakkale strait, have taken their place in Turkish history as 'The Naval Victory of March 18th'. This date has been accepted as 'Memorial Day of the Killed in Action' and has been commemorated each year with various activities.

In this study, the naval battles of Çanakkale are examined through daily and hourly reports based on the Turkish official records of the period. This has been

---

1 This chapter was translated from Turkish to English by Dr Aslı Değirmenci of the Department of English Language and Literature, Faculty of Letters, Hacettepe University, Turkey.

2 Cemil Bilsel, *Lozan, V. I*, İstanbul 1933, p. 138; Armaoğlu, p. 107.

3 Fahir Armaoğlu, *20. Yüzyıl Siyasi Tarihi 1914–1980*, İş Bankası Yayınları, 2nd edn, Ankara, 1984, pp. 107, 108; Cemil Bilsel, *Lozan, V. I*, İstanbul, Ahmet İhsan Matbaası, 1933; pp. 140–42; Yusuf Hikmet Bayur, *Türk İnkılâbı Tarihi, V.II, Part IV*, Ankara, TTK Basımevi, 1952, pp. 549–58. For detailed information see Cemal Pasha, *Hatırat*, eds Metin Martı, Arma Yayınları, İstanbul, 1996.

done in order to shed light on how the records were kept and how the battles were reported on the Turkish side. Furthermore, the chapter reviews the evaluations of this subject by analysing memoirs and secondary works.

Since the military correspondence on the Çanakkale naval battles are mostly in the Archives of the General Staff Military History and Strategic Studies Department (ATASE), the main sources of this chapter are the documents available in these archives. These documents consist of military correspondence, orders, daily reports, maps, overlays, photos, intelligence reports and wartime logs.

While examining these documents, it is evident how precise the Ottoman state was about keeping records during the war. The order the commander of III Army Corps gave about the Çanakkale front was specific in this regard: 'the troops, generally following the instructions as they did in the previous war, will keep wartime logs not only from the first day of the campaign but daily and hourly so as not to have any difficulties at the end.'[4] This was echoed by the Çanakkale Fortified Area Commander: 'it is required to keep wartime logs regularly from the first day of the campaign.'[5] This clearly shows the meticulousness of the Ottoman General Staff on this matter. Accordingly, the wartime logs of the Çanakkale naval battles are a complete record.

Geographical location of the Çanakkale and its evaluation in terms of the assault

'The straits have long confirmed its importance by being the door to the capital and to the caliphate, and it has actually proved its significance many times throughout history.'[6] These words by the Çanakkale Fortified Area Command Chief of Staff, Lieutenant Colonel Selahattin Adil, summarise the significance of the straits for the Ottoman Empire. Besides being considered the way to the heart of the Ottoman regime, due their strategic location, the straits have also been seen by other states as a symbol of power that has to be neutralised, and for this reason the area has been the scene of great battles. One of these actions, which left deep scars, was the bombardment on the Çanakkale coastline during the First World War. At the time, the straits were the means by which the Allied powers could realise their ambitions, while, for the Ottoman state, it was of vital importance as their means of survival.

Geographically speaking, the Çanakkale starts in the north of Gallipoli, on the Çankaya Cape and the arc of Bitlice, and, it extends in a south-westerly direction until it reaches the Aegean Sea. The coasts are wide and parallel to each other until

---

4 General Staff ATASE Archives; Kol. BDH, Kls. 3964, Dos. H-1, Fih. 1–13.

5 Ibid.; Kol. BDH, Kls. 4669, Dos. H-1, Fih. 1–10.

6 Selahattin Adil, *Çanakkale Cephesinden Mektuplar-Hatıralar*, Yeditepe Yayınevi, İstanbul, 2007, p. 21.

the Nagara Point, where they narrow significantly and extend to the south. Around Çanakkale, the strait narrows still further and thus forms the strategically important central military fortification zone. The Çanakkale widens between the Kepez Point and Baykuş, and, after the Erenköy Cape, it continues to broaden in the direction of the Anatolian shores and forms the harbours of Erenköy and Karanlık.

The widest part of the strait is the line between the Erenköy Cape and Tenkerderesi. After the Eskihisarlık Cape, the strait forms the harbour of Morto by making a curve to the west. After the harbours of Karanlık and Morto, the strait narrows again and forms the area of entrance between Kumkale and Sedd el Bahr.

The length of the strait is 60km, and, while the length of shore on the peninsula of Gallipoli is 78km, it is 94km on the peninsula of Biga. Where the width of the strait at its northern mouth is 3.2km, it goes up to 5.8km between Gelibolu and Çardak. It narrows to just 1.2km between Çanakkale and Kilitbahir, and then it widens up again to 8 km around İntepe. The length of the strait, with its oval-shaped trench, exceeds 90km at two points. The longest section reaches up to 100km around Çanakkale.[7]

When evaluated in terms of the possibility of an assault, the entrance of the strait is a location suitable for being besieged any time. On the other hand, the north of the Cape Tekke and the entrance fortifications around Yenişehir are open to possible oblique fire. However, within the strait the situation is reversed. The ships entering the strait become canalised: the width of the strait simply limits the number of ships that can fight side by side.

The Erenköy Cape might have provided a place for shelter and preparation for the fleet of the Allied powers that made it into the strait. It was a dead zone for the Hamidiye fort where the most powerful guns of the central fortification were held. The heavy guns were placed to the east of Erenköy Cape and on the opposite shore to hold the enemy fleet with enfilade fire. The surface current in the strait would also limit the movements of small ships. When the current becomes faster, the activities of laying and searching for mines become far more difficult. On the other hand, the undercurrent in the strait affects the movement of submarines. Nevertheless, the breadth of the strait could not limit the movement of large warships.[8]

Troops in defence on the Çanakkale front

Just before the First World War broke out, the area that contained the Çanakkale front was under the authority of the First Army Inspectorate, the headquarters of which

7 İbrahim Atalay, Kenan Mortan, *Türkiye Bölgesel Coğrafyası*, İnkılap Kitabevi, İstanbul, 1997, p. 92.

8 Hülya Toker, *Birinci Dünya Savaşı'nda Çanakkale Cephesi (Haziran 1914–25 Nisan 1915)* Vol. 5, Book 1, Ankara, Gnkur. Personel Bşk.lığı ATASE Daire Başkanlığı Yay., 2012, pp. 8, 9.

were in İstanbul. The duty of defending the Çanakkale was given to III Army Corps Command which was also under the orders of the First Army Inspectorate. This III Army Corps consisted of Çanakkale Fortified Area Command, 7th, 8th and 9th Infantry Divisions, 3rd Cavalry Brigade, and additional troops of the III Army Corps.[9]

Among the combat forces of Çanakkale Fortified Area Command, there was a small fleet. The four torpedo boats (*Kütahya, Draç, Musul, Akhisar*) that made up this light fleet reached Nagara on 31 July 1914.[10] Later, one gunboat and two destroyers were added to the flotilla.[11]

On 4 September, the Ministry of the Supreme Military Command notified the Fortified Area Command that *Mesudiye*, a warship, would be sent to Çanakkale; that it should anchor at a suitable place so as to attend the defence of the strait with the guns on board; that the guns on the other side of the ship should be taken out to set up batteries on the shore; and that steamboats should be used in the service of patrolling the strait.[12]

Military fortifications and the defence plan of the Çanakkale

On the forts at the entrance to the Çanakkale, there were 20 guns with calibres ranging between 15 and 28cm, and there were just four operable guns of 24 and 25cm. The range of these was some 14,800m while the range of the other guns was 7,500m. In the inner forts there were 78 guns between 15 and 35.5cm, and among these there were five pieces of 35.5 or 35 cm and three of 34 or 35cm. While the former's range was 16,900m, the latter's range was 14,800m. Among the remaining guns, those of 15/40cm had a reach of 9,600m and the 22cm had a range of 7,500m. The first part of the strait from the entrance until Dardanos was empty and defenceless. There were only seven naval guns with the calibre of 7.5/15cm around Dardanos and Kepez.[13]

The General Staff, realising the inadequacy of the defence arrangements for the Çanakkale, had drawn attention to these points:

1 However many reinforcements were sent to the batteries in Sedd el Bahr and Kumkale, they would never be enough to close off the strait against the superior fire of a navy. The enemy would destroy the batteries.
2 The most important point was to reinforce the central group of batteries with available medium guns. Unfortunately, in the case of the enemy entering the

9 Ibid.; Kol. BDH, Kls. 3964, Dos. H-1, Fih. 1–1.*Türk Silahlı Kuvvetleri Tarihi*, Vol. 3, Part 6 (1908–20), Ankara, Gnkur. Basımevi, 1971, pp. 221, 222.

10 Ibid.; Kol. BDH, Kls. 4669, Dos. H-1, Fih. 1–10.

11 Ibid.; Kol. BDH, Kls. 4669, Dos. H-1, Fih. 1–33.

12 *Birinci Dünya Harbinde Türk Harbi, Deniz Harekâtı*, Vol. VIII, Ankara, Gnkur. Basımevi 1976, p. 103.

13 *Cihan Harbinde Osmanlı Harekatı Tarihçesi, Çanakkale Muharebâtı*, Cüz 1, Dersaadet, Matbai Askeriye, 1338, pp. 8, 10.

strait, there was the possibility of the central batteries being destroyed before they could open fire due to the limited range of the guns. In order to prevent this, it was requıred to open fire in such a way that the enemy wouldn't benefit from the fact that the range of their guns was longer.

3 Our batteries should be protected as much as possible so that they could fulfil their role. We have considered forming new groups of batteries for this purpose. It was deemed essential that these groups should keep the enemy ships away from the central group.

4 We have decided to establish a group of howitzers between Erenköy and İntepe. To reinforce the Fortified Area Command, we have asked İstanbul for the howitzer batteries. These were deployed.

5 To be able to use the Kepez Group as an obstacle against minesweepers, quick firing guns were required. We have removed these guns from ships and placed them there.

6 The heavy guns, which would take a lot of time and trouble to move, were not transferred. It was preferred to use them as they were, because it could not be determined when war would break out.[14]

After Austria–Hungary declared war upon Serbia, on 29 July 1914 the Ministry of Defence notified the authorities at the Çanakkale that the general situation had become more unstable and ordered that the shores should be monitored and necessary precautions should be taken.[15] With this order, Çanakkale Fortified Area Command accelerated the activities related to the defence of the sector.

The Ministry of Defence, with a new order issued on 4 August 1914, asked that the Çanakkale should be protected with mines but that the strait should be open to commercial ships. It was ordered that the buoys established during the Balkan Wars should be taken away and the lighthouses should be switched off. Thereupon, a 2,200m-long mine line was laid between Havuzlar and Kepez. On this line, there were 22 mines placed at 80m intervals. The aim was to close off the narrowest section of the strait, but there were a limited number of mines available. Four mines were therefore saved as a precaution to close off the passages.[16]

One day later, 26 more mines were brought in and they were laid as a second line of mines to the east of the first line. The distance between mines was approximately 20m on this line.[17] On 15 August, the third, fourth and fifth lines of mines were laid between Soğanlıdere and Kepez lighthouse.[18]

---

14 *Harb-i Umumide Çanakkale Muharebât-ı Bahriyesi*, İstanbul, Erkanı Harbiye Mektebi Matbaası, 15 February 1336, pp. 7, 8.

15 Ibid.; Kol. BDH, Kls. 4669, Dos. H-1, Fih. 1–8.

16 *Harbi Umumide Çanakkale Muharebatı Bahriyesi*, pp. 7, 8.

17 Ibid.; Kol. BDH, Kls. 4669, Dos. H-1, Fih. 1–33; *Deniz Harekâtı*, vol. VIII., p. 96. In the work titled *Çanakkale Naval Battles in the First World War* (*Harb-i Umumide Çanakkale Muharebât-ı Bahriyesi*) this date is given as 6 August 1914.

18 Ibid.; Kol. BDH, Kls. 4669, Dos. H-1, Fih. 1–45.

Even though the batteries at the entrance were reinforced, these were considered to be inadequate against the superior fire of the Allied fleet, which might position itself beyond the reach of those batteries. So, the inner fortifications were given greater priority and they were strengthened and reinforced with the available medium guns. It was decided that the Allied navy should be confronted in the narrow part of the Çanakkale. In accordance with this, these additional measures were taken:

1 In the case of the Allied navy destroying the entrance forts and entering the strait, it was assumed the interior fortifications with short-range guns would be destroyed before they could open fire. To prevent this, eight howitzer batteries of 15/10.8 cm calibre were placed on both shores of the Karanlık harbour.
2 By using all the available materials, nine lines of mines were placed in the narrowest part of the strait, and a torpedo tube was put on the Namazgah shore.
3 In order to protect the mine lines from minesweepers, a group of gun batteries were brought together and were placed around Kepez, Soğanlı and the Havuzlar Brook. These consisted of small guns removed from the war ships as well as Krupp and Mantelli-brand guns and some Nordenfelt batteries available in Çanakkale.
4 In order for the mine area to be lit at night, eight more searchlights were added to the existing two searchlights on the shoreline.
5 Specific light batteries were brought together, consisting of Krupp guns, and placed in different locations, partly to open fire at Allied aircraft but also to act as harassment fire against enemy shipping. These batteries proved helpful in creating deception against the Allied navy.
6 Against an assault from the sea, the Çanakkale was further strengthened and reinforced. The 7th and 9th divisions as well as six mobile gendarme battalions were appointed to monitor and protect the shores starting from the Gulf of Saros to the Cape of Old İstanbul across from Bozcaada (Tenedos).[19]

The Ministry of the Supreme Military Command stated in an order sent to III Army Corps that: 'In case of an attack against the Çanakkale, Çanakkale Fortified Positions Command might ask directly for additional divisions from the III and IV Army Corps.'[20]

As a result of these orders issued by the Ministry of the Supreme Military Command, we understand that the 11th Division of the IV Army Corps in Aydın and Denizli, and 7th and 8th Divisions of the III Army Corps in Tekirdag and Bandırma were made ready to depart for Çanakkale. Thus, in case of an invasion to the Çanakkale area, the Fortified Area would be reinforced with these three

19 *Çanakkale Muharebatı*, pp. 10, 11.
20 Ibid.; Kol. BDH, Kls. 3964, Dos. H-2, Fih. 1–22.

divisions. In accordance with this plan, the 8th Division moved to Tekirdag from Bandırma,[21] and the troops of the 11th Division were sent to Bandırma.[22]

While these precautions were being taken for the Çanakkale, the Ottoman state officially started negotiations regarding an alliance with Germany on 27 July 1914.[23] These negotiations, that started in İstanbul, were finalised officially on 2 August with the signing the Turkish–German alliance.[24]

The Ottoman state declared its mobilisation immediately, on 2 and 3 August.[25] This call for mobilisation produced an overwhelming response from the people. Sultan Mehmet Reshad V had to ask the elderly and the uneducated volunteers to be sent back home, stating: 'Even before one week is out, so many young people have taken up arms that the army has satisfied its needs. I have been greatly touched by the patriotism and enthusiasm my people have shown.'[26]

In the meantime, Germany started to pressure the Ottoman state into entering the war as soon as possible. Nevertheless, Ottoman officials stated that the agreement was a defensive one, and they were not in a hurry to enter the war. However, two battleships, *Goeben* and *Breslau*, first came to Izmir and later came to Çanakkale on 10 August 1914 while operating against France and its colonies in the Mediterranean, and this accelerated the process of the Ottoman Empire

---

21 Ibid. ; Kol. BDH, Kls. 3964, Dos. H-2, Fih. 1–24.

22 Ibid.; Kol. BDH, Kls. 4857, Dos. H-2, Fih. 1–7.

23 Mahmut Muhtar, *Maziye Bir Nazar*, ed. Nurcan Fidan, Ankara, Gnkur. Basımevi 1999, pp. 118, 119.

24 Yusuf Hikmet Bayur, *Türk İnkılâbı Tarihi*, vol. II, part IV, Ankara, TTK Basımevi, 1952, p. 626. For detailed information on the negotiations see *Talat Paşa'nın Anıları*, ed. Alpay Kabacalı, İletişim Yayınları, İstanbul, 1993, 3rd edn, p. 29. Cemal Pasha states that the negotiations for this alliance started even before the First World War; he knew about this at the last minute; and Enver Pasha had said that the offer came from the Germans.

Cemal Pasha, *Hatırat, ed.* Metin Martı, Arma Yayınları, İstanbul, 1996, p. 117. Cemil Bilsel states that the offer for an alliance first came from Austria (Bilsel; pp. 149, 150). Enver Ziya Karal states that the first offer was made by The Committee of Union and Progress (İttihat ve Terakki Cemiyeti) (Enver Ziya Karal, *Osmanlı tarihi* Vol. IX, Ankara, TTK Basımevi, 1996, p. 379); Mahmut Muhtar Pasha also states that it was made by The Committee of Union and Progress. Mahmut Muhtar, p. 118.

25 Ibid.; Kol. BDH, Kls. 4669, Dos. H-1, Fih. 1–12.

26 *Askeri Tarih Belgeleri Dergisi*, August 1989, Issue 88, Document No: 2124. The Ottoman state had been suffering from the defeat of the Balkan Wars when the First World War broke out. They had declared a partial mobilisation on the Çanakkale on 15 June 1914 against the threat of Greece in order not to lose any territory. With the start of the war, in the face of a bigger threat, they ordered a special mobilisation on 31 July 1914 and the overall mobilisation on 2 August 1914. In the command given by the sultan, it was stated that, except for the 7th Army Corps, 21st and 22nd Independent Divisions, the land army and the navy should be mobilised; all the fortifications should be manned; the first day of the mobilisation was 3 August 1914. Ibid.; BDH Kol., Kls. 3964, Dos. H-1, Fih. 1–11; Kls. 4669, Dos. H-1, Fih. 1–9, 1–12. Aga.; Kol. BDH, Kls. 4669, Dos. H-1, Fih. 1–2; Selahaddin Adil Pasha, p. 21.

entering the war.[27] The Allied powers gave a note to the Ottoman government stating that, according to neutrality agreements, these battleships should leave Turkish territorial waters in 24 hours or should be disarmed immediately.

The response of Enver Pasha, the Deputy Commander in Chief, signalled the Ottoman state's entry to the war on 11 August 1914, because in his reply Enver Pasha stated that the battleships had been duly purchased by the Ottoman state and their names were now *Yavuz* and *Midilli*.[28]

On 29 October 1914, the Turkish forces under the command of German Admiral Souchon bombarded the ports of Odessa, Sevastopol and Novorossiysk in the Black Sea as well as sinking one French and two Russian ships. This incident was the last part of the Ottoman state's process of entering the war. After this incident, Russia crossed the border in the north of Doğubeyazıt while the British bombarded Aqaba.[29] In turn, Russia, on 2 November; Britain, on 5 November, and France, on 6 November, declared war on the Ottoman state. In response, the sultan declared that the state was at war with Russia, Britain, and France on 11 November. The sultan also made a proclamation to the army and the navy explaining the righteousness of the Ottoman state in this war.[30]

The bombardment of 3 November of the Çanakkale's entrance fortifications

Two days after Russia's assault on the Caucasus, Britain started to bombard the entrenchments at the entrance to the Çanakkale.[31] Six warships began to close on the entrance at 6:40 am on 3 November.[32] Two of the ships were alongside the Sedd el Bahr; the others were on the Anatolian side; and French ships were placed at the centre. Around 6:50 am, the assault began from a distance of 16km

---

27 Ibid.; Kol. BDH, Kls. 4669, Dos. H-1, Fih. 1–35. For detailed information see Yusuf Hikmet Bayur, *Türk İnkılâbı Tarihi*, Vol. III, Part I, Ankara, 1953, pp. 74–9.

28 *Askeri Tarih Belgeleri Dergisi*, August 1989, Issue 88, Document No: 2125. *Birinci Dünya Harbinde Türk Harbi Çanakkale Cephesi Harekâtı*, Vol. 5, Part 1 (June 1914–25 April 1915), Ankara, Gnkur. Basımevi, 1993, p. 69; Kadri Perk, *Çanakkale Savaşları Tarihi* 1st and 3rd parts. *Büyük Harpte Çanakkale*, Issue 116 of the *Military Journal* (*Askerî Mecmua*) History Part (Tarih Kısmı), 1 March 1940, pp. 3, 4. In fact, Enver Pasha had already given an order to Çanakkale Fortified Area Command on 7–8 August stating that the German battleships *Goeben* and *Breslau* might have engaged in battles with the enemy and that these ships should be permitted to enter the strait if they take refuge in the Çanakkale. *Askeri Tarih Belgeleri Dergisi*, August 1989, Issue 88, Document No: 2123.

29 Mehmet Emin, *Harbi Umumide Osmanlı Cepheleri Vakayi*, Erkânı Harbiye Mektebi Press, Beylerbeyi, 1 Teşrin-i evvel (October) 1338, p. 38.

30 Bayur, Vol. III, Part I, Ankara 1953, p. 260.

31 Aga.; Kol. BDH, Kls. 4669, Dos. H-3, Fih. 1–80.

32 Aga.; Kol. BDH, Kls. 4669, Dos. H.3, Fih. 1–79, 79a.

and continued for approximately 15 minutes.[33] None of the batteries were able to open fire. Turkish gunners fired just four rounds from the forts of Ertuğrul and Orhaniye. This short duration bombardment had a great impact: it caused significant destruction in Sedd el Bahr. The French had attacked Kumkale and the British had targeted the forts of Sedd el Bahr and Orhaniye. There was little damage done in Ertuğrul, Orhaniye and Kumkale so it was possible to make repairs in a few days. However, there had been an explosion in the fort at Sedd el Bahr. It was noted that the reason for the explosion was two shells striking the magazine. It was pointed out the reason for such a big explosion was that the black powder left from the campaign against Italy (1911) was placed in the magazine as it was not deemed dangerous. Although one or two guns were repaired in a short time, none of the others could be repaired immediately. The total number of casualties was 92: five killed in action and two injured among the officers, and 66 killed in action and 19 injured among the rank and file.

There were inspections in the area. It was established that the destruction in the 1st and 2nd batteries were much greater compared to the other batteries. The forts of Kumkale and Sedd el Bahr were therefore renovated and made more secure.[34]

After this bombardment, the Deputy Commander in Chief Enver Pasha stated that he saluted all the officers and the other ranks, and he asked for the names of those who had been involved in the action who had distinguished themselves.[35] In general, it is understood that the bombardment of 3 November was a demonstration, and the explosion of the magazine had increased the level of destruction, making this bombardment an important warning to the Ottoman state to increase their defensive measures in the straits.

The precautions taken after the bombardment of 3 November

Britain and France officially declared war on the Ottoman state after the bombardment of 3 November, but the political discussions in the British War Council regarding the issue of starting a campaign in Çanakkale started much later.[36] Meanwhile, the Çanakkale Fortified Area Command evaluated the situation by assessing the extent of the damage after the bombardment of 3 November. They outlined the problems:

---

33 Ibid.; Kol. BDH, Kls. 4669, Dos. H.3, Fih. 1–79. In the work titled *Çanakkale Naval Battles in the First World War* (*Harb-i Umumide Çanakkale Muharebât-ı Bahriyesi*) this duration is given as 17 minutes (p.10). In the report that Çanakkale Fortified Area Commander Colonel Cevat gave to the Supreme Military Command, this duration is stated as 20 minutes. *Askerî Tarih Belgeleri Dergisi*, Issue 132, January 2014, p. 33.

34 *Harb-i Umumide Çanakkale Muharebat-ı Bahriyesi* İstanbul, pp. 10, 11.

35 Ibid.; Kol. BDH, Kls. 4669, Dos. H-3, Fih. 1–87.

36 In the meantime, the *Mesudiye* battleship was sunk by a British submarine on 13 December 1914. Ibid.; Kol. BDH, Kls. 4669, Dos. H-3, Fih. 1–129.

> The soldiers must be completely camouflaged, particularly those stationed around the light guns. Attention must be paid to situate these soldiers in a dispersed manner. There should be training in this matter. Because the Mantelli batteries cannot be used against small warships, the guns should be kept in an area that would be safe from long range naval fire.
>
> As soon as there is word that any fort or force is engaged in a battle with the enemy, the necessary arrangements should be made by the troops. The fighting troops should be contacted and all possible support should be given to them. I repeat, that success in war will only be possible with the support of all troops, from the smallest unit to the largest formation.
>
> Success in war is possible if one does not lose fortitude and common sense, and by doing your duty with enthusiasm, and by not impeding it even at a troubled and stressful time. I hope that our military officers will work calmly once informed of the situation; that they will carry out their duties knowing that fighting back, in accordance with the current instructions, will be effective; and that they will set good examples in this matter.[37]

In the meantime the council, previously formed to prepare a defence plan against an attack on the Çanakkale, now prepared to implement the new orders of the Ministry of Supreme Military Command. According to these instructions, prepared on 8 November 1914, the Çanakkale was separated into four districts for defence against naval attack.

The First District would consist of the forts in Kumkale and Orhaniye on the Anatolian side as well as the forts in Sedd el Bahr and Ertuğrul on the Rumelian (European) side. These forts would prevent the Allied fleet from entering the Çanakkale.

The Second District would consist of the batteries that would halt the Allies' ships that were able to enter the strait. These ships would be prevented from anchoring in the Cape of Erenköy to prevent them using the Cape as a base for fresh operations.

The Third District would consist of mine lines that were protected with the batteries of small guns. These batteries would prevent the free movement of the Allied fleet and complicate the long and arduous job of sweeping mines. They would also prevent the actions of the ships that would try to proceed in order to open a route through the mine lines.

The Fourth District would consist of the forts in Anatolia Hamidiye and Kilitbahir, which were the strongest. They would prevent the Allied fleet from entering the Marmara basin. At the farthest end, there would be the forts of Anatolia Mecidiye, Değirmenburnu, and Nagara which cover the narrowest part of the strait.[38]

---

37 Ibid.; Kol. BDH, Kls. 4669, Dos. H.3, Fih. 1–88, 88a

38 Ibid.; Kol. BDH, Kls. 4669, Dos. H-3, Fih. 1–88,1–89.

During this time, the fortifications of the forts were completed and reinforced with heavy guns.[39]

Çanakkale Military Fortifications Command asked for suitable units, particularly the NCOs, to be sent to Kumkale in order for them to see the destruction of the Allied bombardment on the bulwarks and to learn from it.[40]

In an order from the Ministry of Supreme Military Command on 4 February, it was directed that the management of the tasks of sea patrols, security, mines, torpedoes and pilotage were to be given to Admiral Merten; the vehicles used for deployments would stay under the command of the Fortified Area but Admiral Merten would notify the Fortified Area Command of all that he would do and Merten's position in the command chain would stay the same.[41]

While these kinds of precautions were being taken against an attack on the Çanakkale, the ships from the Allied fleet would appear in front of the strait at various times and the information on these ships would be conveyed to the upper posts. There were other measures that evolved through experience. On 15 January 1915, the French submarine *Saphir* went aground at Nagara Point while it was trying to pass through the strait and it was sunk by the batteries on the shore.[42] In order to prevent further submarine activities in the strait, a net sewn together from a few fishermen's nets was tied up between the buoys in front of the last line of mines on the southern side of the strait.[43] This was followed by two more nets being thrown in front of the first line of mines.[44]

Another element used for the defence of the strait was the release of drifting mines. After 10 of the existing 23 drifting mines were sent to İstanbul on 20 September, the remaining 13 mines were supposed to be used against the enemy warships that were able to enter the strait. The necessary arrangements were made for these mines to be left in the parts of the sea with a strong current, ensuring they drifted with maximum effect.[45] Finally, to augment the surface defences, Çanakkale Fortified Area Command was reinforced with the pre-dreadnoughts *Barbaros* and *Turgut Reis*.[46]

The bombardment of 19 February 1915 and the precautions taken afterwards

In the meantime, the Allied powers had formalised their decision to open a front in Çanakkale and had planned to attack the Çanakkale with naval forces. The

---

39 Ibid.; Kol. BDH, Kls. 121, Dos. 572, Fih. 1.
40 Ibid.; Kol. BDH, Kls. 4669, Dos. H.3, Fih. 1–88.
41 *Deniz Harekâtı*, vol. VIII, p. 154.
42 Aga.; Kol. BDH, Kls. 4669, Dos. H-12, F. 1–23.
43 Aga.; Kol. BDH, Kol., Kls. 4669, Dos. H-12, Fih. 1–41.
44 Aga.; Kol. BDH, Kls. 4669, Dos. H-12, Fih. 1–40, 1–41.
45 Aga.; Kol. BDH, Kls. 4669, Dos. H-3, Fih. 1–31,1–32.
46 Deniz Harekâtı, ch. VIII, p. 156.

commander of the Allied fleet, Admiral Carden, prepared a plan for forcing the Çanakkale. He intended:

1 To destroy the four forts protecting the entrance of the strait and the forts on the first joint of the strait;
2 To sweep the mines up to the curve of Kilitbahir and Çanakkale;
3 To move the fleet up to the first curve on the strait and destroy the forts on Kepez Point;
4 To sweep the mines in the middle of Çanakkale and destroy the Çanakkale forts;
5 To pass Çanakkale bend with the fleet and move on to İstanbul.[47]

The Allied fleet attacked in the strait for the first time on 19 February 1915 in order to carry out the first part of this plan. At 09:51, they opened fire on the forts of Orhaniye, Ertuğrul and Kumkale. Since the guns on these forts were short range, they could not fire back. The bombardment from the battleship *Inflexible* was effective against the fort of Ertuğrul, and the same battleship directed its fire at the fort at Sedd el Bahr in the afternoon.

After it was found out by an aerial inspection that the guns in Kumkale and Orhaniye were intact, Admiral Carden started the second phase of the action at 14:00. Nevertheless, because of unfavourable weather conditions, the operation ended at 17:30.[48]

In the battle of 19 February, two Turkish officers and two soldiers fell, killed in action, and 11 soldiers were injured.[49] The bombardment did the greatest damage to the bulwarks of Kumkale. The outer parts of the bulwarks and slopes on all of the forts were destroyed. Some of the platforms and floors in Sedd el Bahr and Kumkale were smashed.[50]

After the bombardment of 19 February it was ordered that the troops of the Engineer Construction battalions in Kirte should go to Sedd el Bahr right away, and the troops in Halileli should depart for Kumkale and Orhaniye. The troops started off towards the evening. As soon as the ships of the Allied fleet withdrew, these troops started to remove the debris of the bulwarks and clear away the collapsed earth. With uninterrupted work until the morning, the damaged bulwarks were filled up with sandbags. The crenulations were repaired. Thus, the batteries in Ertuğrul, Orhaniye and Sedd el Bahr were made ready for battle for the next day. Even though the necessary repairs were made to the walls at Kumkale, the guns were nevertheless inoperable.

---

47 Mirliva Sedat; *Boğazlar Meselesi ve Çanakkale Deniz Savaşı'nda Türk Zaferi*, ed. Mehmet Köçer, Ankara, 2007, p. 137.

48 Ibid.; Kol. BDH, Kls. 121, Dos. 572, Fih. 1–15.

49 Ibid.; Kol. BDH, Kls. 4669, Dos. H-12, Fih. 1–54. Kls. 121, Dos. 572, Fih. 1.

50 Ibid.; Kol. BDH, Kls. 4669, Dos. H-12, Fih. 1–54.

The commander of the Fortified Area evaluated the bombardment in this manner:

> Despite the fact that the bombardment of 19 February lasted a long time and that it was most severe towards the evening, the casualties and the damage we suffered was slight. It was clearly seen in this bombardment that the possibility of the entrance bulwarks being battered by fire creates an inconvenience for us. Three of four ships from the Allied fleet, after they went in between Tekkeburnu and İmroz, were able to get close in and open fire without being affected by our return fire. The ships that went beyond Yenikoy were able to batter Orhaniye beyond our firing range. Our batteries could not open fire, or couldn't return fire, against the Allied battleships that were out of range.
>
> The guns on the bulwarks of Kumkale and Sedd el Bahr could easily be destroyed because their location made them a large and obvious target.
>
> The Allied fleet regulated its fire well and was effective because their aircraft provided reconnaissance. Their hits were numerous and usually clustered around our guns. The large shells opened gaping holes in our forts.
>
> The serenity our divisions showed under the fire of the Allied fleet was worthy of serious appreciation. When there was a chance of bombardment, the soldiers would go back to the protected area. And despite the constant shelling, they would commence firing as soon as the Allied fleet came within range. Taking advantage of every interval in the bombardment, which frequently covered the artillery with earth, the troops were trying their hardest to get the guns out into the open and into action.
>
> The battery that opened fire managed its shots calmly. The Ertuğrul battery started to find and hit the target at its fourth shot. It was particularly pleasing to see its economical approach to ammunition consumption.[51]

Despite all, the bombardment was evaluated as favourable since there was little harm done on the Turkish side. The Deputy Commander in Chief, Enver Pasha, communicated his appreciation to Çanakkale Fortified Area Command:

> I was pleased by the fortitude and effort shown by the soldiers in the batteries of the 5th Regiment despite the violent enemy fire today. I will present to our Commander in Chief in İstanbul that the commanders, officers and soldiers in the Çanakkale are worthy of trust in every way with the courage and zeal they have shown.[52]

The Allied fleet, having had no important success during the 19 February bombardment, could not attempt any other attack until 25 February because of unfavourable weather conditions. However, the repairs on the forts continued.

---

51 Ibid.; Kol. BDH, Kls. 121, Dos. 572, Fih. 1–8.

52 *Askerî Tarih Belgeleri Dergisi*, issue 132, p. 108.

The bombardment of 25 February 1915

It was windy and cloudy on 25 February. All night long, the rain hadn't stopped and the storm only began to abate towards the morning.[53] At 09.45, three French battleships came to the shores of Zığındere, and another cruiser that had previously been stationed near the Hayırsız Islands, and, along with the pre-dreadnought *Agamemnon*, that arrived off the coast near Yenikoy. At 10.00, *Agamemnon* opened fire at the walls of Sedd el Bahr. It also opened up on the fort at Ertuğrul, which returned the fire. Nevertheless, the range from the Orhaniye fort to the Allied ships was 11,000 to 13,000m, which was beyond the distance the guns of the batteries could reach. The ships from the Allied fleet continued the bombardment with a great volume of fire.

The effects were soon apparent on both sides. At 10.50, *Agamemnon* suffered three hits due to the fire from Ertuğrul Fort, and it returned to Merkeb Island. By mid-morning, Ertuğrul Fort was filled with earth and debris from the shelling, which made the movements of the crew harder, until, eventually, fire ceased altogether. At the same time, a shell struck the barrel of a second gun, and it was destroyed. The remainder of the battery was therefore hastily withdrawn to a protected area. In a little while, the bombardment of the Allied fleet intensified and, as their gunners ascertained the range, their fire grew more accurate against the Ottoman positions.

At 13.25, the Allied fleet stopped firing for a while. This gave the Ottoman forces a chance to clear up the forts, but only half an hour later, the bombardment started again on all the positions. Only four rounds were fired from Sedd el Bahr before the Allied fleet responded to the fire and two guns were knocked out. Similarly only four rounds were fired from Kumkale. Moreover it was reported that there was damage to the Orhaniye fort, which hadn't even started firing. The magazine was destroyed.[54] In the meantime, a fire broke out in Sedd el Bahr and the town started to burn.

At 15.30, the bombardment increased in severity and it continued this way until 17:30. After a further half an hour, five of the battleships of the Allied fleet stopped firing and moved back to Kömürburnu. It was reported at 18.30 that these battleships went to Bozcaada (Tenedos), and the others were slowly closing on Sedd el Bahr and Kumkale. Since there were no guns left in action there, the gunners had moved behind the batteries. It was reported that there was music coming from the ships of the Allied fleet. The ships watched the batteries constantly so that there couldn't be any repair work during the night.[55]

There were 13 killed in action as a result of the bombardment, and 18 were injured. It was reported that most of the guns at the bulwarks were buried with

53 Ibid.; Kol. BDH, Kls. 121, Dos. 572, Fih. 1–13.
54 Ibid.; Kol. BDH, Kls. 121, Dos. 572, Fih. 1–14.
55 Ibid.; Kol. BDH, Kls. 121, Dos. 572, Fih. 1–14.

earth; at least 15 to 20 days were required to clear them out; the barracks were partly burned down or half-demolished; and the telephone lines were wrecked. Since the Allied fleet held the entrance, no lights could be used at night. As a result, movement, clearance or repair at the bulwarks was nigh impossible.[56]

The bombardment of 25 February made the Supreme Military Command anxious, and the Deputy Commander in Chief Enver Pasha gave this order to Çanakkale Fortified Area Command:

> If the enemy fleet passes the strait, there must be further precautions taken in İstanbul, which would require at least a period of 12 hours to execute. Thus, if our outer defences are silenced and the enemy fleet starts battering down our inner defences, or if the enemy fleet starts to move along the strait directly without being affected by the fire from the bulwarks, the Main Headquarters should report clearly by this wire: 'The fortifications are finished'. Once the enemy ships pass through the strait and reach the Marmara Sea, the I and II Army Commands as well as the Main Headquarters should be notified directly and right away.[57]

After the 25 February bombardment, the following precautions were taken in the area:

> The battery on the hills at Halileli was moved to a protected site in order not to allow it to be destroyed: its location had clearly been discovered by the Allied forces.
>
> One battery of the 1st Battalion in Tenger was placed secretly on the hills of Kereviztepe. This battery was given the task of firing unexpectedly at the battleships that lingered between Sedd el Bahr and Hisarlik, and preventing any attempts at invasion of Kumkale. Just as with the entrance fortifications, the protected area behind the howitzer batteries was reinforced and fortified so as not to give an opportunity to the Allied fleet to locate the batteries separately and destroy them. Since it had become too difficult for the batteries to continue firing from the open sites, they were taken to a protected area. The number of dummy batteries was increased. Finally, on 26 February 1915, the 10th mine line, consisting of 53 mines, was laid in the strait between Değirmenburnu and the Çanakkale lighthouse.[58]

---

56 Ibid.; Kol. BDH, Kls. 121, Dos. 572, Fih. 1–15

57 *Askerî Tarih Belgeleri Dergisi*, Issue 132, p. 179.

58 Nazmi (Bnb.), *Çanakkale Deniz Savaşları Günlüğü (1914–1922)* Çanakkale Deniz Müzesi Komutanlığı Yayınları, Çanakkale 2004, p. 41.

The bombardment of 27 February 1915

After carrying out the first step of Admiral Carden's attack plan on 25 February, the Allied fleet continued with the bombardment to achieve the next steps. Since the weather was taken into consideration when it came to the bombardments, the next barrage took place on 27 February.

It was reported that at 08.00 that day two cruisers and one battleship were across the entrance; two torpedoes were thus being fired from around Kumkale and Orhaniye; and six minesweepers, one seaplane carrier, and 11 small ferries were located behind the Merkeb islands.

In the meantime, it was reported by the 19th Division that a scouting party of 10 men had landed on Sedd el Bahr by using morning fog to their advantage; that they went forward until Harapkale; and they escaped when confronted, with two of them injured. The division was notified that this scouting party had come as far as Harapkale without being seen, and that the utmost care must be given to observing and defending the area around Sedd el Bahr.

On the other hand, four Allied torpedo boats entered the strait, later followed by two more torpedo vessels and two cruisers. Upon the scouting party being driven back, the Allied fleet came close to Sedd el Bahr and started to give covering fire with machine guns.

At 15.00, they wanted to get closer to Sedd el Bahr again with a small boat under the protection of the battleships but they were driven back. At 16.00, it was reported that three pre-dreadnoughts and six torpedo boats were beyond the entrance on the line between Sedd el Bahr and Kumkale, that there were three pre-dreadnoughts, two cruisers and five ships near Sedd el Bahr, and the torpedo boats at the entrance were slowly backing away.

Against the possibility of the Allied fleet's attempt at seizing the entrance, and for the purpose of keeping the site more secure using the nearby infantry divisions, it was ordered that 1st Battalion of the 5th Heavy Artillery Regiment be transferred to 19th Division, and the battalion should gather in Kirte. It was also decided that the 2nd Battalion should be transferred to the 9th Division and the battalion should assemble in Halileli. It was further ordered that these battalions should be formed into counter-invasion detachments, making use of the entrance fortifications. Their ammunition, provisions and other supplies were to be pooled with the infantry divisions.[59]

Reflection on the war in İstanbul

The bombardments of the Allied fleet against the Çanakkale made the İstanbul government despair for a short while; for it was thought that the fortifications

59 Ibid.; Kol. BDH, Kls. 121, Dos. 572, Fih. 1–20.

were unable to resist such a powerful maritime force. It was even decided that the government should temporarily move away from İstanbul to Eskisehir. The sultan approved this decision. The manager of the imperial furnishings, Hacı Akif Bey, went to Eskisehir and provided places to stay there for the sultan and his cortège. The valuable items from the sultan's treasury were put in chests and sent to Konya as a precaution. If the Allied fleet made it through the strait, the sultan would go immediately to Eskisehir together with the ministers.[60]

With the decisions taken on 28 February, the Ministry of Finance reported that 3,500 gold coins would be given to the Police Director General once the city of İstanbul was exposed to the bombardment. The Director General, who would operate as the governor of the city, would be authorised to spend this money on all the various needs of the city.

The Ministry of Post, Telegraph and Telephone declared that it was necessary to take over the network of İstanbul Telephone Company and all calls should be taken under his control in the event of the enemy passing the Çanakkale. To be able to do this, it was vital to remove the technical employees that were citizens of enemy states. Some 2,000 gold coins were assigned to bring employees from Hungary in order to replace those removed.[61] These concerns ended only after the failure of the 18 March bombardment.

The bombardments until 18 March 1915 and the precautions taken

There was no large-scale bombardment in the Çanakkale between 27 February and 18 March. From the beginning of March, some of the ships from the Allied fleet came to the strait and opened a desultory fire but these were never in the form of a full-blown assault. For instance, at 10.45 on 1 March, some ships from the Allied fleet came near Soganli, and they came under fire from the Mesudiye and Muini Zafer batteries in Rumelia and the Dardanos battery in Anatolia.

On 2 March, at 14.20, the pre-dreadnought battleship *Cornwallis* opened fire at Dardanos battery from the vicinity of Kereviz Brook. The fire from the Allied fleet continued with intervals for a while, until it ceased at 15.00. After a time, the Allied pre-dreadnoughts started to proceed again. The bombardment resumed at 16.00. Three pre-dreadnoughts together with three torpedo boats targeted Dardanos. At 16.20, the rear mast of *Cornwallis* was hit and broken, but Dardanos battery continued to come under naval fire from a distance. Another pre-dreadnought hammered the Erenköy howitzer battery.[62] At 17.40, the ships started to move away slowly. In the next 20 minutes, three pre-dreadnoughts drew

60 Ali Fuat Türkgeldi, *Görüp işittiklerim*, Türk Tarih Kurumu Basımevi, Ankara 1949, p. 130.

61 Yusuf Hikmet Bayur, *Türk İnkılâbı Tarihi*, Vol. 3, Part 2, Ankara, Türk Tarih Kurumu Yay., 1955, pp. 72, 73.

62 Ibid.; Kol. BDH, Kls. 121, Dos. 572, Fih. 1–25.

off. While the larger ships fell back, the torpedo boats stayed at the entrance as a monitoring flotilla.

On 3 March, at 13.00, the first shell was fired towards the hills of Halileli, signalling the start of a barrage. Until 13.50, the hills of Halileli and Tenker were bombarded at intervals. The pre-dreadnoughts opened fire against the howitzers in Erenköy and the guns recently moved onto the hills of Halileli. From 14.30 to 16.30, the fire continued at intervals. At 16.30, the attack started to intensify.[63] But, once again, as evening came, at 18.10, the ships of the Allied fleet started to move away. One pre-dreadnought and five torpedo boats again stayed at the entrance while all the others moved back. On that day, one Turkish soldier fell and 11 others were injured.[64]

On 5 March at 11.30, in the vicinity of Kumkale and Yenişehir, there was yet another bombardment. At the same time, the environs of Sedd el Bahr came under fire. The shelling went on for about two and a half hours. Then, at 14.45, one torpedo boat, one cruiser and five pre-dreadnoughts opened up on Sedd el Bahr from different directions. Three big rowing boats got close to the dock of Sedd el Bahr and around 70 soldiers landed on the shore. Half of the detachment from the 3rd Division of the 27th Regiment started firing right away at this landing and the Allied fleet started to return fire to cover its own forces. The infantry battle went on for about three hours. The infantrymen resisted strongly and had some partial success in driving back the Allied soldiers on land with bayonet charges. The Allied fleet nevertheless pounded Halileli severely. Towards 16.00, the barrage of the Allied forces around Kumkale started to intensify. After bombarding the Kumkale and Orhaniye for a long time, disembarkation started from the side of the dock. Thanks to the strong resistance of the Turkish infantry, the Allied soldiers couldn't get far inland that day.

When the Allied forces couldn't move forward from the side of the docks in Kumkale, they started to disembark between Orhaniye and Kumkale, behind the forts, and adjacent to the town. One squad of a Turkish infantry company entered the area from this direction. They fired with some effect at the Allied forces that had moved around the town. The Allied fleet was covering its infantry with seven pre-dreadnoughts, three cruisers and five torpedo boats and all the areas around Kumkale and Orhaniye up to Yenisehir were engulfed in gun fire. The Allied landing forces that started to come ashore between Kumkale and Orhaniye were nevertheless subjected to retaliatory fire by a company that was detached from the 3rd Battalion of the 64th Regiment. Due to this resistance, the Allied forces couldn't move up to the high ground: they were held on the beaches. At 19.00 hours, the Allied forces evacuated by taking their surviving and injured soldiers off the shore on small boats.[65] During these battles of 5

63 Ibid.; Kol. BDH, Kls. 121, Dos. 572, Fih. 1–26.

64 Ibid.; Kol. BDH, Kls. 121, Dos. 572, Fih. 1–27.

65 Ibid.; Kol. BDH, Kls. 121, Dos. 572, Fih. 1–32a.

March, one Turkish officer and 47 soldiers were wounded, and 16 soldiers were killed in action.[66]

On 6 March, two pre-dreadnoughts – *Cornwallis* and *Majestic* – started to fire at the environs of Halileli, and progressed slowly up the strait. The French battleship *Suffren* also moved up from the entrance. They opened fire at Dardanos at 10.30 to which the guns at Dardanos responded. At 11.00, Rumelia Mecidiye opened fire too but they didn't continue as their shells were falling short.

Around 13.00, the fire slackened. However, indirect fire on Mecidiye started again soon after. There, three pre-dreadnoughts and one torpedo boat were firing at a range of 2km, a fact reported by the commander of the 19th Division, Lieutenant Colonel Mustafa Kemal (Atatürk).

Towards 16.00, the severity of the direct and indirect fire increased. Every now and then Mecidiye returned fire against the approaching ships but their shots still fell short. At 17.00, the Allied ships retreated, ending the engagement for both sides.[67]

On 7 March, at 10.55, shells once again landed around Halileli. The most severe of the bombardments was directed at areas in depth. Many shells hit the front but also fell behind the batteries, on the kitchens and barracks as well as the training areas. At Dardanos, howitzer and field artillery battalions responded to the fire of the Allied fleet. Two shells of the central group hit *Agamemnon* and *Lord Nelson*. One shell from the howitzers hit one of the French ships.[68] At 15.30, the Allied fleet started to leave the strait, with *Lord Nelson* and *Agamemnon* in the lead and the French ships following them. In the bombardment of 7 March, 14 men were injured and five were killed in action.[69]

The next day, the Turkish mine-layer ship *Nusret* went to Karanlık Harbour, and without any incident, left 26 mines at 100m intervals parallel to the shore. At 10.30, four ships came towards the entrance of the strait, and they opened fire at Kumkale at 11.40 hours. After a few salvoes, they fired at Sedd el Bahr more intermittently. At 13.00, *Queen Elizabeth* fired at Mecidiye from a location beyond Kumkale. It moved towards Karanlık Harbour for some time and then came back to Kumkale. At 14.10, it fired again. At 14.30, two of the pre-dreadnoughts returned from Karanlık Harbour and bombarded Erenköy more intermittently. At 15.15, *Queen Elizabeth* slowly moved away and left the strait in front of Kumkale as its rounds were falling short. At 16.00, other ships also stopped firing and left Karanlık Harbour. In the following days, the attacks directed at the strait were not conclusive as they were generally short-lived and ineffective.[70] These bombardments by the Allied fleet were reported in the Turkish press, and the

66 Ibid.; Kol. BDH, Kls. 121, Dos. 572, Fih. 1–33.
67 Ibid.; Kol. BDH, Kls. 121, Dos. 572, Fih. 1–37.
68 Ibid.; Kol. BDH, Kls. 121, Dos. 572, Fih. 1–42.
69 Ibid.; Kol. BDH, Kls. 121, Dos. 572, Fih. 1–42a.
70 Ibid.; Kol. BDH, Kls. 121, Dos. 572, Fih. 1–46, 1–47, 1–50, 1–52.

results of the bombardments raised the hopes of the people. On 17 March 1915, *Tanin* newspaper made this comment:

> This is a very strong fleet. So, the British cannot find any fault in their ships for not being able to force the strait. If the strait isn't forced, it is not because these ships are not capable of forcing them but because the strait is one that cannot be forced. Until now, the enemy has been less giving in terms of the sacrifice it would make for the strait. Even if they couldn't pass the strait, these ships would be able to move and fight more boldly. They didn't do that, which means they are afraid of both the strait and the result[s of attempting to force it]. What they have done so far is examining and investigating, and they have fired thousands of shells, some here and some there.
>
> The enemy has not achieved anything yet, and it looks like it is impossible for them to do so. What has passed until now can be called a demonstration. I wonder how much this demonstration has cost them.
>
> To summarise, it is understood that for a result amounting to 'nothing' the enemy had to leave the firing line with its huge pre-dreadnoughts and other battleships. One of these ships has gone aground hopelessly; two of them have been torpedoed; one carrier ship and a few minesweeping ships have sunk; and at least two torpedo boats have been damaged. We are quite pleased with this result. That's why we would like the attack to go on.[71]

The İstanbul government, in a statement given on this issue, pointed out that in every part of the strait all defence measures required had been taken by the Ottomans; that the chances of the British–French navy forcing the strait were diminishing by the day; that work was continuing at the strait day and night under the surveillance of experienced engineers; and that it would be technically impossible for the Allied fleet to pass the strait now that the density of the mine lines had been increased.[72] News like this made a positive impact on Turkish people; the hope of winning the war increased each day.

The bombardment of 18 March 1915

The main assault of the Allied fleet took place on 18 March. At 10.30, it was observed that the Allied ships were proceeding as before in front of Sedd el Bahr. These ships consisted of the pre-dreadnoughts *Agamemnon*, *Lord Nelson*, *Goliath*, *Majestic* and *Triumph*, in the lead along with the battleship *Queen Elizabeth* and the battle cruiser *Inflexible*. The pre-dreadnoughts started firing at the batteries at 10.58, and they then pushed on towards Karanlık Harbour.[73]

---

71 *Tanin*, 4 Mart 1331 (17 March 1915), p. 1.
72 *Tanin*, 5 Mart 1331 (18 March 1915), p. 1.
73 *Askerî Tarih Belgeleri Dergisi*, Sayı 132, p. 293.

Queen Elizabeth opened fire at Anatolia Hamidiye battery and the bulwark of Cimenlik near Çanakkale while *Agamemnon*, *Inflexible* and *Lord Nelson* opened fire at the batteries of Kilitbahir and Rumelia Mecidiye. Soon after, the French ships separated into two wings with *Suffren* and *Charlemagne* on the Rumelian shore and *Gaulois* and *Bouvet* on the Anatolian shore. While the British ships were firing from a moderate distance, the French ships moved forward and behaved as if they wanted to fire at the batteries more closely and get a result more quickly. Since the main batteries were too far away from the ships to return fire, it was the howitzers that were ordered to fire more rapidly. The 25cm and 35cm guns lining the shore thus opened up. Due to the clouds of dust and smoke resulting from the Allied fleet's firing, the batteries couldn't easily be seen. The rangefinder at Hamidiye battery showed that the ships had got closer than 1,400m.

The gunners were ordered to fire on the largest ships to protect the main artillery group from being destroyed by the Allied attacks; it was also noted that howitzer batteries should fire in such a way as to protect the main group and that their ammunition should be used economically since the battle at hand would be need to be decisive.[74] The fact that howitzer batteries were hitting some targets quite well was understood by *Inflexible* which left the line of battle.

The main Allied group opened fire from a distance of 12.5km. From 11.15 until 14.00, the situation continued with no significant change either way. Hamidiye battery fired intermittently sometimes with just one gun and at other times with two guns, using either the 35.5-cm or the 24-cm pieces. The battery in Rumelia Hamidiye had never fired before. The Mecidiye battery continued to fire intermittently. The telephone connection with the Rumelia post was cut after two hours when a shell hit the telephone exchange.[75] *Queen Elizabeth* was firing at Hamidiye and Çimenlik where the latter took many hits as it was an old-style fort and more easily targeted.

At 12.00, it was found out that the bulwarks overlooking the entrance at Çimenlik were completely destroyed and the guns inside were knocked out. In the meantime, the battleships *Bouvet* and *Gaulois* came as close as 5,000m to the line between Kepez and Soğanlı, and they moved towards the quarantine line. *Bouvet*, once within the range of Ottoman guns, was fired at by the batteries of Anatolia and Rumelia Hamidiye.

At 13.55, the commander of the fort stated they took two hits. However, at this precise moment, it was noticed that *Bouvet* was sinking. The French ships that were following along the Rumelian shore went ahead to help *Bouvet*.[76] The French stopped their firing completely and the British also paused for five minutes.

Making use of this brief lull, the soldiers cleaned the gun rails immediately. The pinions of the guns were also oiled. This was a great opportunity for the forts.

---

74 *Harb-i Umumide Çanakkale Muharebâtı Bahriyesi*, p. 18.

75 Ibid.; p. 19.

76 Ibid.; Kol. BDH, Kls. 4669, Kls. H-13, Fih. 1–14, 14.

The ships *Charlemagne* and *Suffren* that came to save *Bouvet* saw that it was in great danger. Since they were also damaged, they left the battle line. This retreat was quite irregular and the morale of the Ottoman soldiers noticeably increased. However, in place of the four retreating French ships, six British ships came up through the entrance. The firing continued intensely on both sides. At 14.00, the battery at Dardanos stopped firing. This silence was caused by the deaths of the Battery Commander First Lieutenant Hasan and his observation officer Lieutenant Mevsuf. This situation was discovered by an officer that was sent to the battery, and the battery was brought back to an operating condition again under fresh leadership.[77]

Of the six incoming British ships, three headed to Rumelia and three to Anatolia. Around 16.30, a British pre-dreadnought got damaged and stuck in front of Dardanos while another one was seen listing to starboard beyond Tenker. The battle continued until 19.00.[78]

The casualties and results of the bombardment of 18 March

The fact that the Allied fleet couldn't pass the strait and their ships were damaged or sunk was met with enthusiasm by the Turkish people. For the difference between the Ottomans and the Allied fleet in terms of ammunition and strength was too disproportionate to compare. Even though the damage on the Ottoman side was relatively low, despite the heavy fire, their limited ammunition was further reduced, and this made them much weaker in the face of a new attack.

In the bombardment of 18 March, 24 were killed in action on the Ottoman side with 55 wounded while there were three fatalities and 15 wounded amongst the German troops present. Among the ships of the Allied fleet, three of them had sunk and four of them had been crippled. The casualties on the damaged ships were 44, and the overall casualties amounted to 800. The ammunition the Allied states used was much greater than the Turkish expenditure. For instance, it was found out that more than 4,000 shells fell in the Dardanos area alone.[79] Selahattin Adil commented on the battle of 18 March in this way:

> The battle of 18 March has proved – as has been confirmed in many previous battles – that land fortifications built with inadequate materials and tools were still superior to a fleet. In general, the result of this battle can be summarised in one statement: no matter what the value of the materials at hand is, if they

---

77 *Harb-i Umumide Çanakkale Muharebâtı Bahriyesi*, p. 21.

78 Ibid.; Kol. BDH, Kls. 4669, Kls. H-13, Fih. 1–14, 14.

79 Ibid.; Kol., Kls. 4669, Dos. H-13, Fih. 1–13, 1–14, 1–16; Aga.; Kol., Kls. 5283, Dos. H-14, Fih. 1–3, 1–4;. Aga.; Kol., Kls. 5640, Dos. H-9, Fih. 1–2; Aga.; Kol., Kls. 5675, Dos. H-1, Fih. 1–11, 1–12.

are used well with faith and zeal towards the goal, it would be possible to gain success and arrive at a decisive conclusion. The battle of 18 March is a good example that the side with a strong faith will always succeed.[80]

The commander of Çanakkale Fortified Area, Cevat Pasha, expressed his happiness with the success of the battle of the 18 March and rewarded those who contributed to this accomplishment as follows:

1 I congratulate all of our brave soldiers who showed a great deal of success, endurance and sacrifice in the defeat that the enemy fleet suffered. On Friday and Monday nights, the surahs Yasin and Feth will be read for the dear souls of our companions who reached the state of martyrdom for this aim. The legends of these heroic sons which illuminate the glories of Ottoman history will undoubtedly be recounted to the next generations as an example of bravery, and they will be inscribed in our memories with the respect they deserve.
2 I appreciate all of you – the commander of the largest unit as well as the smallest, down to the private soldiers – for the strength and courage you have shown. The paperwork regarding the payments to be given to the families of the deceased, whom they entrusted to us, will be arranged accordingly and sent out with great speed.
3 Due to the effort they have demonstrated, the names listed here are shown particular appreciation for their service and each is awarded with a Silver Medal for Merit in Battle: Transport Officer Major Nuri, First Lieutenant Ali from the Fortified Area Command; the Battery Commander of Rumelia Mecidiye Fortification, Captain Hilmi; the Battery Commander of Rumelia Hamidiye; First Lieutenant Nazmi; the Battery Commander of Namazgah, Captain Mahir; Captain Herşel from Anadolu Hamidiye, and Squad Officer Remzi from the Dardanos Fortification. Three have been awarded the Silver Medal for Merit in Battle with Distinction: the 2nd Heavy Artillery Brigade Commander, Colonel Talat; the Fortification Officer, Colonel Şükrü, and the training officer, Colonel Lieutenant Wossidlo. It is ordered that they are to be notified when their medals are sent.[81]

The relief that the Allied fleet couldn't pass through the Çanakkale in the bombardment of 18 March was echoed in Austria–Hungary and Germany, the allies of the Ottoman state, and the situation was reported in Turkish newspapers. The latter also gave examples from the foreign press. For instance, Austrian newspapers on 19 March congratulated the garrison of Çanakkale for the great success they had achieved.[82] German newspapers also reported the Turkish accomplishment in

---

80 Selahattin Adil, *Çanakkale Cephesinden Mektuplar-Hatıralar*, pp. 45, 46.
81 *Askerî Tarih Belgeleri Dergisi*, Issue 132, p. 267.
82 *Tanin*, 8 Mart 1331 (21 Mart 1915), p. 1.

Çanakkale, remarking that it was a great success that two British pre-dreadnoughts had sunk due to the damage they took, and that one French dreadnought and one torpedo boat had been destroyed.[83]

The celebratory communiqués that were sent by the Ottoman Empire's partners were also printed in the newspapers. The German Emperor Wilhelm wrote: 'I express my sincere congratulations for the brilliant accomplishments shown during the defence of the Çanakkale yesterday and the day before, and I ask that my congratulations are conveyed to the brave Commander Cevat Pasha.'[84] The newspapers also published messages from the German prince and the chief of German General Staff, and Enver Pasha's responses.

These reports made the Turkish feel appreciated by their allies. The trust and appreciation the Central Powers had for the Turkish army was particularly emphasised. This emphasis on a 'brotherhood in arms' – initiated in Germany and replicated everywhere during the First World War – was used as propaganda and was manifest in all kinds of badges, medals, money, postcards and ephemera. Propagandists emphasised that there was an unbroken line of success between Çanakkale and that which continued in Galicia.

Evaluation of the operations

There were several turning points in the Çanakkale naval operations. The first among these was the bombardment of 3 November 1914. This barrage reminded the Turkish high command that the defences of the Çanakkale were inadequate while, for the British, it proved an experiment that would shed light on the possibility of forcing a passage through the Çanakkale.

The bombardment of 3 November painfully reminded the Ottoman regime that batteries placed on the Anatolian and Rumelian shores of the entrance of the strait were out-ranged. The fact that only the forts in Orhaniye and Ertuğrul were able to fire showed how serious the situation was. In fact, when we take into consideration that the Ottoman state had only just ended the Balkan Wars where it had lost considerable amounts of both land and manpower, these might seem to be reasonable justifications for the inadequacies in the precautions taken in the defence of the Çanakkale. However, since the straits were considered to be the entrance to the Ottoman Empire, this short-lived bombardment made it imperative that there should be more effective security precautions at this entrance.

Another important date for the Çanakkale operations was 19 February 1915. This date is significant in that it was the date of the first major attack on the Çanakkale after 3 November. In this bombardment, the batteries at the entrance of the strait couldn't return much fire. The reasons for this might be counted as the

83 *Tanin*, 8 Mart 1331 (21 Mart 1915), p. 1.
84 *Tanin*, 11 Mart 1331 (24 Mart 1915), p. 1.

limited ammunition the Turkish army had and the fact that ships of the Allied fleet did not come within firing range. Contemporary reports confirm this. Local reports indicate that Turkish batteries couldn't use any of their guns when the ships were out of range, but once they came within range, the artillerymen ran to the guns and started firing with some relief. The thanks Cevat Pasha sent to the artillery soldiers is also relevant in this context. Cevat Pasha stated that the Allied fleet was unsuccessful in the attack of 19 February. He also stated that the main reason for this was that the Allied ships were scattered against all of the forts; that they acted too reservedly in general; and that they fired while on the move.

When considered within the larger picture, it is clear that the Allied fleet couldn't carry out its attack plan. Evaluated from the Turkish point of view, this first official attack of the Allied fleet resulted in the prevention of ships entering the strait. However, it also showed the necessity of taking some precautions in terms of the defensive plan because during this attack Turkish bulwarks were destroyed by flanking fire even when Allied ships were prevented from attacking from the front.

On 25 February, the Allied fleet carried out the first part of its attack plan and prevented the forts at the entrance of the strait from firing by inflicting significant damage on them. Moreover, they also succeeded in making frontal attacks. The bombardment of 25 February had increased the hope of success in the Allied fleet while it greatly concerned İstanbul and necessitated new precautions at the straits.

Although the bombardments that lasted periodically until 18 March were not as effective as the others, there were attempts at disembarkation on 27 February and 5 March, and these attempts were driven off by the Turks.

The bombardment of 18 March was more decisive. However, this attack –which featured many Ottoman artillery hits on the ships of the Allied fleet – convinced the Allied powers that the strait couldn't be forced without an amphibious operation.

Evaluation of the sources

Despite the fact that 'Çanakkale Naval Battles' has entered the literature of Turkish history as 'Naval Victory of 18 March', and, due to its significance, it has been accepted as the day of commemorating all killed in action in Turkey, it is with sadness we realise that the works written on this topic are not equal to the importance given to this issue. Notwithstanding that the 'Naval Victory of 18 March' is regarded as a victory gained as the result of all of the Çanakkale operations, it is quite interesting to see that the works written on the Çanakkale naval actions are fewer in number compared to the works on the land battles. It might be thought that the reason for this is that the land operations lasted longer, more divisions took part in these battles, and more of the divisional commanders wrote their memoirs about them. All this draws our attention to the fact that a very limited number of works have been written after consulting the official documents, and the works written lately have been rather critical about the Çanakkale land battles. Since it is mostly official documents that have been used in this chapter, there are some points to dwell upon with regard to the utility of these sources.

When the documents about the Çanakkale naval battles are examined, they are reported minute by minute, hour by hour, day by day and with overlays and maps. They also include the correspondence and orders from all levels, from the commander of the smallest troop, to the highest authorities. They give details of the weather conditions, and why operations were halted by them. The documents include notes of warning as well as messages of appreciation. The reports of shore observations were written in particular detail.

Notwithstanding that most of the reports confirm each other, there are also statements that contradict each other. For instance, it is seen that some numbers don't match up in the reports by some of the troops. This discrepancy (with minor differences) is usually about the ships that enter the strait and the time of their entry. There are contradictions particularly among the reports of 18 March operations. The number of ships that entered the strait on 18 March was recorded variously as 12, 15, and 18 vessels. This is believed to be a result of observing activity since these reports were given by the divisional commanders located in different parts of the strait. These divisions wrote down numbers according to ships that were in their field of vision, and thus we have quite different numbers.

It is noteworthy that there were no warnings about the reports from the higher command. In other campaigns of the First World War, there were orders warning against issues such as the deficiency of reports or misinformation. For instance, in the Galicia Campaign, the commander of the XV Army Corps had often warned the commanders of the troops, and gave instructions about how the reports should be written, and in what way the contents of the report should be arranged. This commander also pointed out to the troops that the orders coming from the divisions were a few minutes late and these minutes might have a significant cost. In the Çanakkale campaign, there are no orders of warning like this. It was only mentioned, sometimes, that the orders were late. The Çanakkale Fortified Area Command Chief of Staff, Selahattin Adil, pointed out the intelligence that the Allied fleet could start an attack on 18 March, but the information had arrived 12 hours later.[85] Delay in orders was seen more often in the Çanakkale land battles. In a situation like this, the commanders of the troops had to use their own initiative. The best example of this is Lieutenant Colonel Mustafa Kemal's intervention against the attack at Arıburnu on 25 April 1915 without waiting for any orders.

The official records mention the deployment of German technical personnel to the area, their inspections, the precautions taken, and that their names were also on the lists of those to be rewarded. The mistakes German officers made – just like the mistakes of Turkish officers – were included in the reports. The main criticism was directed at the German Commander of the Orhaniye battery,

---

85 Selahattin Adil, *Çanakkale Cephesindeki Mektuplar-Hatıralar*, p. 39.

specifically that he used too much ammunition in the bombardment of 19 February but stayed relatively inactive during the bombardment of 25 February, and that this encouraged the Allied fleet.

However, in correspondence sent to the Çanakkale Fortified Area Commander, Nihat Pasha, on 12 March 1916, it was reported that a military ceremony was to be held to commemorate the lives of those fallen during the naval battles of 18 March 1915. It was also noted that there would be a similar religious ceremony for German soldiers as well at the cemetery. This is significant in showing us that the Turkish authorities and higher-level commanders did not forget their friends who supported them in the Çanakkale operations. It is quite noticeable that even though the Turkish official records did not ignore the German contributions, Liman von Sanders only wrote about German officers in his memoirs of the Çanakkale naval battles.

The issues surrounding the Çanakkale naval operations

In many works written on the naval actions of Çanakkale, the issue that was rarely debated was the deficiency of the batteries and fortifications in Çanakkale Fortified Area at the beginning of the war. It was nevertheless noted that these batteries would prove inadequate against the Allied fleet, particularly Britain's Royal Navy, then the largest sea power in the world. The discussion of whether to move the İstanbul government can be seen as evidence of this anxiety. However, when the official records are examined, it appears that the troops in the Çanakkale sector were expecting an attack on the strait from the outset and there was not any hopelessness about their situation: indeed, their morale was quite high.

Another important accepted point was that the Çanakkale had geographical characteristics that were convenient for defence, and that there would be success if these characteristics were assessed correctly and the right precautions taken.

The first of the more debated issues was the defence plan and the measures taken in the Çanakkale naval operations. This debate is not about the Turkish chain of command but rather between Turkish and German officers. In terms of land defence, while Turkish officers based their defence on the shoreline, the commander of the V Army, Liman von Sanders, nevertheless thought it fit to protect the shore with few troops and to have the main defences in depth. As for the naval operations, Turkish officers thought that due to the strategic position at the entrance of the Çanakkale there should be short-range guns in the fortifications here while longer-range pieces should be placed in the inner fortifications that were considered to be the main defences. This way, the long-range guns would not be destroyed right away. The value of this decision was seen clearly during the bombardments.

The Çanakkale Fortified Area Command Chief of Staff, Lieutenant Colonel Selahattin Adil, reported in early 1915 that the German advisors on the fortifications were preparing a report against the views of Turkish officers. Selahattin Adil stated that, with the decision of the Inspectorship of Heavy Artillery, many forts were left out of the Turkish staff assessment. He emphasised the defence plan was based on the entrance of the Çanakkale but that bigger 30.5cm howitzers were on order from Germany. However, there were contradictory decisions about the points for building fortifications, the placement of barbed wire fences, giving up on torpedo observation stations and the positioning of the 9th Infantry Division (which was located in the Fortified Area as mobile forces and was left under the command of III Army Corps, and, as a result, tasks like training were left to various troops that were supervised by separate posts). He also criticised that the Fortified Area Command which was supposed to function together and which had the heaviest responsibility due to the necessity of commanding all assault axes, but which was not given any right of observation. He argued that he was permitted only to fire guns on days determined by higher command, but he was expected to inform the Ministry of Defence of the ships that passed through the strait. This left him unable to fulfil his real duties.[86]

Selahattin Adil also stated that, by the order of the Army Improvement Council which was inspired by Germany after the Balkan Wars, various military categories were attached to the Turkish inspectorship (but under German officers in the Council of Improvement) and each category had been put under the command and management of different inspectors. This resulted in significant delays due to the lack of cooperation particularly between sea and land formations. According to Selahattin Adil, if the plan, prepared by the council, of fortification was put into action, the Fortified Area would be weaker compared with that before the war.[87] Notwithstanding that Selahattin Adil's statements were correct, the new arrangements made after the bombardment of 3 November also turned out to be inadequate, and the situation was re-evaluated after each assault. Liman von Sanders, who was the Inspector of the I Army at the beginning of the war, and the commander of the newly formed V Army during the Çanakkale operations, had criticised Enver Pasha, the Ottoman Minister of Defence and the Deputy Commander in Chief, for the precautions taken in the defence of the Çanakkale. Liman von Sanders wrote that he himself took all the precautions for the strait, but Enver Pasha later made changes in the arrangements. Liman von Sanders thought these changes were quite unwarranted, and he reported the situation to Germany. He later abandoned the plan envisaged by Enver Pasha.[88]

---

86 Selahattin Adil; *Hayat Mücadeleleri Selahattin Adil Paşa'nın Hatıraları*, İstanbul, Zafer Matbaası, 1982, p. 209.

87 Selahattin Adil, *Çanakkale Cephesinden Mektuplar-Hatıralar*, p. 23.

88 *Çanakkale Hatıraları*, vol. 2, ed. Metin Martı, Arma Yayınları, İstanbul 2002, pp. 51, 52.

By contrast, Brigadier General Sedat stated that Liman von Sanders made the changes in the plan by taking advantage of Enver Pasha's travel in Caucasia, and this was criticised in the Main Headquarters.[89]

Debates like this go on. In fact, the controversy between the Turks and the Germans shows its presence not only in the Çanakkale Campaign but also in other campaigns. The reasons for this are to be found in the situation the Ottoman Empire was in after all the defeats it had suffered and Germany's technical superiority compared to its allies. Germany wanted the Ottoman Empire to remain strong against the Allied powers and wear them down. This way, the Allied powers would gradually lose their strength and would be weakened compared to Germany. However, there were different points of view on this matter both at the start and at the end of the war. On the one hand, the propaganda opportunities provided by the Central Powers' 'brotherhood in arms', the power of the Turkish army, especially the benefits it provided Germany in the battles at the Galicia Campaign, was commended. There was particular praise for its conduct in the Çanakkale Campaign. On the other hand, the Ottoman Empire was sometimes compared to a corpse, to which Germany was shackled.

In conclusion, the naval battles of the Çanakkale Campaign, one of the many campaigns the Ottoman state fought during the First World War, can be considered a success. At a time of defeats in other campaigns, the Çanakkale naval operations were seen as a significant outcome facilitated by mines laid in the sea and guns used against the Allied fleet. Ultimately this victory was a source of inspiration for the Turkish troops engaged in the Çanakkale land battles, but it also became a source of spiritual renewal during the Turkish War of Independence.

---

89 Sedat, p. 108.

Chapter 7
Talking to hearts and minds
Influencing strategies in the Gallipoli Campaign

Metin Gürcan

> 'The poet! While the Ottoman soldier was willingly shedding his blood for you, why don't you write a poem for him by dedicating some of your moments?'[1]

Since ancient times, the aim of influencing by shaping and managing perceptions has always been one of the great objectives of strategic thinking. Chinese strategist Sun-Tzu (*c.*500 BC) and Indian Kautilya (sixth century BC) are regarded as the pioneering thinkers of strategic influence. In Sun-Tzu's *Art of War*, for instance, there exist many explicit and implicit references that indicate propaganda is an integral component of strategic thinking. Nevertheless, the beginning of the twentieth century may be regarded as a new era in which strategic influence was introduced through new technological means, such as mass print, newspapers, journals, telegraphy, photography, motion pictures, planes and balloons that made the dissemination of ideas on and beyond the battlefield possible far more rapidly and with much greater effect. It is not hyperbole to assert that the introduction and widespread use of these new technological means and methods that enabled the dissemination of ideas permitted revolutionary developments in traditional propaganda techniques.

This chapter seeks to shed light upon influencing strategies used by the Allies and the Ottoman General Staff on the Ottoman soldiers[2] during the Gallipoli Campaign. It suggests two points. First, among the campaigns the Ottoman military fought in the First World War, the Gallipoli Campaign was the first one in which both the Allies' propaganda and the Ottoman General Staff's counter-propaganda strategies were used on the Ottoman soldiers in a coherent fashion. Second, there

---

1 Ziya Gökalp, 'Soldier and Poem', *Military Journal*, November 1916. In this poem, Ziya Gökalp, the leading figure in the Committee of Union and Progress (CUP) and extremely influential intellectual in the late Ottoman period, admonishes the Ottoman intellectuals for not participating in propaganda activities during the First World War.

2 Despite the fact that the sources both in English and Turkish literature prefer to use 'Turkish' instead of 'Ottoman', I prefer to use 'Ottoman' on the basis that this is the more correct and official form as, in all official documents on the Ottoman side during the Gallipoli Campaign, such as war records, telegraph messages and executive orders, the term 'Ottoman' was used.

is a need to widen and deepen the grasp of the traditional conceptualisation of propaganda in the literature when attempting to understand the war of ideas in this conflict and particularly in the context of Gallipoli. When taking the strategic consequences of the Gallipoli Campaign into account, instead of using the traditional conceptualisation of propaganda, which conceives propaganda as a narrowly defined military means only for tactical and short-term gains, the phrase 'strategic communication efforts to influence the thinking faculties and behaviours of first the Ottoman soldiers and then the whole Ottoman society' may be more appropriate in terms of defining the efforts of both the Allies and the Ottoman General Staff. It is possible, under this wider definition, to suggest that even very minor incidents that occurred during the Gallipoli Campaign do not have one singular and narrow explanation. One should, therefore, take a broader stance when it comes to the interpretation of any event in this campaign and its socio-political consequences. Put simply, both the Allied forces and the Ottoman General Staff sought to communicate with the Ottoman soldiers fighting in Gallipoli to influence their 'hearts and minds'. To elucidate these suggestions, the first section of this chapter provides the definition and attributes of the propaganda used in the Turkish literature for more conceptual clarity, and then presents the socio-political context the Ottoman Empire faced just before the First World War. The second section, concentrating on the themes used by the Allied forces on the Ottoman soldiers, provides the Allied forces' perspective of their strategic communication efforts. This section is the result of meticulous archival research in the Turkish General Staff Main Library and the Military History and Strategic Studies Directorate (hereafter ATASE) in March–April 2014, where 62 original propaganda leaflets and 22 prisoner of war (PoW) letters produced by the Allied forces were analysed. In this section, first, the findings will be provided under thematic classifications, and then a follow-up analysis on the content and style of these texts will be presented.

In the third section, the counter-propaganda strategies used by the Ottoman General Staff to sustain the Ottoman soldiers' morale and motivation are explained. Among these counter-measures, the *War Magazine* (*Harp Mecmuasi*), a monthly photo-journal published and distributed both to the public and to the Ottoman soldiers fighting on the front lines of the Gallipoli Peninsula, and the visit of a group of Ottoman intellectuals (authors, journalists and poets) organised by the Ottoman General Staff, the first example of 'embedded journalism' in Ottoman military history, are analysed. In this section both the content analysis of the articles and photographs published about the Gallipoli Campaign in the *War Magazine* and significant thematic concepts used by the Ottoman intellectuals in their journal articles and poems after their visits are examined in detail. One should note that this cultural literature produced by the Turkish intellectuals through the success story of the Gallipoli Campaign constituted a fertile ground for the production and mass consumption of the strategic narratives which were soon to be employed during the Turkish independence struggle of 1919–23. Moreover, two facts should be mentioned to better understand the scale and depth of the Gallipoli Campaign's impact on the Turkish quest for independence. The first is that the Gallipoli experience had a direct impact on the cognitive and emotional backgrounds of the Turkish high-ranking officers who constituted most of the commanding cadres during the Turkish National Independence War (35 of the 67 [52 per cent of the total] high-ranking commanders in the Turkish Independence War were Gallipoli veterans).[3] Second, when founding the Turkish Republic, 17 of the Turkish Republic's founding fathers were Gallipoli veterans who had benefited from their reputation, fame and prestige gained at the front.[4] Metin Heper, a reputable scholar in the field of contemporary Turkish history, notes that: 'those cadres who looked below at the sharp edges of the Gallipoli cliffs and saw the possibility of a total collapse at the bottom, founded the Republic of Turkey'.[5] This chapter concludes with a section that provides insights on the influencing strategies of the Allies and the Ottoman General Staff in the Gallipoli Campaign.

Propaganda as a concept

Despite the fact that there are many definitions of propaganda in the literature, this study seeks to provide its definition in relation to the Turkish sources. Propaganda is designed 'to infuse and to operate in an organised and continuous way in order to indoctrinate, to gain the mental attention of a targeted group or population and to affect the opponent's psychology in a desired way'.[6] A Turkish Special Warfare Department (TSWD)[7] manual notes that 'propaganda is the intentional effort of a person or a group of people to control or change the behaviours of other individuals or groups by means of communication devices'.[8]

---

3 İsmet Görgülü, 'The Impact of the Gallipoli Campaign on the Commanding Cadres of the Turkish National Struggle (Turkish)', *The Yearbook of Canakkale Researches* (95th Anniversary of the Gallipoli Campaign Special edition, 2010), pp. 13–32.

4 The prominent figures among these founding fathers are as follows: Mustafa Kemal Atatürk, Fevzi Çakmak, İsmet İnönü Kazım Karabekir, Nuri Conker, Yakup Şevki Subaşı, Ali Fuat Cebesoy, Cafer Tayyar Eğilmez, Nazif Kayacık, Fahrettin Altay, Kazim İnanç, İzzettin Çalışlar, Nafiz Gürman.

5 From the class discussion in the PhD course titled 'Turkish Political History' taught by Metin Heper at Bilkent University, 2012.

6 Selahattin Ertürk, *Propaganda ve Beşinci Kolun II. Dünya Harbinde Oynadığı Roller*, (Ankara, Gnkur.Bsk.ligi Basımevi, Ankara 1951 – Turkish) p. 5.

7 The Turkish Special Warfare Department (TSWD) was founded in 1952. After restructuring and reformation in 1998, this special unit changed its name to the Turkish Special Forces.

8 ST 33–1 *Propaganda ve Psikolojik Harp* (Turkish Special Warfare Centre Field Manual entitled *Propaganda and Psychological Warfare*, Özel Harp Dairesi Yayınları, Ankara – Ottoman), p. 26.

With a broader grasp, this study, however, tends to define propaganda as a 'capability package', neither a simple 'means' nor a narrowly defined process, but a wider array of tools and techniques to disseminate the cognitive and emotive messages in the most effective and fastest way to the targeted audience to be influenced.[9] A propaganda strategy is thus expected to put this capability package into a means-ways-ends framework to achieve the strategic objectives, or the desired ends, in a campaign. Propaganda is not only a method which simply dictates to people *what* to think by promoting lies and distorted truths; it also tells people *how* to think by shaping the thinking faculties. That is why propaganda is both directly related to the emotive component (hearts) and cognitive component (minds) of the thinking faculty. It is perhaps because of this fact that the debate on whether propaganda is an art or science has not been settled for hundreds of years. The term 'hearts', or the emotive component, on the one hand, implies the strength of the emotional relationship between an individual and the cause s/he follows. That is why, with a culturalist twist, it may be easier to explain this component with norms and values existing in a society or identities of individuals. The term 'minds', or the cognitive component, on the other hand, implies that 'to be on the winning side or to flee from a life-endangering situation' will best serve the long-term interests (whether material or physical) of the individual. That is why this component could be more satisfactorily explained with a rational choice paradigm. In the use of propaganda as a military strategy directed onto soldiers on a battlefield, however, both calculated self-interests and emotions are what matters when influencing the targeted audience to achieve the objective of behavioural change. This behavioural change (to surrender, to desert, to disobey, or to rebel, for example) on a battlefield, particularly in trench warfare in which soldiers have plenty of time to think and to reflect while sitting idle in trenches for days (even for months in the case of the First World War), could happen in the blink of an eye at the individual level. Anybody who has experienced the *sui generis* conditions of the battlefield, in fact, an arena in which individual soldiers and units perform the art of 'killing before being killed', conscious of their comradeship and cohesion, knows that both courage and fear are highly infectious concepts in battlefields. It is not so easy, however, for an individual act of 'breaking of will' to 'go viral' and to lead to collective action; that is, there should exist some other in-group or inter-group mechanisms for this to happen. It is therefore not easy to establish a clear-cut causal relationship between the effectiveness of a propaganda strategy and victory, the desired end state in a battle. Propaganda has, thus, always been considered an 'accelerator' for the traditional *means* (military techniques) and *ways* (military tactics) of strategy to achieve the desired objectives in battle. Thus, a propaganda strategy in a military campaign may be conceived of as a package of efforts, which proposes a formal methodology that crafts messages through careful deliberation

9 Metin Gürcan, 'The Strategic Communication Model and Its Usability in the Security Field (Turkish)', *The Journal of Security Strategies*, Vol. 15, pp. 99–138

and coordination. It also analyses and prioritises the targeted audience's emotive and cognitive strengths and vulnerabilities, and synchronises the type and time of release of information to the respective audience in a disciplined, premeditated fashion.

The TSWD manual asserts that military propaganda is divided into the following categories with respect to the areas where it is to be directed. First is tactical propaganda which implies a type that is only used on the combatant soldiers on the battlefield. Second is operational propaganda which includes civilians (friendly, hostile and neutral) around the battlefield. Last is strategic propaganda which implies a comprehensive campaign for the whole population of a country and has more political objectives.[10]

For anyone who wants to study the birth and evolution of the influencing strategies in a modern sense after the emergence of new technological assets such as mass print, newspapers, journals and photography, the First World War emerges as the first stop to dig in. This is true for the Turkish case as well.

Propaganda and the Ottoman Empire before the First World War

In 1914, an exhausted Ottoman Empire, which had lost a vast amount of its population and lands after a period of continuous war during the previous three centuries, struggled against its assailants on many fronts. In the First World War, the multi-cultural, multi-lingual and multi-communal Ottoman Empire, which had not benefited from industrialisation and had a weak economy, fell behind the Western powers in every aspect of the military domain including the propaganda production for war. Erol Köroğlu's book titled *Ottoman Propaganda and Ottoman Identity: Literature in Turkey during World War I* constitutes one of the rare examples in the English literature that examine the relationship between literature, propaganda and national identity in the late Ottoman period leading up to and during the First World War. In this book, Köroğlu suggests that the Ottoman war experience differed from those of the Western European nations in respect of propaganda activities.[11] By deploying a cultural materialist analysis to explain the empire's failure to develop an effective propaganda mechanism during 1914–18, Köroğlu notes that there are qualitative differences between the propaganda activities produced by industrialised societies such as the British Empire and Germany, where national identity was already well established and universal education widespread, and those in the Ottoman Empire, then still an agrarian society. First, in the Ottoman Empire, where nationhood was in an early stage

10 *The Official History of the Turkish Military*, Vol. 3 Section. 6. 1st edition (1908–20) (Gnkur. Harp Tarihi Başkanlığı Yayınları, Ankara 1971) pp. 380–81.

11 Erol Köroglu, *Ottoman Propaganda and Ottoman Identity: Literature in Turkey during World War I* (London: I.B. Tauris, 2007), pp. xvi–xviii.

of development, there was a low level of literacy (as of the 1910s, only 10 per cent of the whole population was literate)[12]. In fact, the backward socio-cultural conditions within the empire prevented the CUP, the political party led by the Young Turks ruling the empire throughout the First World War, from achieving the fully fledged Ottoman war propaganda machinery; instead, Ottoman war propaganda sought to promote Ottoman national identity among the population, which would bear its cultural and political 'fruits' just after the First World War; that is, during the foundation of the Republic of Turkey.[13] Emphasising the well-developed Western European propaganda infrastructure and concluding that the high literacy rate in Europe was one of the main constituent factors of propaganda success, Köroğlu suggests that in the Ottoman Empire there was, with the exception of Enver Pasha's personal endeavour and the efforts of very few authors, only a very limited degree of institutionalised war propaganda. One may also attribute this situation to the harsh censorship measures of the CUP regime, according to which virtually everything written on warfare was censored by the CUP government, and also to the political conflicts among the CUP leaders, as well as the insufficient communication and education infrastructure in the empire. In a nutshell, one may conclude that the lack of effective Ottoman propaganda was partly due to historical conditions in the empire, and partly the result of literary nationalists' overriding concern to create a unifying cultural discourse of Ottoman identity as the ideological cement of an imagined national society. One may see this as an index of the relative underdevelopment of the features of a modern nation-state as understood by theorists like Ernest Gellner and Benedict Anderson, including mass literacy, industrialised cultural production and relative democratic openness. The lack of propaganda was also partly due to the intellectual malaise created by the 'exceptional . . . irrationality and rigidity'[14] of the wartime censorship exercised by the CUP government, whereby exile and assassination were employed to suppress all opposition, and press freedom was drastically curtailed.[15]

It can be asserted, then, that just before the First World War the Ottoman Empire was very weak in terms of its propaganda strategies mainly due to: the underdevelopment of the means of cultural production in the empire; the still fledgling nature of the educational infrastructure, the literacy rate of approximately 10 per cent, the underdevelopment of the publishing industry; the inability to produce paper on an industrial scale, and the absence of strategic success stories to disseminate. In the midst of things, the campaign on the Gallipoli Peninsula, however, was to provide the crucial and much-needed 'strategic success story', and was soon to be translated by the Turkish intellectuals into one of the main socio-cultural pillars of the Turkish state and its nation-building efforts.

---

12 Ibid., p. 22.

13 Ibid., pp. xx–xxi.

14 Ibid., p. 21.

15 Ibid., pp. 12–13.

Allied Forces' propaganda towards the Ottoman soldiers

In the archives of the Turkish General Staff Military History and Strategic Studies Directorate (ATASE), there are original documents providing valuable insights into the Allies' propaganda strategies that were intended to influence the hearts and minds of the Ottoman soldiers. In the Gallipoli Campaign, the Allied forces, having more effective capabilities and greater resources than the Ottoman military, used leaflets, propaganda cards and letters, which were dropped on the trenches by means of aircraft and balloons. Noticing the low level of literacy among the Ottoman soldiers, the Allied forces also used caricatures, pictures and photographs on their leaflets and propaganda cards.

The main objective of the Allies' propaganda strategy was to weaken the Ottoman 5th Army, which was then responsible for the defence of the whole Gallipoli Peninsula. The Allies, therefore, sought to attack the Ottoman soldiers' determination to fight by persuading them to surrender, to desert or to disobey their orders individually or in groups. To achieve this objective, the Allies attempted first to analyse and then to exploit the emotive and cognitive vulnerabilities of the Ottoman soldiers to initiate the decision to desert, surrender or disobey at the individual level and then to spread panic or encourage hesitation at the unit level. Both ploys related to the cognitive domain such as the material shortages affecting the physical comfort of the Ottoman soldiers, particularly poor clothing, or food and drink shortages, access to clean water and sanitation, infectious diseases, such as malaria and typhus; while issues related to the emotive domain, such as homesickness, curiosity about the fate of loved ones and religious sentiments, were also used shrewdly in the same text.

Themes on the allied forces' propaganda texts: 'PoWs are treated well'

The fact that this theme exists on the 32 leaflets (53 per cent of the total) and 14 of the letters (63 per cent of the total) indicates the significance attributed to it by the Allies when tailoring their propaganda strategies. This theme belongs to the cognitive domain as it seeks a behavioural change (to surrender) after a rational process of calculating the pros and cons of surrendering and continuing fighting. To increase the pros of surrendering in the Ottoman soldiers' strategic calculations, the first thing the Allies did was to disseminate the message that Ottoman PoWs were treated well and that they were living in comfortable conditions. In the leaflets, written in Ottoman Turkish and German, distributed across the 5th Ottoman Military Region, and on the cards dropped to the 3rd Army Corps Region on 28 April 1915, and on the declarations dropped into the trenches of the 57th Regiment on 5 June 1915, the same remarks were written:

> Our dear Ottoman brothers!
>
> Rumours that Englishmen behave badly to the PoWs and even that they kill them brutally, is a German lie. Ottoman soldiers who were hungry, bare

> and miserable when they are captured, are treated marvellously by the British Government. Do not pay attention to these lies and join your captured friends' prosperity.[16]

On a leaflet which was found on 9 May 1915 in the East Group Command in the vicinity of a farm named Süleymanoğlu Farm, the humanity and helpfulness of the Allied soldiers are mentioned:

> . . . the captured Ottoman officers and soldiers are thankful and appreciated the good behaviour shown to them. The treatment by British soldiers is also taken well by wounded Ottoman soldiers.[17]

On a letter thrown into the 24th trench in the North Group Command Region on 20 July 1915, it was written:

> Fellow Turkish Friend! How do you spend time there? I claim that you do not spend time better than half of what we spend here. I claim that you want to come to our side and stay here. Most of your friends who support us also want to be with us.[18]

The Allies, to promote the theme of 'the PoWs are treated well', disseminated letters written in the words of the Ottoman PoWs. In these letters, the Ottoman PoWs state that they are living in excessively comfortable and restful conditions, and look forward to seeing their fellow friends among them. The original letter presented below, which was dropped on the North Group Region on 27 May 1915, and addressed to the Ottoman soldiers in trenches, is a good example of this.

The letter states:

> To my brothers in arms,
>
> Somehow I was captured by a British man a few days ago. The treatment we are subjected to is totally different from which we presumed there. I conscientiously consider informing you about this, as this is a debt [of gratitude] for me. When I surrendered, they took me to some commanders. They rewarded me with different gifts. They presented cigarette boxes, tea, jam, etc. On the road, officers and soldiers saluted me closely like a brother. Even they were asking me how to please me. At the end, we were propelled to the Imbros Island. There are many of our friends [here]. All of them were given new clothes and shoes. They share special tents with just five soldiers in each one. Some three blankets are dispensed for each person. The British man does not nurse any grudge against the Ottomans. They only say that we are the victims of the Germans. They have

16 ATASE Archive ; K. 3438, D. 26, F. 1, 1–1, 1–2; 9,g, 9–1, 9–2.

17 ATASE Archive; K. 3438, D. 26, F. 3–2.

18 ATASE Archive; K. 3438, D. 26, F. 14, 14–1.

prepared equipment and ammunitions. Some friends were afraid of punishment when we return as prisoners after the end of the battle. British men will surely solve this problem. Never worry about this.

The list of daily supplies given to each soldier. (Drachma)

Sugar	50	Tea	20
Rice	75	Meat	150
Potato	60	Vegetables	75

One bread, one box of jam per two days, etc. Briefly, all of my friends are living a comfortable life here and greeting you with the wishes that you will be saved soon.

Of the Ottoman Prisoners
Medical Master-Sergeant M.C.[19]

The Allies, fully recognising the extremely low levels of literacy among Ottoman soldiers, did not neglect to distribute visual images, such as caricatures and photographs, alongside letters like this. On the leaflets dropped to the Ottoman trenches in the Gallipoli Peninsula, the life in an Ottoman PoW camp on the Nile River in Egypt is depicted as sweet, and the cheerful soldiers (some in military uniforms and some in civilian clothes to show that they can go out freely), with their names and their units, pleased with their lives, are pictured boozing, singing, smoking, hugging each other, and eating abundant food on the tables on which there are also roses and other flowers. To attract the attention of Ottoman soldiers and to lure them to surrender, the Allies used the authenticity of Egypt and aimed to portray the PoW camps as a 'prisoners' paradise'. On 28 July 1915, the leaflet distributed to the Kumkale region stated:

> The Ottoman prisoners are dwelling in a wonderful garden beside the Nile River. Individual beds are reserved for each. Everybody is given various foods on different dishes and tobacco, etc. everyday . . . . Prisoners are educated, and, in order to have fun, they are provided with musical instruments and musicians which are in their tradition. Toys like musical instruments are presented by their Egyptian friends. Prisoners are allowed to be visited. Dedicated individual departments are devoted to prisoner military officers and they are given bedstead, blankets, sheets, chairs, sofas and tables. Their food and drinks are prepared by private workers. Prisoners' daily wages are about 4 and 4.5 Shillings. Every kind of fruit and sweets are sold at a suitable price in the shops which are opened in the garden prisoners dwell in. There is a very close friendship between prisoner military officers, prisoner soldiers and the guards who protect the prisoners.[20]

19 ATASE Archive; K. 3438, D. 26, F. 6–1, 6–4.
20 ATASE Archive; D: 643-A/1559, F:1–65, 1–66.

Another theme used by the Allies to lure the Ottoman soldiers towards surrender was hatred towards the CUP's suppression and the desire for liberty.[21] In a leaflet dropped in the North Command Region, the emphasis on liberty and 'the provision of freedom by the Allies to discuss the political future of the Empire in the PoWs camps in Egypt' is striking.[22]

The theme 'Ill-intentioned Germans are deceiving and exploiting you'

Some 16 leaflets (26 per cent of the total) and 20 letters (45 per cent of the total) include the idea of 'German deception'. The high ratio indicates the significance of this theme for the Allies. One of the objectives of the Allies was to plant the seeds of suspicion between the Ottoman and German soldiers by promoting the idea that the Germans had secret ambitions against the Ottoman soldiers.[23] In particular, by exploiting the failures of the German commanding officers, the Allies sought to drive a wedge between Ottoman and German soldiers and foment resentment. The remarks on a leaflet dropped onto the 15th Army Corps region on 30 April 1915 are a good example, indicating the Allies' intention of shaking the Ottoman soldiers' confidence in their German commanders by flattering the Ottoman Army. The leaflet states: 'Due to the mistakes and bad decisions of the German commanders, Ottoman soldiers had to withdraw 25 km without resisting the Allied soldiers' attack.'[24] On a leaflet dated 9 May 1915, Ottoman soldiers are praised: 'Your bravery and courage is known all over the world. Why are you trying to extend the duration of this meaningless conflict which started solely for the particular interests of Germany?'[25] In some leaflets, the Allies sought to create a perception that they were saddened by the campaign and their reason for coming to Gallipoli was to save the Turks from the Germans' control. In the leaflet dated 9 May 1915 is it stated:

> . . . They [English soldiers] are saddened that they are forced to fight with you. Please understand that the Government of England is obliged to conduct the Gallipoli Campaign in order to save you from the pressure of the Germans and the Committee of Union and Progress, which, in fact, belongs to the Germans . . . .[26]

---

21 Sadık Sarısaman, *The Psychological Warfare in the Turkish Fronts in WWI* (Turkish) (The General Staff Printing House, Ankara, 1999), p. 15.

22 ATASE Archive; K. 3438, D. 26, F. 19, 19–1, 19–3.

23 Terence H. Qualter, *Propaganda ve Psikolojik Harp* (Turkish Special Warfare Department Publications, 1972, Ankara) p. 102.

24 ATASE Archive; K. 3438, D. 26, F. 2, 2–2.

25 ATASE Archive; K. 3438, D. 26, F. 3, 3–2. The same leaflets were also found in different regions in the Gallipoli Peninsula.

26 ATASE Archive; K. 3438, D. 26, F. 3, 3–2.

In their propaganda strategy, the Allies tried to combine the theme of 'the Allies treat PoWs well' with the theme of 'hatred towards the Germans'. In a letter written by an Ottoman PoW, the Allies emphasised that the Ottoman soldiers came to fight for their homeland but, it continues: '. . . in this battle, do not spill your blood for the sake of the Germans, and please leave the battlefield, since this is a battle not for the benefit of the Ottoman people but only for the benefits and advantages of the Germans . . . . '[27] In the same vein, a leaflet dated 5 June 1915, which was dropped on the 57th Regiment trenches, tried to encourage apathy amongst Ottoman soldiers towards the Germans: 'Why do you sacrifice yourself for the plots of Germans and their allies, who caused the unnecessary death of your Muslim brothers by endangering your nation?'[28]

The Allies, seeking to exploit the religious feelings and the sense of Muslim brotherhood, continued their propaganda efforts towards the Ottoman soldiers through not only the letters written by Ottoman PoWs, but also by distributing leaflets containing the thoughts of Indian and Egyptian Muslims who came to the Gallipoli Peninsula to fight on the Allied side. In a letter written in the words of an Indian Muslim, which was dropped onto the Asia Group Region at Gallipoli on 11 June 1915, it is stated:

> . . . We, Muslims, know well that the Germans are a lying nation. History is the witness to this fact. So the Germans are deceiving you and ruining your country. Furthermore, their sole objective is to control your homeland and colonise her with Germans. Be sure that all your Muslim brothers in the world are feeling pain when you are deceived by Germany and praying deeply for you to get rid of the Germans and their tricks.[29]

While the Allies endeavoured to divide the Germans and Turks by addressing the Turks' liability towards their homeland, the idea that the Germans were an expansionist and unreliable partner was reinforced by reminding them of the German Empire's plans to extend their influence into the Ottoman-controlled Balkan regions. The same leaflet continues:

> Up 'til now, what sort of help have you had from the Germans? Didn't your land of Bosnia-Herzegovina get taken from you by Austria–Hungary? Did Germany help you against this? On the contrary, they left you on your own and did nothing until you lost these lands. The Germans violated the agreements which they had signed and they broke their promises . . . . [It was the] Germans who drove Belgium into blood [and who] will not be ashamed of destroying the Ottoman Government.

27 ATASE Archive; K. 3438, D. 2, F. 6–1, 6–3.
28 ATASE Archive; K. 3438, D. 26, F. 9–2, 5.
29 ATASE Archive; K. 3438, D. 26, F. 11, 11–3, 11–6, 11–7.

> Our Dear Ottoman Brothers! You should not trust the Germans. If Germans occupy your country, you will see and understand how they consume all of your country's crops. You will not have independence and safety.[30]

A message sent to the Ottoman General Staff in İstanbul from the 5th Army headquarters noted:

> To the Supreme Military Command,
>
> One copy of each leaflet dropped by an enemy aeroplane to the village of *Büyükanafarta* and by the Allied soldiers to *Suvla* are enclosed:
>
> 'Oh Ottomans!
>
> What do you think about the Germans and German Emperor?
>
> Who promises the safekeeping of Turkey?
>
> How many cities did Turkey lose, after Wilhelm promised the safekeeping of Turkey?
>
> – Twelve.
>
> What is the number of soldiers who died due to illnesses and injuries after the arrival of generals sent to sabotage the Ottoman Military by Wilhelm?
>
> – 800,000.
>
> Who did grease Enver Pasha's palm in order to force Turkey to battle with England?
>
> – Wilhelm.
>
> What did Turkey earn from the battle except corpses and devastated regions?
>
> – Nothing.'

> Invitation for the prosperity of Ottoman citizens:
>
> 'Dear Friends!
>
> I take it as my holy duty to inform you fraternally that I have spent a comfortable and happy life especially in these cold days after the day I was captured.
>
> My Brothers, my friends! I quiver with fear when I remember the days in the trenches. I cannot prevent myself from feeling sad whenever I remember the lack of food in the trenches, the cold weather and the sequential barbarous behaviour of our commanders; in short the attacks and the misery that you live through now. I'm completely feeling dejected. When I came here, immediately I'm given hot tea, plenty of food, sweets and tobacco. There is no limit of blankets and wool clothes. Finally I reached the comfort which I have never seen before. A father cannot desire or do more than this for his children! They treat us fraternally. They respect our religious beliefs and practices. The allies are actually our best friends, and far from being our enemy. Brothers who

30 Ibid.

unfortunately do not have that happiness, if I have anything to wish, it is for them to provide the same comfort for you, to be like me. Therefore, try to get out of your miserable situation. Do not miss this chance and come here! Fall into the arms of the supreme and humanist British nation! I entrust you to Almighty God and pray for your welfare and comfort.

6 November 1915A.D.,

One of the prisoners in the Imbros Island'

The theme 'Germany and Austria are in trouble: they, therefore, cannot help you'

To demoralise Ottoman soldiers and officers, another theme raised by the Allies was that the Germans and Austrians were on the ropes. Because the Ottoman Empire waged war by relying on Germany and its material support, British leaflets carried news about those countries waging war against Germany. In a leaflet dated 2 June 1915, which was dropped onto the 57th Regimental Region, is written: 'Romania and Bulgaria waged war against Austria. Goodness be upon them.'[31] Again, a leaflet which was dropped into the same region explains that Germany and its allies are isolated in the world: 'Even Italians, who are not deceived despite all efforts of the Germans, defeated the Austrians, and you Ottomans unfortunately have become Germany's sole ally in the world.'[32]

The theme 'Holy war (*jihad-i ekber*) is meaningless'

Some 11 leaflets (18 per cent of the total) and four letters (18 per cent of the total) include the theme that 'holy war' was a hollow expression. The Ottoman Empire declared 'Holy War (*Jihad*)' against the Allies hoping a global Muslim insurgency would break out particularly in the Muslim-dominated colonies.[33] There was no doubt in their minds that the invitation would strengthen the spiritual power of the Ottoman Empire over the Muslim populations who had been 'forced' into the front lines by the Allies. When the Allies, especially the British Empire, were taking precautions in their colonies against this call to Holy Jihad, they also attempted to create doubt and shake the confidence of the Ottoman soldiers by their own declarations. As a result *fetwas* (religious decrees) explaining the error of the Ottoman call to 'Holy Jihad' were distributed as leaflets. In the leaflets, written by Indian and Egyptian Muslims, the nature of *jihad* was explained to the Ottoman soldiers on the Gallipoli Peninsula. In one dated 11 June 1915, which was found in the Asia Group Command region, was stated: '. . . you want to make religious

31 ATASE Archive; K. 3438, D. 26, F. 8, 8–2.

32 ATASE Archive; K. 3438, D. 26, F. 9, 9–2.

war for the sake and benefits of foreigners. The war is not holy, in other words, it is not jihad. It is regretful to say that Muslim Brothers kill each other for the sake of the German Emperor.'[33] In another leaflet, there are explanations of the true definition of *jihad.* It writes:

> Holy *Jihad* can only be declared in case of attack and violation of *Shariah* [Islamic law] and the honour of the people. Because the Allies do not have ill feelings towards *Shariah*, a Holy *Jihad* cannot be declared. A battle which is declared for the victory of the German Empire can never be holy. How can Muslims' murder of another Muslim be accepted just to satisfy the German Emperor? Your brothers in holy cities of Mecca *(Mekke-i Mükerreme*) and Medina *(Medine-i Münevvere*) have been rebelling against you and are angry with you since you participated in just such a battle in which Muslims kill Muslims. It is shameful for you to fall into such a great humiliation.[34]

The message that 'the British Empire is loved by Muslims so much that they will die for it, and she fights for the rights of the Muslims' was the theme of a leaflet dropped onto the 57th Regimental Region on 2 June 1915. It states:

> . . . by means of the British Government's effort, today millions of Muslims are living a happy life and thousands of Muslim young men participate voluntarily and fight against our opponents with great effort thus proving their thankfulness and sincerity.[35]

The British government supported these ideas through leaflets explaining that the Indian and Egyptian Muslims accepted that the Allies were protecting Muslim nations. The Allies, therefore, intended to influence the Ottoman Muslim soldiers in the trenches through these particular messages. A leaflet dated 11 June 1915, dropped onto the Asia Group Command Region, states:

> Our Fellow Ottoman Brothers!
>
> Please hear the voices of your Muslim brothers in Egypt and India. They are comfortable and happy as Muslims living under the protection of the British in Egypt. Indian princes and soldiers devote their lives for the sake of the British Empire, the real friend of Islam's nations . . . . Our Ottoman brothers, you are the sons of our almighty religion. Please know that millions of Muslims are praying to *Allah* to keep his blessing on the British Empire. In the Muslim countries, the *Ezan* (the holy call to prayer) and the *Holy Quran* are protected by the British Empire. Don't you see that the princes, officers and all the Indian people

33 ATASE Archive; K. 3438, D. 26, F. 11–11–3.

34 ATASE Archive; K. 3438, D. 26, F. 11, 11–7.

35 ATASE Archive; K. 3438, D. 26, F. 9 9–2.

> sacrifice themselves and spend their wealth, spill their blood and sacrifice their souls for the sake of helping the British Empire, the real friend of Muslims? . . . . It makes us upset to see that you are deceived by the Germans despite the fact that all Muslims are willingly fighting alongside British soldiers, the oldest and the most honest supporters of all Muslims in the world. Hence, please brothers! Pray and strive for God's keeping you safe from misdeeds and tricks. May God help you to wake up from your sleep.[36]

The theme 'Ottoman armies are being defeated in other fronts'

As well as demoralising Ottoman soldiers on the Gallipoli Peninsula, the Allies aimed to benefit from the deteriorating condition of the CUP government and the failure of the Ottoman armies fighting on other fronts. By these means, the Allies intended to break the resistance of Ottoman soldiers fighting at Gallipoli. On 27 May 1915, a leaflet dropped into *Yenişehir* trenches by an Allied aircraft states:

> Ottoman army of 18,000 soldiers, which was moving on the east of the city of Van and between the straits of Diman and Koçka, lost and failed totally in the battle that continued for 3 days. Ottoman soldiers withdrew in desperate conditions leaving 3,500 casualties behind.[37]

The theme of 'homesickness'

Some 21 leaflets (31 per cent of the total) and six letters (26 per cent) include this theme. Belonging to the emotive domain, this theme would affect most Ottoman soldiers, the great majority of whom had been under arms since the Balkan Wars and had not seen their families for four or five years. To agitate the feelings of longing for home, the Allies incessantly reminded the soldiers of their families and children. In a leaflet found in the South Group Command region on 9 May 1915, this theme is emphasised strongly. It states: 'If you put down your weapons to avoid the continuation of the fighting, you will be able to return to your wives and children.'[38] One should note that in trench life the soldiers, who had plenty of time to think about their loved ones, were sensitive to this theme. The Allies, taking this fact into account, wrote in a leaflet which was dropped onto the 19th Division on 2 June 1915: 'Oh soldiers! Wake up! We will accept every private soldier who attempts to surrender, except the ones who want to go to their families. We will let them go to their families freely.'[39] In another leaflet, dated 11 June 1915, the

36 ATASE Archive; K. 3438, D. 26, F. 11, 11–3, 11–6.
37 ATASE Archive; K. 3438, D. 26, F. 5, 5–3.
38 ATASE Archive; K. 3438, D. 26, F. 3, 3–2.
39 ATASE Archive; K. 3438, D. 26, F. 9 9–1.

same persuasive message of 'reuniting with your family is only possible after your surrender' was employed:

> . . . You were living a comfortable life with your family and children. Before the calamity of the Balkan War, you were farming and living a happy life with your family. Why did you wage war for the benefit of the German Government and at the expense of your family? If you want to reunite with them, please join your friends enjoying their lives in our camps.[40]

The theme 'internal political turmoil in the Ottoman Empire'

Internal political turmoil in a country may constitute a useful area for foreign exploitation, which was certainly the case during the Gallipoli Campaign. Some seven leaflets (12 per cent of the total) and four letters (18 per cent) focus on this vulnerability. Worth noting is that this theme was presented in such a manner that the officers affiliated to the Party of Independence and Agreement, the representatives of the political opposition to the ruling CUP, were divided against the Unionist officers. On 2 June 1915, in a publication dropped onto the 19th Division front line, the policy of the CUP and its handling of the First World War were criticised with the question: 'Can you see any probability for victory?'[41] The message of the leaflet implied that there is no need to resist during such an unnecessary war, and all soldiers should question the CUP's war policies. A leaflet dated 11 June 2015 dropped into the Asia Command Region asserts:

> We know very well that Young Turks [CUP's leadership cadre] deceived you due to their inclination for German money. Here we tell you the reality and say our opinion. We hope you give up fighting against the Allies and put down your weapons to punish the CUP, [which is] the only remedy for the safety of your country.[42]

In a related manner, ethnic and religious minorities were also the target of Allied propaganda efforts. The fact that there were Kurds from the east and southeast of Anatolia fighting in the Ottoman Army made the soldiers vulnerable to the exploitation of nationalist feelings. In a leaflet dropped on 29 July 1915 into the North Group Command Region, this theme of ethnic division was suggested in the following way: '. . . Kurds rebelled against the Ottoman military and occupied the southeastern cities of Muş and Harput during a Kurdish insurgency.

40 ATASE Archive; K. 3438, D. 26, F. 11, 11–3, 11–7.

41 ATASE Archive; K. 3438, D. 26, F. 9–2.

42 ATASE Archive; K. 3438, D. 26, F. 11, 11–7.

The insurgents assigned the respected Abdurrıza Bedirhan as their chief. My Kurdish Brother, what are you waiting for?'[43]

The theme 'Corrupted political leaders will lead the Ottoman Empire to a total defeat'

Rumours about the political elites of the CUP were exploited in Allied leaflets. The rumours that stated that the CUP leaders were having a prosperous life, embezzling funds and making profits through personal connections and illegal commerce, were expressed in the leaflets. On one, for instance, the text starts with the following remark: 'While you are fighting under terrible conditions and your family is living in misery, your ruling leaders are busy with their personal trade and robbery'.[44] Furthermore, it went on:

> The CUP leaders, Enver Pasha, the Minister of War, Talat Pasha, the Grand *Vizier*, and Hayri Bey, *Sheik-ul Islam* [the clergyman representing the highest religious authority in the Ottoman Empire], accepted a bribe of 2,000,000 Liras, in order to bring the Ottoman Government into the war. It is also pointed out that Enver Pasha and Tal'ât Pasha enriched other people close to them through their corruption.[45]

Furthermore, on another leaflet, the idea that Enver Pasha wanted to be the Sultan of the Ottoman Empire was propagated, attacking Enver Pasha's personality. One stated: 'as long as such a merciless killer commands the Ottoman soldiers, can God bestow victory on his soldiers?'[46]

A thematic analysis of the Allies' propaganda leaflets and letters

The first thing one may infer from the analysis of the leaflets and letters dropped by the Allies on the Ottoman fronts on Gallipoli is the latent assumption that the leading cadres of the CUP, or the 'Young Turks', used physical violence in their political revolution in 1909, abolished the Sultanate, then became corrupt and failed, to manage the Ottoman nation. When combining this assumption with other accurate details – such as the fact that many Ottoman soldiers had been unpaid for months and that they had been serving under tough conditions – the Allies thought

43 ATASE Archive; K. 3438, D. 26, F. 20, 20–2.
44 BDH., K:3443,D:195/45,F:4–4
45 BDH., K:404,D:189/1592,F:21--1
46 BDH., K:3443, D:195/45, F:7–2; K:394, D:643-A/1559, F:1–15.

that the Ottoman armies were on the verge of mutiny.[47] This myth that the Ottoman soldiers could not adequately defend themselves and they were ready to surrender, desert or rebel when threatened with a gentle fist constituted the reference point of the influence strategies of the Allies. That is why the Allies seemed to tailor these strategies to appeal to the reasoning faculties of the Ottoman soldiers expecting that, as rational beings appraising all the negative points in the policies of the CUP, the Germans' manipulations, the deceptions of the CUP leaders and their extremely impoverished living conditions, the Ottoman soldiers would reach the right decision of surrendering, deserting or rebelling.

Coming to the thematic structures of all the leaflets and letters, both in terms of style and content, it is striking that they are professionally chosen and produced. The themes were buried into the texts and were concealed under the 'cordial tone' of the texts to such an extent that all the works examined could be defined as kind, written requests from a close friend garnished with warnings, but were never overtly threatening. The common pattern, for instance, that exists in all the texts about the Germans is the tone that a cordial friend (the Allies) was trying to warn his 'deceived' fellow friends (the Ottoman soldiers) against the misdeeds and manipulations of a wolf in sheep's clothing (the Germans).

Propaganda texts should ensure that explicit messages will guide the masses in the desired direction. When organising propaganda, characteristics like theoretical depth, complexity or literary language are not required. Since the main aim is to introduce certain ideas, all strategies and plans are established on the basis of a common minimum standard. Messages are communicated to their recipients in the simplest manner possible. The important point of a message is its capacity to be easily remembered, and its persuasiveness *vis à vis* the largest possible mass of people. All the fundamental points of propaganda are based on common minimums, but such minimums can be reached only if a national culture with obvious and common points of reference is present. To influence audiences in the emotive domain, the selection of the words can be deemed successful in the Allies' propaganda texts. In the leaflets, for instance, the word 'joining' is used frequently, rather than the word 'surrender', which would imply a negative meaning for Ottoman soldiers. By combining 'unification' with 'courage', 'friends' and 'families' the Allies, instead of simply saying 'come and surrender', disseminate a patterned message in the texts, namely: 'be brave: come and join your friends enjoying their lives in Egypt's paradise.' This unification is presented as the first step for the Ottoman soldiers who made the 'right' decision to surrender in order to reach their families.

It is also interesting to note that, in all of the examined 84 original documents, there exists no conditional sentence starting with 'if'. Conditional sentences are preferred in propaganda texts only when the strategy of threat and the spread

47 Alan Moorehead, *Gallipoli* (New York: Harper & Brothers Publishers, 1956), p. 47.

of fear are sought through direct messaging, which is not the case in the Allies' texts. In the same vein, it is noticeable that the words which imply cowardice and humiliation are deliberately omitted from the texts. In the leaflets and letters, the Ottoman soldiers are always portrayed as 'heroes' fulfilling their tasks bravely; there is a lack of any provocative, disturbing words such as 'coward', 'traitor' and 'enemy'. It is also significant to note that, in the texts, personal and religious concepts are never attacked; instead a latent directive is felt in the sense that a 'caring' friend is guiding the Ottoman soldier by helping him to find his way. It is evident that, in all texts questioning the socio-political condition of the Ottoman Empire, the deliberate intention is not to degrade the Ottoman soldiers' honour and personal pride. The other observations are that:

1 Challenging questions are asked in a kind manner but Ottoman soldiers are not given the chance to find the right answer by themselves.
2 In the texts, if the theme belongs to the cognitive domain, a simple cause–effect relationship is constructed, blaming the Germans when explaining the catastrophic events the Ottoman Empire was exposed to just before and during the war. If, however, the theme belongs to the emotive domain, the Allies seemed to deliberately refrain from proposing strong causal explanations, and instead preferred to put tentative open-ended questions to make the Ottoman soldiers think and reflect about this particular theme by themselves.
3 The influential phrases reflecting Islamic terminology are commonly used and Ottoman-Turkish was chosen in the texts. For instance, the preferred phrases were 'digging the grave of the country' when describing the CUP government's policies, and the phrase 'they are calling for the Ottoman Empire's funeral pray' (*salat-al janazah*) when portraying the 'misdeeds and mismanagements' of the CUP leaders. Ottoman soldiers were warned not to participate in this '*great sin*' conducted by the CUP leaders.
4 An appropriate amount of humour was put into the texts. In those depicting the Ottoman PoWs' conditions in Egypt, the Allies preferred to decorate the PoWs' 'fascinating living conditions' with a sense of humour.
5 To make the texts eye-catching at first glance, up-to-date titles and emotional introductory sentences were commonly used. By arousing curiosity with these introductions, the Allies aimed to make the target audience feel obliged to read the text to the end.
6 The words 'homeland, nation, honesty, and honour' and polished expressions like 'honourable country', 'heroic nation', 'Oh, little Ottoman pure and noble children', 'Oh, our soldier brothers', 'Our brothers', 'Oh innocent soldiers', and 'Oh honourable soldiers' etc. were preferred in order to establish an emotional attachment between the text and the soldier reading or hearing about it.
7 The expressions used in the texts included simple, short, meaningful and concise words and phrases which were easy for the Ottoman soldiers to

understand. Similarly, repetitive statements and reassuring expressions aiming to be more persuasive were employed frequently in the texts.

The Ottoman General Staff's influencing efforts

It was difficult for the Ottoman General Staff to develop an effective powerful counter-propaganda machine to neutralise the Allies' efforts towards the Ottoman soldiers due to the deficiencies stated in the introduction. This, however, does not necessarily mean that the Ottoman General Staff sat idle. The *War Magazine* (*Harp Mecmuası*), for instance, publication of which began during the Gallipoli Campaign, could be acknowledged as the most successful influencing effort of the Ottoman General Staff in preserving the morale and fighting will of the Ottoman soldiers in the area of visual propaganda.[48] The aim of the magazine was to publish photographs that would show the *grandeur* of the state and of the army that would convince people of the fact that everything was all right, which would serve the purpose of raising the spirits both of the soldiers at the front and of the civilians on the home front. All publication processes of the magazine, from the first stage to the very last, were carried out in the Ottoman General Staff headquarters located in İstanbul.

The *War Magazine* (*Harp Mecmuası*)

The *War Magazine* was a photographic publication, meaning that the articles were simply used for garnishing the images. More than half of the magazine was allocated for pictures and photos, and the images were of quite a high quality. The magazine claimed it was published with the aim of 'perpetuating the golden story of the magnificent Ottoman armies battling courageously against their enemies and to reveal this heroic stance of the Ottoman Military to all of the world'.[49] The magazine began its publication life on Teşrinisani 1331 (November 1915) and closed down on Ramadan 1334 (June 1918) after publishing its 27th issue.

Although the phrase 'twice a month' existed in the first issue, the magazine was usually published in a monthly fashion. That the magazine was printed on glossy paper of good quality in an environment where other magazines and newspapers published around the same time could not even provide basic paper indicates the priority, care and attention paid by the Ottoman General Staff to their own works. However, low quality paper was used towards the end of the war due to financial

48 Niyazi A. Banoğlu, *Türk Basınında Çanakkale Günleri*, (İstanbul, 1982 – Turkish), p. 100.

49 (Military Journal) 'Niçin Çıkıyor' *MJ*, Sayı 1, p. 3. Please note that *MJ* refers to the *Military Journal* hereafter.

Figure 7.1 The cover of the first issue of the *War Magazine*.

difficulties caused by the longevity of the war.[50] Printing presses, equipment, paper and ink were brought from Vienna through the connections of the CUP government, which, in fact, illustrates that the magazine was supported directly by

50 Ali Fuat Bilkan-Ömer Çakır, *Harp Mecmuası*, (Kaynak Kitablığı yay., İstanbul, 2006 – Turkish)

the government.[51] Yet, curiously, the distribution centre of the magazine was stated as Number 77 of the student dormitory *Servet-i Fünun* printing house on the street of *Bab-ı Ali*.[52] On the last two pages of the magazine, advertisements were taken. These advertisements usually belonged to corporations supplying materials to the military and semi-official aid organisations like the community of *Hilal-i Ahmer*, the Incorporated Trade Company of *Eşya-yı Askeriye*, the Commerce Office of Great Fur, and the Commerce Office of *Bekirzade Hacı*.[53]

In an unsigned article entitled: 'Why is *War Magazine* Published?' in the first issue, the Ottoman government's reasons for waging the war, the explanations for the alliance with Germany and the righteousness of this alliance are explained. The article suggests that the Russians, the implacable enemy of the Ottoman Empire, first attacked the Muslim Ottoman lands. Interestingly, the article asserts that the period of decline which started after the Vienna retreat in 1699 stopped with the First World War and the Ottoman Army reared up in defiance in this war. The centuries-old withdrawal of the Ottoman Empire which epitomised the disgrace of the Balkan War was cleansed away in the Gallipoli Campaign.[54] Similarly, in another article written by Ağaoğlu Ahmet in the first issue, the reasons why the CUP government joined the war are explained in the following manner:

> First of all, countries like the Ottoman Empire, which are geographically in the middle of the world, cannot be kept out of the war. It is a must that we join the fighting sooner or later . . . . It was not possible for a country like the Ottoman Empire to be neutral until the end of the war. There were two sides fighting in the war. One of them was the Entente Powers aligning with Russia which has been fighting with Turkey for two centuries. The other side was the Germany and Austria–Hungary alliance which has no domination and no negative sentiments towards Muslim nations. It is wrong to consider that neither the British government nor one of her allies are the Ottomans' protector as they were keeping more than a hundred and thirty million Muslims in Africa, India and Asia under their fierce domination.[55]

Ağaoğlu Ahmet also expressed the view that the war would create a window of opportunity for more prosperity in the Ottoman Empire and thus 'a brilliant future is waiting for all Ottomans'.[56] At the end of his article, Ahmet concluded that the reason for the British government and her allies' entry into the First World War

51 Ibid.

52 *MJ*, Vol. 1, p. 17.

53 Please see *MJ*, Vol 1, p. 17; *MJ*, Vol. 19, p. 405.

54 (Harp Mecmuası) 'Niçin Çıkıyor? (Why we publish?)' *MJ*, Vol. 1, p. 3.

55 Ağaoğlu Ahmet, 'Türkiye'nin ve İslam Âleminin Kurtuluşu (The Salvation of Turkey and Muslim Nation)', *MJ*, Vol.1, pp. 7–9.

56 Ibid.

Figure 7.2 Photo of three Ottoman soldiers from the *War Magazine*. The caption reads 'Sergeant Wrestler Ismail (blackish), the son of Ahmet, Şükrü the son of Mustafa, and Hüseyin the son of Hasan grabbed the enemy's machine guns and took them to our front lines under fire'.

was to 'rescue' the Christians living in the Ottoman domains. That is why, siding with the German government, the Ottoman Empire should strive to become the rescuer of all the world's Turks and Muslims. Photos of guns, aircraft and weapons which had been captured from the enemy were the most important thematic photos of each issue of the magazine.[57] Through these photos, the intention was to raise

57 *MJ*, Vol. 19, p. 291.

Figure 7.3 Photo of the captured French submarine *Turquoise*.

the spirit of Ottoman soldiers, to activate patriotic sentiments, develop a sense of national solidarity, and to release the news to the people that the Ottomans had won significant victories.

The story of a French submarine named *Turquoise* (*Turkuaz*) constitutes one of the most interesting capture stories in the campaign.[58]

Turquoise, which was captured with all its crew, was renamed *Müstecip Onbaşı*, to commemorate the artillery corporal (onbaşı) named Müstecip who shot it up. Pictures of Corporal Müstecip and the submarine's renaming ceremony were provided in the *War Magazine*.[59] The article on the capture of the *Turquoise* submarine was placed in *Tanin*, a leading newspaper published in İstanbul, explaining its capture and the heroic story of Corporal Müstecip with an announcement that, for two days, the submarine would be visited by the people living in İstanbul for one Ottoman lira thanks to the permission of the Ottoman General Staff.[60] Put simply, both the capture and the exhibition of a French submarine became an important propaganda instrument for the CUP government.

One should note that thematic messages are also used in the photos, and these messages are strengthened with explanations in the subtitles. To spread the message that 'the Ottoman Military is a civilised one and it treats its PoWs well',

58 *MJ*, Vol. 2, p. 25.
59 *MJ*, Vol. 2, p. 20.
60 *Tanin*, 29 Teşrinievvel 1331 (11 November 1915).

Figure 7.4 Photo of Müstecip and his friends from the *War Magazine*. The caption reads: 'Gunner Müstecip, who shot *Turquoise* and enabled its capture, is sitting triumphantly on his targeting chair near his cannon . . .'.

for instance, the picture presented below with a short subtitle, published in the *War Magazine*'s second issue, is a good example. Note two latent messages in the arrangement: first is the 'bravery of the Ottoman officer who risked his life by jumping into the sea to rescue the enemy personnel from *Safire*' emphasised in the subtitle; and the second is the proper religious ceremony organised by the Ottoman military to honour the death of a Christian soldier.

In another photo, Senegalese, Australian, British, French and Indian PoW soldiers are pictured in the same frame. On some photos, prisoners numbering between 100 and 150 were taken and aligned side by side.[61] Through these photos, it was intended to portray the message that the Allied PoWs were well treated.

Another significant theme continuously emphasised in the magazine was that the Ottoman Army was equipped with modern and powerful weapons and the latest military equipment. These symbols are supported via tens of photos and subtitles. Almost all modern weaponry included in the Ottoman military inventory was presented in the magazine.

61 *MJ*, Vol. 4, p. 62.

Figure 7.5 **Photo of the Ottoman soldiers to honour the funeral. The caption reads: 'Funeral ceremony with priest and imprisoned friends of Engineer Bone, engineer of the submarine *Safire* sunk in the Dardanelles Strait and who could not be rescued even by one of the Turkish officers who jumped into the sea . . .'.**

Figure 7.6 **Photo of the Allied PoWs from the *War Magazine*. The caption reads: 'A picture of a group of English and French PoWs from various front lines'.**

Figure 7.7 Photo of the Ottoman soldiers in the trench from the *War Magazine*. The caption reads: 'A new weapon used by our powerful soldiers'.

Figure 7.8 Photo of Lieutenant Hilmi from the *War Magazine*. The caption reads: 'Lieutenant Hilmi, the commander of Artillery Battery who hit and blew apart the armoured *Bouvet*, standing before his cannon proudly'.

Furthermore, in the magazine, the success of the unit of commanders and units garnished with their heroic stories was often provided.

The photos of the ceremonies organised to award medals of war and regimental banners to the units were a common theme in the *War Magazine*.

The prime function of the *War Magazine* was to present visual materials with the help of patriotic articles and poems, and to transfer the updates of news about the fronts to the reader within the framework of the government's policy. Hence, the magazine presented the news about the First World War with visual materials, prose and poetry which inflamed the Ottoman soldiers' emotions of heroism and transmitted only as much as the public needed to hear and in the form that the public understood. In some of the photos published in the magazine, images are provided of a 'military unit relaxing before the attack', 'aircraft shot down by Ottoman shooters', 'soldier who is feeling enthused with the love of war and blowing a trumpet for the attack', 'British soldiers running away after a fire fight', 'soldiers who are sleeping with bombs on their laps and waiting for their enemies behind the trenches', 'praying soldiers', and 'soldiers sledging to their trenches in the snow'. One of the important symbols of frontline propaganda in the First World War is conditions in the trenches. Although the daily life in the trenches was hard and had many physical and psychological difficulties, it is significant to note that this negative aspect of trench life was almost

Figure 7.9 Photo of a regimental ceremony from the *War Magazine*. The caption reads: 'Ceremony of golden medal of war decoration and concession of regimental banner to 27th Regiment for their sacrifice and bravery in the Arıburnu Battle'.

never reflected in the magazine's photos. Although some deficiencies of the soldiers were shown in some photos published in the magazine, such as physical exhaustion and improper sanitation, the more common theme that exists in all these photos is the dedication of Ottoman youths to their country and people.

İstanbul Literary Society's (*İstanbul Heyet-i Edebiyesi*) visit to the Gallipoli front

In his book titled *The First Casualty: From the Crimea to Vietnam: The War Correspondent as Hero, Propagandist and Myth-Maker*, Phillip Knightley suggests that in order to start or perpetuate a war a nation has to produce its version of truth, and the process of bending truth starts with the approved war correspondent or 'embedded' journalist who obediently only tells pre-approved versions of what is really happening in the war zone.[62] This was exactly the case concerning the visit of the İstanbul Literary Society (*İstanbul Heyet-i Edebiyesi*) to the Gallipoli front, a large-scale press tour to Gallipoli that constituted the first ever example of 'embedded' journalism in Turkish military history. The Ottoman General Staff, accepting the Ottoman intellectuals' request, organised a field trip to the Gallipoli Peninsula during the campaign. The observations and feelings of those intellectuals who participated in the trip were published in the *War Magazine*'s third issue in the form of articles and poems. On the 22nd page of this issue, a photo was taken of the visiting group between the soldiers' tents in Arıburnu.[63] In fact, the explanation written under photos, 'İstanbul Heyet-i Edebiyesi who will write the victory in Çanakkale (Dardanelles) for the public', reveals clearly why the group came to the front line: this was not to be impartial journalism.

One of the prominent newspapers then published in İstanbul, called *Ikdam*, released news about the invitation of the Ottoman General Staff in its issue dated Sunday 11 July 1915. In this item, the editorial office of *Ikdam* announced that: 'the poets, writers, and composers will arrange their poetry, feelings, and other works inspired by heroes, respectively, and the painters will try to capture events that they have witnessed during their visit to the Gallipoli front.' In his book entitled *The Traces of Çanakkale*, İbrahim Alaattin Gövsa notes that the intellectuals who went to the Gallipoli front were: İbrahim Alaattin (Gövsa), Hamdullah Suphi (Tanrıöver), Ağaoğlu Ahmet, Enis Behiç (Koryürek), Ali Canip (Yöntem), Celal Sahir (Erozon), Mehmet Emin (Yurdakul), Orhan Seyfi (Orhon), Hakkı Süha (Gezgin), Yekta Madran (Bestekar), Yusuf Razi (Bel), Hıfsı Tevfik (Gönensay), Muhiddin (Birgen) (journalist), Nazmi Ziya (Güran) (painter), Selahaddin (Öksüzcü), Ömer Seyfettin, İbrahim Çallı (painter), and a photographer and a cinematographer.

After the visit of the İstanbul Literary Society, there were also authors who were taken personally to the front lines. Hüseyin Cahit, for instance, was shown around by the Ottoman General Staff during the fiercest fighting. The author wrote his observations about the front line in an article entitled 'Two Days on the Front Line' and published this piece in the newspaper *Tanin*.[64]

Particularly during the Gallipoli Campaign, the poems and articles that aimed to arouse heroic feelings by addressing themes such as love of country and nation, the national flag, the idea of self-sacrifice, a sense of duty, bravery, patriotism, the merits of martyrdom, respect for the veterans, protecting national integrity and honour, and the high character of the Ottoman Empire appeared frequently

62 Phillip Knightley, *The First Casualty: From the Crimea to Vietnam: The War Correspondent as Hero, Propagandist and Myth-Maker* (Andre Deutsch Ltd, 2003). See also David Welch and Jo Fox, (eds), *Justifying War* (Routledge, 2012).

63 *MJ*, Vol. 3, pp. 42–3.

64 Hüseyin Cahit, 'Cephe-i Harpte İki Gün (Two Days on the Front Line)', *Tanin*, 23 June 1331.

سد البحر غروب قوماندانی وهیب پاشا دشمندن اغتنام اولنان ماکنه‌لی تفنکاری
استانبول هیئت ادبیه‌سنه تشهیر ایدرکن

Figure 7.10 Photo of the committee from the *War Magazine*. Caption reads: 'While the Group Commander Vehip Pasha was presenting the machine guns captured from the Allies to İstanbul Committee of Literature'.

in the *War Magazine* after the intellectuals' visits to the front lines.[65] The type of prose that commonly appeared in the magazine comprised short emotional articles written like sincere conversations, war anecdotes about heroism and the dedication of the soldiers, biographies of some prominent officers, letters sent from soldiers, and stories of military units fighting on the front line. In one article, the Ottoman Empire is presented as a 'living being' that has a spiritual personality, or a soul, and 'tries to survive' with the support and sacrifice of the Ottoman people. The

65 'Kahramanlık ve Kahramanlar (Heroism and Heroes)', *MJ*, Vol. 2, p. 123.

emphasis on the holiness of land is also prominent. In a short article featuring nationalist feelings flavoured with Islamic sentiments, the author tells the story of six heroes martyred in Koca Çimentepe battle (Hill of the Great Pasture) on the Gallipoli front during fierce fighting:

> Oh citizen! Oh Brother! Do not forget Koca Çimentepe! In the duration of your life, accept holy hajj [pilgrimage] to Koca Çimentepe as your debt of gratitude for hajj . . . . While I am writing these lines, I hear the voices of their soul saying: Hold our capital city, we are the everlasting defenders of Koca Çimentepe! . . .[66]

The equation of a visit to Koca Çimentepe with *hajj* (the Islamic pilgrimage to the holy city of Mecca) in the article indicates the author's intention to bless the Gallipoli Peninsula as a 'holy site'. This attempt to amalgamate nationalist feeling and Islamic sentiment, when disseminating the strategic narrative of the Gallipoli Campaign, is most striking in the work of Mehmet Akif Ersoy, one of the greatest Turkish poets of the twentieth century. Mehmet Akif Ersoy, in his poem titled 'To the Martyrs of Çanakkale' written just after he had been informed about the victory in Gallipoli in 1916 in Hejaz, wrote:

> Dear soldier, who fell for the sake of this land,
> How great you are, your blood saves the Muslims!
> Only the lions of Bedr[67] rival your glory!
> Who then can dig the grave wide enough to hold you, and your story?
> If we try to consign you to history, you will not fit!
> No book can contain the eras you shook!
> Only eternities can encompass you! . . .
> Oh martyr, son of the martyr, do not ask me about the grave:
> The Prophet awaits you now, his arms flung wide open, to save!

This time, Mehmet Akif Ersoy equates the soldiers who fought in Gallipoli with the companions (*Sahabe*) of the Prophet. For him, the soldiers' blood spilled in Gallipoli saved the whole Muslim nation (*ummah*), and thus should be equal to the blood of the Prophet's companions in the Battle of Badr as only these two battles saved the Muslims in the world, and none except for these in Islamic history.

Another interesting piece of prose published in the *War Magazine* is a short article written for the Ottoman mothers who sent their sons to the front line. The

---

66 Süleyman Nazif, 'Çimentepe'de', *MJ*, Vol. 3, pp. 34–6.

67 The Battle of Badr is the first battle fought by the Prophet and 305 companions (*Sahabe*) against the infidels in 624. As the Battle of Badr is a battle explicitly discussed in the Quran, this battle and those *Sahabes* that participated in it are considered excessively 'blessed' by the Muslims.

article, entitled 'What do Ottoman mothers think?', is written as an emotional imaginary speech at a train station of a mother who is sending her only son Hüseyin to front line. This is in fact a message to those hesitating to go to the front. The event is reported as follows:

> The commander sees a black silhouette on the opposite side of the train. This silhouette is a compassionate person who is keeping a tab on the sons of the country. When he comes closer, he notices that she is a mother who is sending her son to the front line. She is an Ottoman mother whose tall length stooped forward with an essential droop resembling the prostrating shape of her waist bent by spiritual destinies and whose sorrowful silence became an interpreter to her heart, shedding tears, like a silent language, standing at the front like a living monument for a holy cause. The mother's advice to her last son before his travel by train was as: '. . . your uncle, your father and your brothers are buried in *Şıpka*, in *Dökme* and in Gallipoli respectively. We have not buried a man in our village cemetery for almost 50 years. You're my last son! If the call to prayer will be stopped and the oil lamps of the mosques will be extinguished, do not come back to our village. I forbid my milk to you if you return. Even if you die, go and serve for your country . . .
>
> This is the mother who gave birth to the Ottoman nation, waiting in that train station for the departure of the train . . .[68]

When the whole text of this highly emotional article is analysed, one notices that the text of the message is aimed at mothers who hesitate to send their sons to the front and their sons who are unwilling to join the army.

In the magazine there were also articles and poems which contained propaganda on political issues. The articles entitled 'French Politics and Ottomans',[69] 'Tricks of Englishmen',[70] 'Occupation of Prussia',[71] 'To whoever escaped from Gallipoli (The British Empire)',[72] and 'To whoever escaped from Gallipoli (France)',[73] are good examples of these. One should, however, note that the overall mission of the magazine was the announcing of the Ottoman military's success, often with poems. The Ottoman General Staff supplied authors with a rich flow of documents in order to prove the military's bravery and its heroic stance. Although, for instance, Ziya Gökalp, a leading figure in the CUP and extremely influential intellectual in the late Ottoman period, had never been to the battlefield, he composed a poem:

---

68 'Türk Anası Ne Düşünüyor (What do Ottoman mothers think?)', *MJ*, Vol.17, pp. 267–9.

69 'Fransız Siyaseti ve Osmanlılar', *MJ*, Vol.23, pp. 359–62.

70 Ağaoğlu Ahmet, 'İngiliz Oyunları', *MJ*, Vol. 2, pp. 22–4.

71 'Prusya'nın İstilası', *MJ*, Sayı 17, pp. 260–65.

72 Mithat Cemal, Çanakkale'den Kaçanlara-İngiltere-, *MJ*, Vol. 5, p.68.

73 Mithat Cemal, Çanakkale'den Kaçanlara-Fransızlara-, *MJ*, Vol. 5, p.68.

Figure 7.11 'The soldier sleeping with a grenade' photo cited by Ziya Gökalp.

'Soldier and Poetry'.[74] It starts with a photograph published on the cover of the same issue, showing a Turkish soldier on the Galicia front, sleeping in a trench while holding a hand grenade to his chest.

In the poem, Gökalp, annoyed, calls for all those 'ignorant' poets to look carefully at this photograph, because, for Gökalp, this soldier was the real poet: he was the one who 'felt and heard'. With his grenade, which he did not let go of even when sleeping, this 'unknown soldier' was writing 'a poem' inspired by his motherland and dreaming of war. Gökalp stated that perhaps this soldier was about to be martyred for his country and would thus become part of history. Gökalp then suggests that this sacrifice was in complete contrast to the laziness of the traditional poet who could not even be bothered to write an epic on the heroism of this soldier. Gökalp, then, ends this poem with an interesting threat: 'The pen of the lazy poet should be taken away from him and he should be sent to the front and made to dig the graves of the martyred soldiers.'[75]

Mithat Cemal, another influential thinker of the late Ottoman period, dedicated his poem, published in the *War Magazine*, 'To the soldier who left his arm on the battlefield',[76] having been inspired by the true story of Lieutenant Hasan Dursun.

It is also worth mentioning that, aiming to defuse the critics asking why the best Ottoman soldiers went to the Galicia front to support the Austrian–Hungarians against the Russians, the *War Magazine* published a great number of articles. To justify the deployment here, there were articles entitled 'From Galicia to Homaland-1',[77] 'From Galicia to Homaland-2', 'To Glorious Ottoman Soldiers in Galicia',[78] 'To those fighting in Galicia', [79] 'The Galicia Legend',[80] and 'From Gallipoli to Galicia'. [81]

Conclusion

Whether in an explicit or implicit fashion, for centuries political entities have applied various strategies to influence their own public opinions and to shape others' thoughts in the way they want. These strategies become more significant in times of war, when more coherent national solidarity and higher morale, particularly for

74 In this poem, Ziya Gökalp calls for poems to be written, dedicated to the Ottoman soldiers. Ziya Gökalp, 'Asker ve Şair', *MJ*, Vol. 14, p. 214.

75 Erol Köroglu, *Ottoman Propaganda and Ottoman Identity: Literature in Turkey during World War I*, p. 9.

76 Mithat Cemal, 'Kolunu Harp Meydanında Bırakmış Bir Askere', *MJ*, Vol.8, p. 122.

77 Ahmet Refik, 'Galiçya'dan Anavatana 1', *MJ*, Vol. 12, pp. 178–81.

78 Ahmet Refik, 'Galiçya'daki Şanlı Osmanlı Askerine', *MJ*, Vol. 13, pp. 196–9.

79 Cenab Şahabbeddin, 'Galiçyadakilere', *MJ*, Vol. 13, pp. 200–02.

80 Mehmet Rifat, 'Galiçya Mefahirinden', *MJ*, Vol. 15, pp. 227–33.

81 Süleyman Nazif, 'Çanakkale'den Galiçya'ya', *MJ*, Vol.20, pp. 316–17.

the soldiers fighting on the battlefield, are needed. The First World War thus could be defined as a context in which all states sought to mobilise influencing strategies to shape the adversaries' and neutral nations' perceptions, and developed counter-propaganda strategies to protect both morale and the motivation of their soldiers fighting in the field and the nations supporting them.

The Gallipoli Campaign may be defined as a battle between the Allies, who had expected a swift and clean victory hoping to change the course of the First World War by relying on their superior modern military assets, and the Ottoman Empire, a strategically exhausted country on the brink of total collapse with a threat that appeared very close to İstanbul. That is why the Gallipoli Peninsula, from the perspective of the Ottomans, was the scene of a struggle for extinction or survival.

This campaign was also one of those first contexts in which influencing strategies with modern means were introduced. Particularly on the Turkish side, the Gallipoli Campaign may be defined as the first case in which photography, cinema, the delivery of the leaflets through air means (planes and balloons) and artillery rounds, press tours of the intellectuals (as the first example of embedded journalism), the use of literary works such as poems and prose, and their dissemination thorough journals, newspapers and photo magazines for mass consumption were used in a coherent and effective fashion.

In this campaign, the Allies concentrated on influencing efforts that paved the way for individual surrender and desertion, hoping that these single acts might become widespread, and then turn into total erosion in the defensive lines of the Ottoman 5th Army. That is why, in the leaflets and PoWs' letters, the themes enabling surrender and desertion were used extensively. The thematic analysis of the leaflets and letters indicates that the Allies, to lure the Ottoman soldiers towards surrender, were inclined, to a greater extent, to talk to the rational minds of those soldiers by choosing themes belonging to the cognitive domain. With themes such as 'the PoWs are treated well', 'the Germans are deceiving you', 'the CUP leaders are traitors and leading you to a total defeat with the wrong policies' the Allies hoped to reach the reasoning faculties of the Ottoman soldiers and sought to make them apply a rational calculation. The Allies also used, to a lesser extent, themes belonging to the emotive domain on the Ottoman soldiers such as 'homesickness' and 'the meaningless of the Ottoman government's call for Holy Jihad' to touch their hearts, hoping that they would surrender or desert. Did the Allies' influencing strategies in the Gallipoli Campaign work? The answer to this question is surely 'No' if we rely on two facts. First is that there was no record of unit replacement on the Gallipoli front.[82] In this campaign that lasted almost a year, despite surrenders and desertions on the Ottoman fronts, these acts stayed at the individual level and did not become widespread in any stage of the campaign. That is why the

82 ATASE Archive; K. 4174, D. 61, F. 2–5.

Ottoman General Staff did not need the option of a unit replacement on Gallipoli, in contrast to the Sinai and Caucasus fronts. Second, the Official History of the Turkish Military suggests that, in total, 2,850,000 soldiers were mobilised in the four-year-long First World War, and there were a total of 202,152 Ottoman PoWs on all fronts, constituting 7 per cent of their soldiers.[83] According to the official war record of the Ottoman General Staff, which was prepared in light of the official war records of the 128 different units that fought on the Gallipoli front, of 315,500 soldiers who fought in the Gallipoli, only 10,022 soldiers (around 8,000 of the British forces and around 2,000 of the French forces) surrendered and became PoWs, constituting 3.1 per cent of the total. Although there is no consensus among the scholars with regard to the exact numbers and percentages of the Ottoman PoWs on all fronts at which the Ottoman soldiers fought in the First World War, one thing is agreed: with around 85,000 PoWs, the Sinai–Palestine front came first in the list of surrendered personnel, and, with around 60,000 PoWs, the Caucasus front came second.[84] In light of these numbers, we may assert that the percentage of the Ottoman PoWs on Gallipoli was relatively low when compared with the percentages on other fronts.

The CUP government running the Ottoman Empire during the First World War applied influencing strategies both to the Ottoman people and in order to influence public opinion of other states during the war. The *War Magazine* used by the leaders of the CUP clearly shows that while propaganda could be useful for motivating the soldiers on the Gallipoli front and the public at home, it could also be a means of preventing the public from receiving accurate and unpalatable information by censorship and by misinformation. The *War Magazine* was also useful in the sense that propaganda is also a field in which fictitious texts could be used intensively to shape the targeted audiences' perceptions. To create the 'illusion that we are marching towards victory', the CUP leaders aptly utilised photographs, visual materials and texts to focus on the 'success story' of the Gallipoli Campaign. This uncovering of the success story of the Gallipoli Campaign would also mean it could conceal the deteriorating conditions and grim losses on all the other fronts in the First World War. We may therefore assert that the deteriorating Ottoman military position on the fronts of Sinai, Iraq and Caucasus, for instance, as well as the growing depression among the population due to material hardships, forced the regime to promote even more energetically 'patriotic' propaganda and publications with the aim of pacifying popular discontent and to provide moral encouragement for its officers and soldiers. That is why the Ottoman government's influencing

83 Official History of the Turkish Military, Vol. 5, 3rd edn (Turkish General Staff Printing House, 2012), p. 463.

84 Cemil KUTLU, *I. Dünya Savaşı'nda Rusya'daki Türk Savaş Esirleri ve Bunların Yurda Döndürülmeleri Faaliyetleri* (Turkish) (Erzurum: Atatürk İlkeleri ve İnkılap Tarihi Enstitüsü, 1997) (Unpublished PhD Dissertation).

strategies mainly targeted the emotive domain to keep the 'hyphen' between the Ottoman people and the cause tight.

As I argued in the introduction, it may be a mistake to define the Ottoman government's influencing strategies as simple propaganda tactics that looked only for short-term gains, meaning that the inclination to narrowly define influencing strategies in the Gallipoli Campaign as merely a set of counter-propaganda tactics by the Ottoman General Staff may be misleading. These efforts constituted benchmarks for the production of strategic narratives which were ultimately transformed into a long-term engineering of national culture.

It can also be argued that the propaganda experience gained by the state machinery and the Ottoman intellectuals, thanks to the campaigns, particularly Gallipoli, were not in vain. Propaganda activities after the Balkan Wars' defeats meant that ideas of Ottomanism and Islamism were weakened, and Turkism was empowered instead. Turkish discourse, which started to gain momentum in 1912 and was slightly diminished towards the end of the First World War due to military defeats, could nevertheless recover and regain momentum. In July 1917, Ziya Gökalp, for instance, the voice of the CUP in the cultural and literary arena, started to publish *New Magazine* (*Yeni Mecmua*) and the authors of this magazine produced articles intended for the development of national identity and national culture instead of producing works of propaganda merely in order to arouse public awareness in the direction of the war.

Chapter 8
Recognising the other
Contested identities at Gallipoli[1]

Alev Karaduman

Besides its political, diplomatic and military consequences, the Gallipoli Campaign also brought different national and cultural identities into confrontation. As can be clearly seen in the memoirs, diaries and letters of the Turkish and Allied soldiers, both sides 'othered' the enemy and, with prejudice, antagonism, and cultural solipsism, failed to recognise each other's identity. The British and ANZAC soldiers depicted the Turkish identity in their writings in a stereotypical and antagonistic manner. Turkish identity was misrepresented especially by the ANZACs who were highly affected by the concept of Orientalism from the Western perspective. However, in time, as a result of the cultural experience shared on the battlefield, this prejudice was turned, not only into mutual respect for each other, but also into a new understanding of their own nations. So, the purpose of this chapter is to discuss and demonstrate, on the basis of memoirs, diaries and letters as primary material, how the fighting at Gallipoli was also metaphorically a war of identities, especially between Turkish and ANZAC soldiers.

Contrary to the general belief, as Kevin Forster has clearly pointed out, 'the 1915 Gallipoli battles have [. . .] been the major factor in fostering closer ties of friendship between [Australians], New Zealanders and Turks both at national and local levels over the past decade.'[2] It is paradoxically true that, out of severe and bloody battles, the Turks and the ANZACs managed to bury their enmities and construct an unforgettable bond between themselves. The major factor that should not be forgotten here is the expectation of the ANZACs who came to Gallipoli with the hope of becoming a stronger part of the British Empire.

In fact, for the British, French, Canadians, Indians and Germans, the Gallipoli Campaign '[was . . .] one of a long tragic list of World War I battles, but for the Turks, Australians and New Zealanders, Gallipoli has been something apart – a

1 This chapter is a revised and expanded version of the paper presented at the EACLALS Triennial Conference: 'Under Construction: Gateways and Walls', Boğaziçi University, İstanbul, 26–30 April 2011.

2 K. Forster et al., *Gallipoli: The Turkish Story* (London: George Allen and Unwin, 2003), p. 12.

significant event in the self-development of their individual nations'.[3] Australians and New Zealanders really recognised the meaning of defending one's own country. Their great losses and their own experiences at Gallipoli made them aware, not only of their own national identities but also of the Turkish national identity. It was these experiences which led them to give up their traditional antagonistic and solipsistic manners. What was the scale of their losses in these battles? Historian J. Macleod wrote:

> Throughout 1915, Ottoman and German troops turned back repeated sea and land assaults from British, French, Indian, Newfoundland, Australian and New Zealand forces. In all, nearly a million men fought there. The battlefields were tiny, the casualties enormous. The Ottomans threw almost half a million men into the battle, of whom 250,000 became casualties. Although no accurate records are available, 86,000 Ottoman troops died there. The German contingent was very small and lost fewer men. British and Indian casualties totalled almost 120,000; [. . .] Australia's wounded numbered 27,700, of whom 8,700 were killed, while the New Zealanders lost 7,521 men (2,701 killed). It seems almost incomprehensible that such casualties could be sustained in this small area. Almost 50,000 Australians subsequently died on the Western Front [. . .] The Ottomans, by comparison, suffered more casualties [here] than in any other campaign of the war.[4]

The British Imperial forces in Egypt trained 20,000 Australian and 8,000 New Zealander troops whose name was soon abbreviated as ANZAC, and who had expected to be shipped directly to Europe, there to join other British armies on the Western Front in the First World War.[5] But, directed by the British authorities, the diversion of the convoy to Egypt and then to Gallipoli left the ANZACs disappointed as they believed, 'they might not get their chance to win fame and glory on the battlefields'.[6]

The ANZACs were sent to Gallipoli without being aware of the realities of the campaign and against whom they were going to fight. An Australian veteran explained why he enlisted the army in an interview: '. . . I wanted to enlist like all the others, you know. Well, lots of the others. I should say, because I thought I was . . . well, I was . . . should enlist. Being a member of . . . being an Australian.'[7]

---

3 Cyril Lawrence and Sir Roland East, eds, *The Gallipoli Diary of Sergeant Lawrence of the Australian Engineers-1st A.I.F., 1915* (Carlton, Victoria: Melbourne University Press, 1981), p. 7.

4 J. Macleod, ed., *Gallipoli: Making History* (London: Frank Cass, 2004), p. 6.

5 Macleod, *Gallipoli: Making History*, 88.

6 J. Murray, *Gallipoli As I Saw It* (London: William Kimber and Co., 1965), p. 40.

7 Alistair Thomson, *Anzac Memories: Living with the Legend* (Melbourne; New York: Oxford University Press, 1995), p. 74.

As Thomson further elaborated on the issue of enlisting in the army in his book entitled *Anzac Memoirs: Living with the Legend*:

> In the memories of most [veterans], the story of enlistment is highly significant and fraught with contradictions. It reveals a struggle to make a sense of a decision that may have been difficult at the time, which sometimes had disastrous personal consequences, and for which public regard has shifted dramatically, from wartime enthusiasm through to doubt, ambivalence and even opposition.[8]

Not only this, but there were also many other ANZAC soldiers who did not have any notion of the realities of war and they thought they were being sent on a romantic adventure. J.G. Gillam who served as 'the supply officer' with the so-called 'immortal 29th division'[9] at Gallipoli wrote in the preface to his *Gallipoli Diary* published in 1918 that he regarded the campaign as the 'most romantic part in the Great War'[10] and that he dreamed of conquering İstanbul. Like many of the ANZACs, he also considered that the Gallipoli Campaign seemed to him 'so romantic and full of adventure'.[11] He again re-stated this perception in the following statement: 'the campaign, I surmised, was likely to be more romantic than any other military undertaking of modern times.'[12] This is indeed a very important point in the ANZAC as well as British soldiers' perception of the war.

As the veteran's interview indicates, and as Thomson's comment and J.G. Gillam's treatment of the war seem to echo, neither the Australian and ANZAC soldiers, nor the public, was aware of the crude realities and devastating effects of the 'Great' war. This would result not only in frustration and disillusionment, as they had to endure miserable conditions and all the difficulties of war, but also a realisation of the misrepresentation of the Turks against whom they were forced to fight.

Just before the war, the troops were trained in Egypt by the British imperial forces for a short time and there they were 'warned' against the Turks who were described as 'a cruel and ignorant race . . . . [They are] one of the most fanatical of the Mohammedan races, the ferocity of the unspeakable Turk in gaining converts being unsurpassed by any other race.'[13] It was not long before the local papers were reprinting stories of '[Turkish] and German alleged barbarity, bayoneting babies, raping and killing women, severing prisoners' hands and a host of similar

---

8 Thomson, *Anzac Memories*, p. 74.

9 John Graham Gillam, *Gallipoli Diary* (London: George Allen and Unwin, 1918), p. 8.

10 Gillam, *Gallipoli Diary*, p. 5.

11 Gillam, *Gallipoli Diary*, p. 16.

12 Gillam, *Gallipoli Diary*, p. 23.

13 R. Koebner et al., *Imperialism: The Story and Significance of a Political Word, 1840–1960* (London: Cambridge University Press, 1965), p. 125.

fabrication.'[14] Largely in response to these stories, many Australians instantly turned against anyone around them of German-Turkish origin.

Australia and New Zealand were members of the British Empire and maintained close economic, social and cultural links with the 'mother country'. In addition, although Australia had gained the status of nation in 1901 when the six colonies combined to form the Commonwealth of Australia, in many respects, this political independence was a 'misnomer'[15] since many Australians, especially the wealthy ones, relied heavily on Britain as their mentor, chief source of inspiration and supplier of continuing financial benefits. At its core British imperialism was a vigorous practice of capitalism, having evolved from its beginnings through the rise of free trade in the late seventeenth and early eighteenth centuries into a hegemonic economic system that flourished in proportion to its expansion on a worldwide scale.[16] This might have been another reason why Britain's trials and triumphs were seen as theirs by the ANZACs. Thus, it was not surprising to observe that the Australian colonies had quickly dispatched military contingents to fight for Britain's wars. Ten thousand men were enlisted in Sydney in a week to join the army on Britain's side. 'Great wars were rare, and short, and many eagerly seized a fleeting opportunity' commented Australian historian E.M. Andrews.[17] Those who were accepted considered themselves lucky. War was glamorous, soldiering was romantic and death was glorious. Their prejudiced and antagonistic attitude towards the so-called 'barbaric Turks' nevertheless changed during the Gallipoli Campaign. The more the ANZACs fought against the Turks and had experience of them, and shared the same conditions, the more they realised how they had been unfairly prejudiced against the Turks. Later on, after the war, they began to regard Gallipoli as the war that made the ANZACs and Turks friends.

In the Australian veterans' letters, this issue was treated as follows: 'Contrary to all negative propaganda and promptings that had been made, we understood by our experiences through events how Turkish soldiers were gallant warriors'.[18] Similarly, the same issue was covered in similar words by another veteran's letter: 'We understood by our experiences and by events how Turkish soldiers were gallant warriors, contrary to all negative propaganda and promptings that had been made while we were going to Gallipoli, about how badly Turkish soldiers might treat.[19]

---

14 G.K. Kerr, *Lost Anzacs: the Story of Two Brothers* (Singapore: Oxford University Press, 1998), p. 53.

15 H. Magdoff, *Imperialism: From the Colonial Age to the Present* (New York: Monthly Review Press, 1978), p. 67.

16 O. Owen et al., *Studies in the Theory of Imperialism* (London: Longman, 1972), p. 52.

17 E.M. Andrews, *The Anzac Illusion: Anglo-Australian Relations During World War I* (Cambridge: Cambridge University Press, 1993), p. 217.

18 B.V. Karatay, *Mehmetçik ve Anzaklar* (İstanbul: Türkiye İş Bankası Yayınları, 1987), p. 104.

19 N. Sezen et al., eds, *Çanakkale Cephesinden Anzak Günlükleri* (Çanakkale: Çanakkale Savaşları Araştırma ve Tanıtım Topluluğu, 2008), p. 115.

What were these experiences which made the ANZACs change their antagonism and cultural solipsism, and recognise the Turkish identity that they earlier considered as the 'Other'? As can be seen from the Australian veterans' letters, the answer is simple, in fact. It was the humane values of the Turkish soldiers, which they experienced in their meetings during truces for the mutual burial of their own soldiers. Another veteran wrote:

> One of the situations that affected us most is the gentlemanliness of the Turkish soldiers . . . The Turkish artillerist, when there was a possibility that the artillery shooting will harm our hospital ship, always ceased fire . . . Our hospital ship that was anchored offshore of the Anzac Bay was protected carefully by the Turkish artillerists. From time to time when our battleship got near to our hospital ship, the artillerists would cease fire in order not to harm the ship with a Red Cross symbol on it . . . These and suchlike events immediately awakened respect and sympathy among every other member of our unit.[20]

The ANZACs realised that what was written in history books and ideas forced on them about the Turks fell far short of representing the truth. Admiration and respect gradually replaced hatred and enmity. In spite of heavy fighting and many devastating battles, there was born a mutual respect and love between the ANZACs and the Turks. It is also reflected in a diary of an ANZAC soldier who relates a story of mutual caring for 'the other':

> I set to work in the light of a torch I have found in the bag of a wounded officer. In the meantime, a Turkish soldier, who was wounded at his knee just like me approached me. He tried to convey that he wanted to cooperate. We immediately took action. We started to cover the wounds with the bandages we can find together and to drop the water that is left in the flasks into the dried mouths of those who were in the agony of death . . . That lasted pretty long. In the end both my friend and I became weary. Before I collapsed there I had to drag myself to the bandage place. Two enemy friends left after having shaken each other's hands.[21]

When the ANZACs recognised the humanity of the so-called 'barbaric' Turks, they understood the fallacies fabricated for them through British imperial ideology which generally ignored, devalued and humiliated the colonised. The humanity of the Turkish soldiers was also emphasised in a memoir of an Australian soldier:

> During our period of being comrades in arms for years, I didn't see any cruelty towards the ones who came to kill themselves and to take their lands. They carried the wounded enemy soldiers on their backs to the battlements and they tended them, if they couldn't find gauze bandages they would tear their shirts, if they had no other substitute to tend them.[22]

---

20 Kerr, *Lost Anzacs*, pp. 99–100.
21 Kerr, *Lost Anzacs*, p. 90.
22 Thomson, *Anzac Memories*, p. 89.

The ANZACs were surprised, shocked and, to some extent, ashamed, because they really became aware of the fact that the Turks were defending their own land and their nation bravely and resolutely despite all their difficulties. For the ANZACs, what made the Turks powerful was neither their financial nor military power but their faith in their mission to defend themselves and their country. An Australian soldier wrote that: ‘what I understood in time was that we fought against a gallant and a brave nation who defended its country against the invasion of the enemy in Gallipoli resolutely . . . . It is impossible to find an equal to Turkish soldiers especially in the battles of the world’.[23] Another veteran described the courage of the Turks in these terms:

> They would sleep on the stones, in spite of the sun, storms, cold and rain; they spend their days in the dust and mud in the unsheltered battlements but they would fight with their enemies, who had every facility in the world, with a lion’s heart. What a humble and calm patriotism was that . . . . There is no other soldier in Europe comparable to Turkish soldiers in defence in Gallipoli. Any other troops, if they had such great losses from the fires from our ships, wouldn’t stay where they were, and would have been withdrawn immediately. However, the Turks never left the battlements throughout the campaign.[24]

The ANZACs appreciated the self-sacrifice, the firmness, and the bravery of the Turkish troops, their determination, and that of the chief commander, Mustafa Kemal Atatürk. The change of heart was induced partly by the need to explain why the Allies had not been able to defeat the Turks as quickly or as easily as had been expected. From the letters and diaries of the ANZAC soldiers it was understood that the Turks were ‘a determined, resourceful fighting force’.[25] An Ottoman general proudly reported in a letter to his father that: ‘The allies are astonished at the bravery and self-sacrifice of our soldiers’.[26] An ANZAC soldier also commented on the same point stating that ‘the Turkish soldiers were determined not to accept the authority of the superiors. They followed the leader unconditionally and went ahead into the enemy.’[27] In the memoirs of the ANZACs, a very interesting remark was made, as follows:

> We observed the courage they showed and their beliefs of ‘either victory or death’ during the war with admiration . . . . Being sure of expressing the ideas and thoughts of most of us, I want to state that we desired by heart that the Turks weren’t fighting against us but beside us.[28]

---

23 Sezen, *Çanakkale Cephesinden*, p. 93.
24 Thomson, *Anzac Memories*, p. 22.
25 Kerr, *Lost Anzacs*, p. 79.
26 R. Eşref, *Mustafa Kemal Çanakkale'yi Anlatıyor* (İstanbul: Şema, 2010), p. 39.
27 Eşref, *Mustafa Kemal Çanakkale'yi Anlatıyor*, p. 40.
28 Murray, *Gallipoli As I Saw It*, pp. 89, 100.

The Allies were really most impressed by the high sense of honour and virtue, boundless bravery, humanity and loyalty, and outstanding patriotism of the Turkish soldiers, and they recognised the value and meaning of all those qualities for the Turks. This was specified in a letter of an ANZAC veteran:

> With the cries of 'Allah – Allah' and with the power of faith in their brave hearts they attacked with the bayonet in such a way that no one in the British history might have showed more bravery than them . . . . They attacked the assailer crying out loud the name of 'Allah' . . . . I couldn't encounter any equal to the courage and humanity of the Turkish soldiers.[29]

The Turkish soldiers were always ready to obey the command of their leader, Mustafa Kemal. That is, 'to defend their country to the death'. Their loyalty and dedication to their country and commander can be traced in their memoirs as well.

> We were firing from our local in Arıburnu. I pulled the trigger of the rifle but it didn't fire. I thought 'Probably, the rifle is faulty'. I turned to my friend next to me: 'Look! I think my rifle is broken, it doesn't fire.' He looked at it and he turned to me saying 'It is not broken, your finger is gone, and that's why it doesn't fire.' I suddenly looked at my finger and it was bleeding. Only then I began to feel the pain.[30]

This incident shows that, for the Turkish soldiers, not just their fingers, but even their lives were of no importance in the defence of their country. That's why all the soldiers were called 'Mehmetçik' to show that they were one and same and ready to die to save their country.

In the memoir of another Mehmetçik, this sacrifice was illustrated in a very emotional, touching but at the same time realistic manner. He wrote:

> One night, I was walking about the stream bed of the Karayürek River. I was very thirsty. The river was flashing. I filled my flask; however, when I drank a sip of water, I thought that its taste was different. When the moon got rid of the shade of the cloud, I took some water in my hand and then I realised it was the blood with which I filled my flask.[31]

The common point shared between the ANZACs and the Mehmetçik was that it was impossible to describe the bloody battles in Gallipoli. It was also undeniable that both sides suffered very heavy losses. From this agony, they managed to construct a mutual friendship between themselves. On the battlefield, during the ceasefire, paradoxically enough, they helped each other and even exchanged cigarettes, water, and other goods. An ANZAC soldier wrote:

---

29 Kerr, *Lost Anzacs*, pp. 23, 22.

30 Sezen, *Çanakkale Cephesinden*, p. 126.

31 G. Tezcan, *Gazilerin Dilinden Çanakkale* (İstanbul: Yarımada, 2007), p. 41.

> Five days after this bloody battle, a period of ceasefire took place between the sides. In those hours we tried to bury the corpses, [and] we have found an opportunity to be in touch with wounded enemy soldiers . . . . While I was going to the bandage place, to the rear, I saw that the position we had just passed over was full of dead bodies and wounded soldiers. The situation of the majority of the wounded was serious. I forgot about my wound and pain. I wanted to help those people. It was of no importance if they are from our side or not anymore . . . . There happened to be times when we exchanged food and cigarettes with them.[32]

This extract shows both sides were respectful to each other. They were not the enemies who tried to destroy each other but mutual comrades. The ANZACs attributed a name to the Mehmetçiks suitable to their own culture and called them 'Johnny Turk'[33] to show their mate-ship with them.

This may also indicate that the ANZACs began to appreciate the patriotic soul of the Turkish soldiers. A veteran explained in his diary why they called the Turks Johnny Turk. 'We were addressing them "Johnny Turk" sincerely . . . . "Johnny Turk" was loved for being a perfect soldier as well as being honest and noble. We agreed that no other army could defend its country better than the Turkish soldiers.'[34] They developed great respect towards the enemy they faced at Gallipoli. Moreover, this emotion deepened in time and turned into a mutual friendship. As can be observed in the letters and memoirs, while the ANZACs were leaving Gallipoli having lost the campaign, they were happy to have an endless friendship with the Turks, as they indicated in their letters:

> We left that peninsula with the admiration we felt towards gallant Turkish soldiers. I want to indicate that you are the offspring of a nation who is as brave as it is humane and civilized . . . if our troops were allies, they would happen to be the most powerful fighting power of the world. And surely, today's map of Europe would have a different composition . . . . I can say depending on what I have seen in Gallipoli that Turkish soldiers and Anzac soldiers are the most superior soldiers in the world . . . . We didn't ever nurse a grudge and hatred towards Turkish soldiers whom we met in Gallipoli in blood and smoke.[35]

As can be understood from all those letters, it would not be wrong to state as a conclusion that, after Gallipoli, generations of Australians 'perceived the Turks as determined people'[36] and learned many things from these experiences. The war changed their antagonistic attitude toward the Turks. This maturity helped in

32 Kerr, *Lost Anzacs*, pp. 90, 88.
33 Murray, *Gallipoli As I Saw It*, p. 85.
34 Murray, *Gallipoli As I Saw It*, pp. 90, 84.
35 Forster, *Gallipoli: The Turkish Story*, pp. 84, 88, 102.
36 Forster, *Gallipoli: The Turkish Story*, p. 67.

the further evolution of their independence as a nation. As an Australian veteran indicated, 'we, old generation, evaluated the Gallipoli war as a great event which shows Australia is not a colony anymore but a country, a nation that is bound to be strengthening in the future.'[37] So, to justify and substantiate this perception, the impact of Mustafa Kemal Atatürk's immortal speech, which was delivered on Anzac Day in 1934, on the Australians and New Zealanders is undeniable:

> Those heroes that shed their blood and lost their lives! You are now living in the soil of a friendly country, therefore rest in peace. There is no difference between the Johnnies and the Mehmets to us where they lie side by side, here in this country of ours. You, the mothers, who sent their sons from faraway countries, wipe away your tears; your sons are now lying in our bosom and are in peace. After having lost their lives on this land, they have become our sons as well.[38]

37 Koebner, *Imperialism: The Story and Significance*, p. 105.
38 Forster, *Gallipoli: The Turkish Story*, p. 79.

Chapter 9
The meaning of Gallipoli in Turkish national identity

Mehmet Akif Okur

As a monumental historical event, the Dardanelles Campaign retains its vivid place in the public memory and the imagination of the Turkish people. But we should note that, during the last century, the story of this catastrophic campaign has been rewritten as part of a great power struggle and debate over national identity. Who was the architect of this victory? Who should have the biggest share of honour? Hitherto, the answers given to these questions about relative importance were determined by the ruling figures of the empire. The 'owner of the victory' would gain enormous prestige that could empower him against his challengers in the Ottoman Palace. Additionally, identification of the true architects of victory was also significant for international players, since any possible shift in the political balance of power would affect the foreign allies of the Ottoman state at this critical juncture.

Thus, from the very beginning, the struggles in the Dardanelles were interpreted carefully both within and outside Turkey. For instance, even while the war was going on, not only the İstanbul newspapers, but also the world press declared Enver Pasha, then strongman of the empire, as the individual who was behind the Turkish achievements in the Dardanelles. Only when the political situation changed did the nature of the arguments relating to Gallipoli take a dramatically different turn. One of the significant consequences of the First World War was the collapse of the Ottoman Empire. At the end of the war, the old ruling cadres of the empire could not survive among the ruins of the defeat and left the country. Then, the successive struggles which would open the way for the Republican regime in Turkey began. After the 'Independence War', the new ideological apparatus of the state emphasised that there was a radical rupture from the past both in policies and discourse. Historiography was among the important tools that were used by the regime, while designing a 'new society' that offered a convenient new ideological orientation for the Republican elites.

During this process, the historical memory of the people was reshaped to fit with the new content of Turkish national identity. The Dardanelles Campaign was among the national myths which, it was hoped, would function as the psychological building blocks of a 'new' Turkishness.[1] During the Republican

---

1 On different interpretations of Turkishness see: Mehmet Akif Okur, 'On the Track of Great Identity: Calls for Expansions, Ergenekons and Turkishness', in *Islam in Central Asia*, Muhammed Savaş Kafkasyalı, Vol. I, pp. 305–34.

period, a variant of the story which underlined the name of Mustafa Kemal Atatürk as the 'Hero of Dardanelles' dominated the Turkish literature of the war.[2] In some extreme versions, the Kemalist narrative nearly reduced the whole story of the war to Atatürk's presence and achievements on the battlefield.

Although the Kemalist definition of Turkishness was endorsed by the state apparatus and was successful in winning over a sizable social base of adherents, it could not obtain a complete consensus or hegemonic position. Some sections of society felt culturally marginalised because the nation-building project identified them with an alternative historical memory. Gallipoli has been among the most popular topics of the counter narrative.[3] In this narrative, the names of Ottoman statesmen were positioned as not merely political rivals, but as symbols of different visions about the future of Turkish society.[4] Similar to its 'Kemalist' version, public and vulgarised versions of this discourse strategy strongly emphasised the positive or negative aspects of the respective 'heroes' as representatives of seemingly antagonistic societal poles. And besides the heroes, two conflicting narratives represented the main precepts of rival world visions and lifestyles. One was secular, and the other religious. They asked: What was the real cause of the victory in the Dardanelles? Was it Reason or the Grace of God?

The use of the conceptual framework produced by Katherine Verdery can help us to formulate more precisely the logic which lies behind the 'competing Turkish narratives on the Dardanelles Campaign' summarised above as the struggle of rival parties trying to dominate the 'national symbolisation' processes. From an anthropological perspective, Verdery looks to the nation as a symbol rather than as an entity. By doing this, she directs our attention to national rhetoric, competing to define the meaning of national symbols and the nation-as-symbol itself. According to Verdery, through the struggles between the rival parties, a single symbol, the nation, takes on multiple meanings:

> . . . Groups orienting to it all take the nation to be the paramount symbol, but they have different intentions for it. Various things enter into their conflicts – contrasting ideas about authenticity, about the nation's true mission, about cultural patrimony or heritage, about national character, and so forth . . . .[5]

---

2 For an example of a Kemalist version of the Dardanelles War, look to this widely read historical novel: Turgut Özakman, *Diriliş: Çanakkale 1915*, Bilgi Yayınevi, Ankara: 2008.

3 Özdemir's historical novel on the Dardanelles War is the most significant example of non-Kemalist nationalist narrative on the war: Mehmed Niyazi Özdemir, *Çanakkale Mahşeri*, Ötüken Yayınevi, İstanbul, 2007.

4 An influential book which has revived the name of Enver Pasha as an idol of the non-Kemalist version of Turkish nationalism should be cited here: Nevzat Kösoğlu, *Şehit Enver Paşa*, Ötüken Yayınevi, İstanbul 2008.

5 Katherine Verdery, 'Whither "Nation" and "Nationalism"?', in *Mapping the Nation*, Gopal Balakrishnan, (ed.) (Verso, New York: 1999), p. 230.

Furthermore, Verdery's perspective focuses on how ideas about nation and identity are produced and reproduced as central elements in a political struggle. Defining 'nation' as a construct implies that its meaning is never stable, but shifts with the changing balance of social forces. And groups competing for power want to construct national identity in a way which affords them a leverage over their rivals.[6]

During the late 1990s and early 2000s, Turkey has become a forum of intense debate on national identity over deeply rooted themes linked to decades-old cleavages in Turkish society. During those years of great political transformations, rival groups have attempted to define 'nation' in a similar way to that explained by Verdery's model. While the old guard elites were trying to preserve their ruling positions in the system, newcomers were trying to create space for themselves in the political economy.

One of the interesting contexts for the tension among the different interpretations of Turkishness, between westernised secular and more religiously oriented understandings of national identity, was the public debate on the tour guides' way of telling stories about the Dardanelles Campaign. Breaking down this debate helps us understand the significant dynamics which are shaping the Turkish political arena.

On 29 July 2004, just four months after the tense local elections, secular-leaning daily *Milliyet* published a report entitled 'Spiritual Rush to Dardanelles'.[7] According to journalist Yetkin İşcen, one of the people cited in the report, religious people were settled in the Dardanelles. He claimed that mayors of AKP, the conservative party of Turkey, had carried people aboard buses to Gallipoli and told them totally false stories about the war: 'People who wear skull caps, harem pants and veils spread out everywhere. They were praying at the war cemeteries and picnicking on the foreign graves. During those tours, developments occurred there in which tales were told that this was the campaign in which Mustafa Kemal deserted.' By highlighting the traditional-religious dress, and religious practices like praying, İşcen uses the stereotypes which divide Turkish society to criticise the efforts of rival groups to interpret this important national symbol according to their own set of values. He shows religious people's alleged disrespect against the memory of Mustafa Kemal as the proof of the denial of Kemalist principles. The sensitivities derived from the centrality of Atatürk in the secular definition of Turkishness can also be seen in the words of others who have become part of this debate on identity.

For example, according to the same report, Tolga Örnek, director of a documentary on Gallipoli, made complaints about the 'intentions' of religious groups. He claimed that the pro-religious sector had been trying to make the Dardanelles an alternative place to Anıtkabir, the monumental grave of Atatürk. Religious tour guides had told the story of the Gallipoli Campaign with purely

6 Ibid., p. 230.

7 'Çanakkale'ye Ruhani Akın', *Milliyet*, 29.07.2004.

spiritual terms as if the war was a jihad won under the command of the caliph. For him, the aim of this narrative is to erase Atatürk's name from the Dardanelles. Documentary producer Savaş Karakaş's cited comments were not dissimilar to Örnek's:

> . . . those reactionary groups wearing skull caps and harem pants were a little further ahead. Those guides who do not know anything about the history of the Dardanelles were telling unbelievable things to visiting groups. They were saying that clouds dropped to earth and the enemy disappeared within it, and birds and bugs destroyed the enemies of God. Setting Mustafa Kemal aside, even the name of Mehmetçik was not mentioned.[8]

The Leader of Dardanelles Tourism Association, Ahmet Kaşıkçı, who also spoke to *Milliyet*, told similar testimonials. Kaşıkçı claims that religious tour guides tell people: '. . . At nights, cries of 'Allah', 'Allah' come from the trenches. Victory in the Dardanelles Campaign could be achieved with the help of saints. Those saints caught and destroyed the cannonballs while they were in the air . . . . '[9]

The language used in these testimonials gives us an idea about the secular-Kemalist symbolisation of the nation and its symbolic understanding of the Other. All the people who spoke to *Milliyet* criticised the tour guides because they de-emphasise Atatürk and overemphasise religious themes at the expense of reason and rationality. Non-Western traditional dress identified with religiosity was underlined as an alarm signal and a kind of supporting evidence for their accusations. According to the people cited in the *Milliyet* report, there was a systematic 'danger' of alternative symbolisation. The aim of those systematic efforts is, allegedly, to redefine Turkishness with religious terms. Because of this it was thought they were trying both to undermine the prestige of Atatürk and to reshape the national memory by retelling a religiously oriented story of this important national myth in a way contrary to secular qualities of reason and rationality.

This report started a hot debate in the Turkish media. One of the important answers came from Ömer Lütfi Mete who was a prestigious conservative nationalist commentator. The title of his article published in *Sabah* was 'Dardanelles and Desire for Nationality-lessness' implying that *Milliyet*'s report could damage Turkish nationality by aggravating the already strained relations between secular and religious Turks.[10] Although he used objective language in rejecting the extremist perspectives of both sides, he strongly criticised *Milliyet*'s report on the basis of its vulgar secularist rhetoric which rejected all religious symbolism, even if widely accepted, by labelling it as superstitious (*hurafe*).

8 'Çanakkale'ye Ruhani Akın', *Milliyet*, 29.07.2004.
9 'Çanakkale'ye Ruhani Akın', *Milliyet*, 29.07.2004.
10 Ömer Lütfi Mete, 'Çanakkale ve Milliyet'sizlik Özlemi', *Sabah*, 24.08.2014.

Another columnist from the same newspaper, Ahmet Hakan, also criticised *Milliyet*'s report by showing that the intention of the tour guides' references to saints is to diminish the role of commanders or soldiers who fought on the battlefields of the Dardanelles.[11] They just use the symbols and values that are embedded in the tradition to more easily internalise the meaning of the war. For him, this reinterpretation supports the love of the army in the hearts of the public, although it uses a different kind of narrative and symbols to do so. Hasan Suat from *Zaman* indicated the stereotypes used by the secular-Kemalist camp by taking double standards into consideration. While consumption of alcohol by the descendants of the ANZACS during their annual visit to the battlefields of the Dardanelles was not seen as disrespectful to the fallen, the dress code of religious people was subject to complaints. In the eyes of the secular Kemalists, the only problem was the possibility of the revival of Ottoman heritage.[12] In another comment published by *Zaman*, Dr Tuncay Yılmazer claimed that without giving the necessary weight to spirituality, it is impossible to understand the Dardanelles. He cited the official historian of the Ottoman state for the Dardanelles Campaign, Mehmed Nihad: 'In fact, the fight is among the spiritualities of the confronting parties . . . . To contradict this is equal to an acceptance that the defence of the Dardanelles is madness.'[13]

The war of words was not limited to journalists or directors. Local residents of Gallipoli also became part of the debate. The headman of the most visited village in Gallipoli, Mümin Devrilmez, denied the claims that tour guides tell stories of superstition to visitor groups: 'Here is Turkish territory. Veiled or unveiled, everybody comes here to visit.'[14] Some other people whose opinions were expressed in the pages of the newspapers cited the popular story of Troy as an example of a perfect myth. They were comparing the reactions of secular Turks against Western and Islamic tales. If the argument is: because stories about unusual events that allegedly occurred in favour of the Turkish army during the Dardanelles Campaign cannot be validated scientifically, they must not be told as truth; the same logic should be adapted to the legend of Troy. There is no exact scientific evidence confirming the story of Troy, but symbolic signs of this mythic war still exist in the Dardanelles. So, if the source of secular Turks' sensibility is pure reason and rationality, why doesn't the story of the Trojan horse irritate them?[15]

---

11 Ahmet Hakan Coşkun, 'Yine Bölündük', *Sabah*, 24.08.2014.

12 Hasan Sutay, 'Gelibolu'da Delidolu İşler', *Zaman*, 15.08.2014.

13 Tuncay Yılmazer, 'Çanakkale Maneviyat Olmadan Anlaşılamaz', *Zaman*, 03.08.2014.

14 Muzaffer Altunay, 'Çanakkaleliler: Asıl hurafe gazetelerin halkı bölmeye çalışan haberleri', *Zaman*, 15.08.2004.

15 Erkan Acar vd., 'Çanakkale, bu ülkede herkesin değer verdiği kutsal bir mekan', *Zaman*, 09.08.2004.

Activated by those polemics in the media, Kemalist NGOs like the Atatürkist Thought Association and the Association of Retired Army Officers made press releases to protect the 'true' story of the Dardanelles War from religiously motivated tour guides' 'unscientific' perspectives.[16] According to media records, those pressures yielded results and the Governorate took some measures against the people who had told religiously coloured stories which did not fit the official narrative. With the support of the gendarme, certain controls, inspections and penalisations began. In a report published by *Milliyet*, we learn that officials prepared criminal complaints about some tour guides with a threat of a prison sentence of up to six years.[17]

News archives showed that the Ministry of Culture followed the line and published a declaration underlying the importance of human factors against the help of supernatural forces: 'It is clear that the Dardanelles Campaign has a legendary aspect. But the source of this legendary component is not unrealistic rumours, but the heroism of the Mehmetçik (Turkish soldier), the genius of Atatürk and the Turkish people's love of their country.'[18]

But this was not the last word on the symbolic interpretation of the Dardanelles. One year later, debates were revived, prompted by a law passed with the votes of the conservative ruling party of Turkey. AKP opened the way for the inhabitants of Gallipoli to become 'area guides'. Because of the villagers' putative religiosity, *Radikal* informed its readers with this subtitle: 'Saints Won the War'.[19] The preparation process of the law was full of controversies. The main opposition party, CHP, put together an investigative commission composed of its parliamentarians. When we look at the report prepared by this commission, we see the superstition issue in different contexts.[20] Meetings held in the Environment Commission of the Grand National Assembly of Turkey to discuss this law became an important ground in which reverse images of nationality once again came face to face. While opposing the draft law, Ahmet Küçük, a CHP member of parliament from Çanakkale, said: 'Visits to Gallipoli National Park should not be like a visit to a tomb, or a religious visit. People should not return to their home with some kind of superstition.' Another member of parliament from Çanakkale, İbrahim Köşdere of AKP, made another controversial speech showing the other side of the coin: 'Using expressions like a tomb and Kaaba does no benefit to anybody. We would be delighted if we could give to our nation the excitement of a second Kaaba.' But perspectives were not limited with those two poles. Records of the meeting show

16 Burak Gezen, 'Hurafe Turizmi', *Radikal*, 08.08.2004.

17 'Hurafeye Suç Üstü', *Milliyet*, 11.08.2204.

18 'Hurafe Anlatan Suç İşliyor', *Milliyet*, 13.08.2004.

19 İsmet Demirdöğen ve Zihni Erdem, 'Rehber mi? Hurafeci mi?', *Radikal*, 07.07.2005.

20 CHP, 'TBMM CHP Grubu, Gelibolu Tarihi Milli Parkı Araştırma Komisyonu Raporu', http://www.gallipoli-1915.org/CHP.htm (accessed 10 June 2014).

that some other members of the commission criticised both MPs because of their extreme statements.[21]

The law on tour guides did not cut off the debate. On 20 November 2005 *Milliyet* printed the headline: 'History Lesson with Superstitions'.[22] According to the newspaper, the Ümraniye Municipality of AKP produced an animation about the Dardanelles Campaign to show to nearly 2,000 schools. *Milliyet*'s claim was a familiar one. The animation was propagating the idea that victory in the Dardanelles was obtained thanks to divine powers. This claim was also carried into the Grand National Assembly of Turkey. MP Ahmet Küçük of CHP prepared a [Parliamentary] Question asking the Minister of National Education whether he approved of the animation's content and whether he had given permission for it to be shown in the schools.[23]

The struggle has continued on different platforms. Secular opposing groups went to court to prevent 'area guides' from working in Gallipoli and other places. In response, the Ministry of Environment prepared a regulation to jump over the legal barriers.[24] In 2008, fines imposed on people for telling the story of Gallipoli 'unrealistically' were again brought up as an issue. Another MP of CHP, Hulusi Güvel, put forward a [Parliamentary] Question similar to previous ones. The answer given by the Ministry of Environment is important in terms of its data showing the number of people punished with a fine. According to the Ministry, criminal records were drawn up against 12 of the 'area guides'. Two of them were because of hyperbolic and unrealistic retellings of the Gallipoli Campaign. Additionally, necessary legal steps were also taken against 52 'undocumented' area guides.[25] A well-known writer who has written a book on the Dardanelles Campaign was also among the people who were subjected to a fine because of their remarks about Gallipoli.[26]

While concluding the chapter, we should not forget to say that the debates and news relating to the tour guides of Dardanelles lost its momentum in parallel with the consolidation of AKP's power over the state apparatus. Perhaps the only meaningful exception was the reports about Kurdish-speaking area guides.[27]

---

21 TBMM Basın Açıklamaları, 'Milli Parklara Alan Kılavuzu . . .', *Meclis Haber*, 17.05.2005, http://www.tbmm.gov.tr/develop/owa/haber_portal.aciklama?p1=26022 (accessed 10 June 2014).

22 *Milliyet*, 'Hurafelerle Tarih Dersi', 20.11.2005.

23 Ahmet Küçük, Yazılı Soru Önergesi, http://www2.tbmm.gov.tr/d22/7/7–11434s.pdf (accessed 8 June 2014), 28.11.2005.

24 Muzaffer Altunay, 'Çanakkal'deki kılavuzlar hurafecilik yapmakla suçlanamayacak', *Zaman*, 02. Nisan, 2006.

25 Hulusi Güvel'in 7/3486 sayılı yazılı soru önergesine verilen cevap, 11.06.2008, http://www2.tbmm.gov.tr/d23/7/7–3486c.pdf (accessed 8 June 2014).

26 Mehmed Niyazi Özdemir, 'Ayıptır, ayıp', *Zaman*, 04.08.2008.

27 Mehmet Güler, 'Çanakkale'de Kürtçe Rehberlik', *Zaman*, 03.04.2013.

Actually, this last picture logically completes the analysis of the nation as a symbol in the Turkish context in the Dardanelles case which fits with reference to Verdery's conceptions. Victory in Gallipoli, which came at the expense of great sacrifices, has a unique place in the positive, shared memory of Turkish citizens. Because of its importance as a living national myth, groups struggling against each other to obtain power have wanted to define and interpret it in a way to support their vision of national identity. For many of the intellectuals in the Kemalist – secularist camp, its main importance comes from Atatürk's presence on the battlefield. But, because Kemalists accepted the Independence War as the founding myth, they did not want to see Gallipoli in the centre of the national symbolisation process.

On the other side, we see the opposition forces that had not shared the Kemalist conceptualisation of Turkish national identity. The main conflicting points between those two camps have been the place of religion, and, to a lesser degree, the position of ethnic identities within the system. While challenging the rule of Kemalist elites they have tried to produce an alternative understanding of nation and nationality through the deconstruction of the old conceptions and through building new ones. So, some of them have looked to the Dardanelles Campaign as a new founding myth because of the advantages it offers to legitimise Islamic discourse in the public realm.[28] To reach this aim, the production of a new narrative, which was different from the Kemalist version in terms of its approach to religious tones in the war stories and the place of Mustafa Kemal on the battlefield, was necessary. As the debates on tour guides indicated, the most recent representation of the Kurds, with their unique characteristics such as their language in the narrative on the Dardanelles operations, is just the latest phase of the new national symbolisation process and its disputes.

28 There are some Islamist intellectuals who have challenged the mystification of the Dardanelles War. Because they claim to be against nationalism, they refuse to approve a new nationalism with Islamic content. Abdurrahman Dilipak is one of them. After an American operation in Necef (Najaf), Dilipak said that 'Necef is a thousand times more virtuous for me than Dardanelles.' Diner Şeref, 'Bu Kez Ölçüyü Kaçırdı', *Milliyet*, 28.08.2004.

Chapter 10
Contemporary Turkish perceptions of the Gallipoli Campaign

Kahraman Şakul

In the 'Gezi Days' [unrest] of 2013, the chief of the riot police department in İstanbul congratulated his men with a text message for 'repeating the Çanakkale epic' when they triumphed over the protestors at Taksim Square.[1] Many were shocked by the ominous metaphor since the riot police were publicly condemned for killing seven and wounding several protestors. A university vice-dean repeated the inopportune remark when likening the government reaction against the 'Gezi Uprising' to the Çanakkale victory.[2] It seems that anyone who criticises or protests against the Turkish Prime Minister R. Tayyip Erdoğan deserves to get a figurative beating with the stick of Çanakkale, if not a real punch from the prime minister himself.[3]

There has always been room for the Çanakkale victory in Turkey's contentious power politics. It left a huge imprint in social memory and became a significant building block in the making of the modern nation-state based on Turkishness. Nevertheless, despite this political utility, little has been written on the popular perceptions of the fighting on the Gallipoli front. This chapter will outline the phases of the evolution of the place of Gallipoli in Turkish politics, society and culture. It contends that disputes over the meaning of the 'spirit of Çanakkale' are emblematic of the general trends in the identity politics of Turkey.

Creating a nation-state, 1923–34: whose territory?

A recent survey revealed that the majority of the Turkish middle-school students supposed the Çanakkale Battle was part of the War of Independence (1919–22).[4]

1 Fatih Sarıyıldız, Chief of İstanbul Riot Police, texted the message on 13 June 2013. Erdoğan approved of the message, http://www.ntvmsnbc.com/id/25450862 [Accessed 18 May 2014].

2 Speech by Prof. Ertuğrul Oral (İstanbul Sebahattin Zaim University): http://www.izu.edu.tr/en-US/iybf/News/assist-prof-dr-ertugrul-oral-spoke-during-the-victory-of-canakkale-battle-commemoration-day-program/1437/NewsDetail.aspx [Accessed 18 May 2014].

3 After the Soma mining tragedy (12 May 2014), Erdoğan punched a protester in the face and threatened to slap another, http://www.cumhuriyet.com.tr/video/video/72569/ [Accessed 18 May 2014].

4 A third of the 1914 students did not know that the Ottomans were defeated, while three-quarters presumed 18 March was the date of the end of the conflict, see Fatma Çoban, 'Orta Öğretim Öğrencilerinin Çanakkale Savaşları ve Öğretimine İlişkin Biliş ve Algılama Düzeyleri' (Master's thesis, Çanakkale Onsekiz Mart University, 2011), pp. 94–6.

Early Republican politics and diplomacy has partly accounted for this apparent confusion. The Treaty of Lausanne recognised Turkey in return for territorial compromises. The straits were demilitarised and generous provisions were made for administration of the graveyards, monuments and memorials of the Allied powers on the Gallipoli Peninsula. While Mosul and its vicinity were ceded to the British (1926), Turkish sovereignty was established in the straits (Montreux Convention, 1936), and in Antioch (1939). Public interest in the Gallipoli Campaign was low until the 1930s because of the concerns over the Kurdish question and religious reactionism.

One can find in the early literature on the Battle of Çanakkale all the main threads that prevail in the modern social memory about the victory. A brief thematic list would include heroism and self-sacrifice of the religious Anatolian peasantry, ethnic nationalism, fear of expulsion from Anatolia, reinforcement of the nation's self-confidence, and anti-imperialism. Groups of intellectuals and parliamentarians were taken to the front during the war as means of propaganda. Various stories from the battlefields, testimonies of heroic deeds, and on-site observations were published in *Harp Mecmuası* [War Magazine] in wartime. The Ottoman government encouraged the visitors to glorify the ordinary soldiers rather than the commanders in their artistic depictions. 'The sword guided the pen' in the 'fulfilment of the national duty' in wartime.[5] Professor Ismail Hakkı argued that the Gallipoli Campaign was over only for the army while it was just about to start for writers, poets, painters and sculptors who should immortalise the victory with their artistic production.[6]

The illustrious poet Mehmet Akif created the official canon on the victory in verse when he published his epic poem 'Boğaz Harbi' ['The Straits War', 1915] in 1924. Praise for self-sacrifice, the emphasis on religious motivation, and patriotism against the imperialist menace were all laid down in beautiful verse, which resonated in more than a thousand poems on the War of Gallipoli. Ömer Seyfeddin set the pattern in prose with four stories that celebrated the victory as the awakening of the Muslim Turkish nation.[7]

5 İbrahim A. Gövsa, *Çanakkale İzleri –Anafartalar'ın Müebbet Kahramanına-* (Ankara: TTK, 1989) [reprint 1922]. See pp. 7–15.

6 *Harb Mecmuası* [War Magazine] (Ankara, TTK, 2013) [reprint]. A special issue of *Yeni Mecmua* [New Magazine] commemorated the third anniversary of the Gallipoli Battles, Murat Çulcu (ed.), *Çanakkale 18 Mart 1915. Yeni Mecmua'nın Nüsha-ı Fevkaledesi* (İstanbul: E Yay., 2006).

7 Akif's poem (trans. by Michael R. Burch): '. . . *Seven nations marching in unison!; Australia goose-stepping with Canada!; Different faces, languages, skin tones!; . . . ; Some warriors Hindu, some African, some nameless, unknown!; This disgraceful invasion, baser than the Black Earth!; . . . ; Who needs steel fortresses? Who fears the enemy?; How can the shield of faith not prevail?; . . . ; Dear soldier, who fell for the sake of this land; How great you are, your blood saves the Muslims!; Only the lions of Bedr rival your glory!;*

The Turkish educated public was familiar with the Allied perspective on the Gallipoli Campaign through the Turkish translations of influential books and reports.[8] In the early Republican era the publication of the first studies from the Turkish perspective on the sea and land battles of the Çanakkale front were then produced. History textbooks issued in 1930/1931 narrated the Gallipoli Campaign as a victory for of the Turks under the leadership of Mustafa Kemal Atatürk as part of a long-term national struggle for the first time.[9] The German ally was excluded from the victory.[10] The 1918 interview with Mustafa Kemal would be republished as a booklet several times, laying the foundational stone of the official narrative centred on the role of Atatürk in the victory.[11] Thus, one of the common objectives in this period was the appropriation of the victory from the Ottoman past. This explains the apparent difficulty experienced by Turkish school children in the proper contextualisation of the 'Çanakkale Campaign'.

Constructing a nation, 1934–60: whose victory?

The Gallipoli victory had been commemorated for the first time in 1916 and official commemorations were regularly conducted even during the Allied occupation of the peninsula. Small groups of Turkish veterans as well as others visited the Gallipoli battlefields regularly before 1934.[12] Public awareness regarding

---

Who then can dig the grave wide enough to hold you, and your story?; If we try to consign you to history, you will not fit!; No book can contain the eras you shook!; Only eternities can encompass you! . . . ; Oh martyr, son of the martyr, do not ask me about the grave; The Prophet awaits you now, his arms flung wide open, to save!', http://www.thehypertexts.com/Mehmet%20Akif%20Ersoy%20English%20Translations%20Turkish%20Poet.htm [23 May 2014]; Ö. Seyfeddin had a secularist vision, 'Bir Çocuk: Aleko' [A Child: Aleko], 'Müjde' [The Harbinger], 'Çanakkale'den Sonra' [After Çanakkale], 'Kaç Yerinden' [How Many Wounds?], Ö. Seyfeddin, *Bütün Hikayeleri* (İstanbul: YKY, 2011), pp. 721–5, 1379–97, 486–92, 513–22.

8 Burhan Sayılır (ed.), *Çanakkale, Ümitler, Yanılgılar, Gerçekler* (Ankara: Yeni Türkiye Yayınları 2005) contains works of Fortescue (1916), Moseley (1917), Bartlett (1916), Robeck & Wemyss (1917), and Monro (1917).

9 Mehmet Ö. Alkan, 'Mustafa Kemal Paşa'nın Bir Lider Olarak İnşası', Bülent Bilmez (ed.), *Cumhuriyet Tarihinin Tartışmalı Konuları* (İstanbul: TV Yurt, 2013), pp. 3–36.

10 Liman von Sanders, *Fünf Jahre Turkei* (Berlin, 1920). *Türkiye'de Beş Yıl*, (E. B. Özbilen trans.) (İstanbul: İş Bankası Kültür, 2010) contains a refutation of Liman von Sanders by the Ottoman Military History Commission, pp. 435–61; Bursalı Mehmed Nihad, *Büyük Harpte Çanakkale Seferi*, Murat Karataş (ed.) (İstanbul: Türk Şehitleri İmar Vakfı, 2012), contains an English translation.

11 Ruşen Eşref, *Anafartalar Kumandanı Mustafa Kemal ile Mülakat* (İstanbul, İş Bankası Kültür, 2009) [reprint 1930]; first published in 1918 issue of *Yeni Mecmua*.

12 Mehmet İrdesel, *Çanakkale Savaşları ve Harp Sahaları Rehberi* (İstanbul: Baha, 1973), pp. 80–90; George F. Davis, 'Anzac Days meanings and memories: New Zealand,

Çanakkale, however, gained a new momentum in 1934 when Turkey revived the 18 March Naval Victory Day. Atatürk also declared the fallen ANZACs 'our sons lying side by side with our Mehmets' in the same year. Often understood as a message of universal friendship growing out of Atatürk's magnanimity,[13] these politically motivated words actually underlined the Turkish sovereignty over Gallipoli while seeking reconciliation with Britain against the rising tide of Italian fascism.[14] Changes have been wrought since. The 1985 translation inscription on the Anzac Cove monolith reworded the original: the words 'over our Turkish home . . . our native land . . . in this soil of ours' were softened to 'the soil of a friendly country . . . in this country of ours . . . lying in our bosom'.[15]

Not until the Montreux Convention did Turkey gain the right to remilitarise Çanakkale. Alongside the diplomatic campaign to revise the straits' regime was the increasing xenophobia that eventually led to the state-backed Jewish pogroms and their deportation from Thrace to other regions.[16] The Turkish apprehension about Çanakkale was partly based on the fact that Thrace had been invaded four times between 1878 and 1922: it was said: 'were that Thrace, İstanbul and the Straits not in our hands, Turkey would be somewhere like Afghanistan'.[17] The diplomatic process undoubtedly aroused intellectual interest in the Gallipoli Campaign. It took more than Turkification policies to build a nation-state and the appropriation of the historical legacy was just as important. Perk, for instance,

---

Australian and Turkish perspectives on a day of commemoration in the twentieth century' (PhD thesis, University of Otago, 2008), 205, 213; Mithat Atabay, 'İtilaf Devletlerinin en kara günü olmuştu', *Çanakkale 1915* 15 (2013): pp. 10–4; Barış Borlat, 'Şehitlere saygı belirli kurallara tabi', *Çanakkale 1915* 19 (2014): pp. 40–43.

13 For a recapitulation of the Turkish public opinion see A. Mete Tuncoku, 'Atatürk, Çanakkale ve Anzaklar', *Çanakkale 1915: Buzdağının Altı* (Ankara: TBMM, Basımevi, 2005), pp. 113–21. Atatürk's statements of 1931 and 1934 are familiar, see Davis, pp. 212–3.

14 E. Zeynep Güler, 'Bir Ulusal Hafıza Mekanı Olarak Gelibolu Yarımadası', İnci Ö. Kerestecioğlu-Güven G. Öztan, *Türk Sağı: Mitler, Fetişler, Düşman İmgeleri* (İstanbul: Iletişim, 2012), p. 316; Davis, pp. 182, 213, 216–7.

15 Davis, p. 215. For the discrepancy between the original statement and the 1985 translation, see Adrian Jones, 'A Note on Atatürk's Words about Gallipoli', *History Australia* 2:1 (2004).

16 Ayhan Aktar, 'Trakya Yahudi Olaylarını 'Doğru' Yorumlamak', *Tarih ve Toplum* 155 (Nov. 1996): pp. 45–56; Özüm Arzık, 'Political Instrumentalization of Commemorations of Çanakkale Victory' (MA thesis, İstanbul Bilgi University, 2012), pp. 47–54. For a summary see, Ö. Arzık Erzurumlu, 'The Commemoration of the Gallipoli Victory in Turkey', in Yumuşak-İlhan (eds), *Gelibolu: Tarih, Efsane ve Anı* (İstanbul Medeniyet UP), pp. 329–36; Rifat N. Bali, *Cumhuriyet Yıllarında Türkiye Yahudileri: Bir Türkleştirme Serüveni (1923–1945)* (İstanbul: İletişim Yay., 2010), pp. 243–65.

17 Press conference by Şükrü Kaya, Minister of the Interior, in 1935 see Bali, pp. 253–4; In 1934, Atatürk dismissed a Jewish citizen in Çanakkale who complained about harassment by the 'people' by saying, 'people can send me away, as well, if they would like to', see Arzık, p. 53.

attempted to present all the wars in the Gallipoli Peninsula since time immemorial as a struggle between races in which the Pelaggians, Mycenaeans, and Thracians, who appeared to be Turkic, had fought against the non-Turkic invaders.[18]

Nihal Atsız, the renowned pan-Turkist thinker, led a group of youths in a study trip to Gallipoli in 1933. He believed that the members of the Turkic race should join in an annual march to Çanakkale as a ritual marking 'the nation's religion'. It was said that Çanakkale must be cleared of the Jews, Gypsies, and Greeks by massacre if necessary.[19] He detested the defeated for the offensively tall and numerous monuments and offered apologies to the victor for the shameful absence of proper memorials. Before the modest Mehmet Çavuş Monument, he cursed the Treaty of Lausanne and 'consoled the martyrs' by the words echoing the eternal rhymes of Mehmet Akif:[20] 'Mehmet Çavuş! Why would you need a monument? . . . Is the land of Turks not the holiest monument for you? You are already eternal (*ebedi*), no need to erect a stone monument (*abide*) to prove it.' Atsız was not alone in feeling irritated. That 'the entire peninsula was a monument to the army' was posited by Fahrettin Altay – a Gallipoli veteran – to Edward VIII during his post-Montreux visit to Gallipoli in September 1936.[21]

Debates regarding monument construction in the Gallipoli Peninsula did not loom large in public opinion until the 1950s. Although the financial constraints were the usual pretext against any monument-building project after 1922, Turkey in all likelihood refrained from causing further rifts with Britain with whom the future of Mosul was to be negotiated. Nevertheless, Mustafa Kemal declared Gelibolu a city on 19 September 1923 so as to scrutinise the memorial-building projects of the French and British. Nonetheless, the Gallipoli Campaign no doubt left an indelible hallmark in the identity formation of the young nation from the outset.[22] Debates on the offensiveness of the Allied memorials and lack of Turkish monuments were never absent in the deliberations of the National Assembly.[23] Evident in these discussions was the Akifesque idea of Çanakkale as the epitome of patriotism, the bastion of the fatherland where the Turkish bosom had been a

---

18 Kadri Perk (major), *Çanakkale Savaşları Tarihi (Miladdan evvel dört bin, miladdan sonra bin sekiz yüz yedi)* (İstanbul, 1935), pp. 16, 56, 93.

19 Nihal Atsız, *Çanakkale'ye Yürüyüş. Türkçilüğe Karşı Haçlı Seferleri* (İstanbul: Irfan, 2009), pp. 2–3, 7–8, 17, available at http://www.nihal-atsiz.com [Accessed 20 May 2014].

20 Atsız, p. 10.

21 During King Edward's visit to Çanakkale, '20 Temmuz [July] 1936' and '18 Mart 1915'were inscribed written on two ridges facing each other at Çanakkale, see Murat Karataş, 'Çanakkale'den bir kral geçmişti', *Çanakkale 1915* 1 (March 2008): pp. 50–56.

22 Arzık, 64; Catherine E. Bobbitt, 'Monument to the Nation: The Changing Face of War Memorials in Gallipoli' (MA thesis, Sabancı University, 2011), pp. 54, 65, 86–8; Gelibolu remained a city until 1925, Osman Macit Söylemez, 'Tarihten Bir Yaprak . . . Fikriye Hanım Gelibolu'da', *Çanakkale 1915* 1 (March 2008): pp. 18–25.

23 Ramazan Balcı, 'Çanakkale Şehitleri ve Biz', http://www.sizinti.com.tr/konular/ayrinti/canakkale-sehitleri-ve-biz-mart-2011.html [Accessed 22 May 2014].

shield against the armies of the Great Powers comprising all the races of the world. Süleyman Nazif called for the erection of a memorial at the entrance of the straits at Çanakkale in 1925 in commemoration of all the martyrs of the Great War and the War of Independence.[24]

The direct connection between the signing of the Montreux Convention and the 'rehabilitation' of the victory at Çanakkale was most obvious in a pamphlet by Tevetoğlu. He accused the authorities of thwarting the unofficial commemorations in the past and celebrated Montreux as a new departure. He called on the Turkish youth to build the highest monument of the world, 'the Great Mehmetçik'[25] on a lofty hillside. Students were to worship the monument on their knees in annual ceremonies to be held on 20 July – the date of the Montreux settlement, 'the new Çanakkale victory'.[26]

Apart from a number of studies that analysed the Gallipoli Campaign from the Turkish perspective, the first war-related memoirs were also published in the 1930s. *Türk Çanakkale* by Yazman set out the official line: Atatürk saved the peninsula on three different occasions, acting on his own initiative. The victory 'totally belonged to the Turks, it is entirely ours'. It was a phenomenal moment in world history since it had brought down the tsarist regime in Russia.[27] Popular folktales and epic anecdotes from Gallipoli would reappear in the 1930s as part of the nation-building process.[28] A most original contribution was *Keloğlan at the Çanakkale Battles*. Kaloghlan Mehmet, the bald boy with a frail and thin composition, was a substitute for the Anatolian Turkish peasantry. With a father killed in Yemen and a brother in the Balkan Wars, the shrewd boy was the fittest

24 Klaus Kreiser, 'War Memorials and Cemeteries in Turkey', in Olaf Farschid, Manfred Kropp, Stephan Dähne, *The First World War as Remembered in the Countries of the Eastern Mediterranean* (Beirut: Orient-Institut, 2006), pp. 188–9.

25 *Mehmetçik* (little Mehmet) may have been coined at the Battle of Tobruk (January 1912) in Libya, see Yetkin İşcen, 'Türk Askeri Ne Zaman 'Mehmetçik' Oldu? Trablusgarp'tan Çanakkale'ye', *Çanakkale 1915* 4 (2009): pp. 6–7. Mehmet Çavuş from Biga, the first Çanakkale hero to be covered in the news, is also a possible source for the nickname, see Şerafettin Turan, *Mustafa Kemal Atatürk. Kendine Özgü Bir Yaşam ve Kişilik* (İstanbul: Bilgi, 2004), p. 133.

26 Fethi Tevetoğlu [Atsız'a Yoldaş], *Çanakkale Abidesi* (İstanbul, 1936).

27 Tuncay Yılmazer (ed.), *Bir Subayın Kaleminden 'Türk Çanakkale': cephaneniz yoksa süngünüz var* (İstanbul: Yeditepe, 2008) [reprint: 1938], introduction, xiii–xvi. Aspinall-Oglander eulogised Atatürk in the official British history of the Gallipoli Campaign. He may have influenced the image-makers of Atatürk see, Aktar, 'The Making of Mustafa Kemal's Saga at Gallipoli: A British Imperial and Turkish Joint Operation, 1921–1932' conference paper, 'The British Empire and the Great War: Colonial Societies/ Cultural Responses', Nanyang Technological University, Singapore, 19–22 February 2014. I am grateful to Aktar for sharing his unpublished paper with me.

28 Yılmazer (ed.), *Türk Çanakkale*, pp. 1–3, 445; *Kahramanlık Destanları*, (İstanbul Askeri Matbaa, 1938).

man to perform all the miraculous deeds at Çanakkale that are commonplace in the popular literature. He, nevertheless, did not breed hatred in his heart even when he learned that his beloved British nurse was actually the fiancé of the injured British soldier he saved.[29]

The installation of the plaque reading 'Long live Atatürk' on the 18 March Hill (Çanakkale) in 1936 declared Turkish sovereignty over the landscape.[30] It was now time to glorify the Turkish victory with the construction of a war memorial dominating the area. Gone were the times of reciting from M. Akif, '*Oh martyr, son of the martyr, do not ask me about the grave; The Prophet awaits you now, his arms flung wide open, to save*' by way of an excuse for the nation's ingratitude. The ideal spot for the overbearing M-shaped monument (standing for Mehmetçik) was the Eski Hisarlık Hill looking down Morto Bay towards the boundless horizon. It would announce to all that the 'the owners and the gatekeepers of the straits will always be the Turks'.[31]

The ceremony for laying the foundation of the monument was held on 17 April 1954, a full decade after its approval in 1944. Quran recitations, eulogies to the Prophet (*Mevlid*), communal prayers in Turkish, and sheep-sacrifices, preceded the speeches and poems by, among others, two women and an infant girl. Those present on the occasion felt like 'visiting the Ka'ba' at the end of the day. The metaphor of a secular and national pilgrimage was not unprecedented, as suggested by Tevetoğlu's aforementioned proposal. Was not Dumlupınar 'the new Arafat' where the 'national *hacıs* [pilgrims]' should wrap themselves in red garments when circumambulating the monument to the Martyred Standard-bearer (*Şehit Sancaktar*)?[32] Nevertheless, the construction of the war memorial came to a halt in 1958 due to financial problems. According to Kreiser, Atatürk's 'colossal mausoleum in Ankara (completed in 1953) overshadowed the importance of the war monuments'.[33] Delayed as it was, the war memorial project was a significant factor in the renewal of public interest in the Gallipoli Campaign. The monument was not erected immediately after the war as part of a mourning process; it would rather serve as a means of unification-building efforts afterwards.[34]

29 He offered a mule-load of water to the British foe and intercepted the enemy telegrams behind the lines, see F. Celaliddin Göktulga, *Keloğlan Çanakkale Muharebelerinde. Uzun Masal* (İstanbul: Ülkü Matbaası, 1939).

30 M. Atabay, 'Çanakkale'yi Aydınlatan Profil', *Çanakkale 1915* issue 19 (April 2014), pp. 58–61.

31 Kadri Ener (ed.), *Çanakkale'den Hatıralar* (İstanbul: MMV İstanbul Temsil Bürosu, 1953), 4, (quotation: 64); Bobbitt, p. 37.

32 Ener (ed.), 75; Güler, 324; Klaus Kreiser, 'Public Monuments in Kemalist and Post-Kemalist Turkey', *Journal of Turkish Studies* 26/II (2002), pp. 47–8.

33 Kreiser, 'War Memorials', 192; Bobbitt, p. 66.

34 The 1940s were, rather, characterized by the construction of symbolic cemeteries on the Gallipoli Peninsula, Bobbitt, pp. 35, 60–1, 86–8.

Turkish identification with Western democracies, however, was the real departure in the Gallipoli commemorations. In 1952, the first Turkish 'postwar pilgrimage' was organised with the participation of 400 citizens as well as British and French ex-servicemen living in Turkey.[35] In 1936 and until 1945, Turkey had prevented local observation of Anzac Day on the pretext of neutrality. The Korean War transformed Anzac Day into the day of celebration of friendship and alliance. Turkish officers have attended the local Anzac Day since 1953. Turkish and Australian veterans met each other for the first time in the 40th anniversary in 1955.[36] The German contribution to the victory also received favourable treatment in line with the reinvigorated enthusiasm for military cooperation with the Western allies through NATO membership.[37]

The possession of İstanbul and the straits had always come to the fore in the press in relation to the commemoration in the post-Montreux era. The 500th anniversary of the conquest of İstanbul (1953) and the 40th anniversary of the Gallipoli Campaign (1955) were happy coincidences for the first democratically elected government of Turkey under Adnan Menderes. The popular government organised nationwide commemorative ceremonies in 1955. The two anniversaries were to end the 'days of humble reticence of intellectuals about Turkish miracles'.[38]

Search for a new world, 1960–80: whose war?

The first military takeover in Turkey occurred on 27 May 1960, ushering in a new era in the understanding of the Gallipoli Campaign. Due to political polarisation in Turkey, leftists, rightists, and the army came up with conflicting interpretations. The hasty inauguration of the incomplete Çanakkale War Memorial on 21 August 1960 demonstrated the willingness of the army to offer the 'Turkish Armed Forces' (TAF – the new name of the army) as the guardian of the secular Republic against 'religious reactionaries'. The famous quatrain from the poem 'Bir Yolcuya' (To a Traveller) by Necmettin Halil Onan was inscribed on the Çanakkale landscape immediately after the 1960 coup.[39] The 12 March Memorandum (1971) issued by

---

35 Ener, 3–4; Şemsettin Çamoğlu, *Çanakkale Boğazı ve Savaşları* (İstanbul: Eski Muharipler Cemiyeti Çanakkale Şubesi, 1962), p. 231.

36 Davis, pp. 30, 76, 82, 182–3, 219, 272–5, 282–3, 302–3.

37 *1915'de Çanakkale'de Türk* (Ankara: Genelkurmay, 1957), pp. 11–13.

38 Tuncay Yılmazer (ed.), *Çanakkale Zaferi 18 Mart 1915. Düşman Geliyor Top Başına* (İstanbul: Yeditepe Yay., 2007), pp. 11–6. [reprint: Ahmet C. Saraçoğlu, *Çanakkale Zaferi: 5–18 Mart 1915* (İstanbul, 1953)].

39 Gürel Göncü, Şahin Aldoğan, *Çanakkale Muharebe Alanları Gezi Rehberi* (İstanbul: MB, 2006), 147; 'Dur Yolcu, bilmeden gelip bastığın; Bu toprak, bir devrin battığı yerdir; . . . '[Stop, wayfarer! Unbeknownst to you this ground; You come and tread on, is where an epoch sank down . . .] Modified from the English translation by Tanwir Wasti,

the TAF was the second military coup in Turkey. The commemoration held a week later turned into a show of power: 'the speeches and messages conveyed by the military stole the victory from the Ottomans for the Turkish army'.[40]

From the 1960s onwards, the commemorations on the sites of the battle turned into an open forum for current political debates. Two rival student organisations, the nationalistic and religiously conservative MTTB (National Turkish Student Association) and the leftist TMTF (the National Turkish Students' Federation) contested the meaning of the victory. Throughout the 1970s, the MTTB used the commemoration ceremony to propagate against the communists, masons, and Zionists. It presented the victory as the triumph of the crescent over the cross and capitalised on it to win 'the second Çanakkale victory' over 'internal enemies'. Conversely, the leftist TMTF and TMGT (Turkish National Youth Organisation) tended to view the TAF as the protector of the Republican regime and condemned the MTTB's exclusion about the role of Atatürk in the victory.[41] The unfading folk song that epitomised the Gallipoli Campaign turned into a revolutionary slogan 'In Çanakkale is the Market with the Mirror; I am off to fight fascism [the enemy], Mother.'[42]

The contest for the possession of the Gallipoli saga crystallised in a curious affair that occurred on the eve of the 1962 commemoration aboard the ship *Kadeş* that carried university students from İstanbul to Çanakkale. Tales of debauchery aboard the ship involving drinking, dancing and free love abounded in the Islamic press. The religious conservatives launched a public campaign for a more religious commemoration for the martyrs and insulted the female passengers as '*Kadeşçi*' (i.e., *Kadeş*-girls). Many student unions, including the rightist MTTB, condemned such accusations while a group of five female university students filed a complaint with the mayor of İstanbul. Nevertheless, the MTTB would later blame the leftist TMTF in 1970 for the *Kadeş* scandal. This demonstrated the sharp ideological split that gave rise to a reign of violence in the 1970s.[43]

A perusal of publications reveals the consolidation of the popular views of Gallipoli that occurred in the 1960s and the 1970s; *Çanakkale Destanı* by

Çanakkale Araştırmaları Türk Yıllığı 1 (2003); the poem praised the decisive victory over the Greek army in August 1922, see Turgut Özakman, *Diriliş. Çanakkale 1915* (İstanbul: Bilgi Yayınevi, 2013) [Resurrection: Çanakkale 1915], p. 669.

40 Arzık, 78–88. In 1979. Now even the chief-of-staff sent a message to the local garrison commander in Çanakkale in order to celebrate him for the victory.

41 Opening of the war memorial was 'a second Çanakkale victory' according to the rightist MTTB the Arzık, pp. 56–7, 81–93.

42 Güler, 327; *Aynalı Çarşı* (Market with the Mirror) refers to the giant mirrors of *Passage Hallio*, a landmark of Çanakkale, built in 1890 by the prominent Jewish resident Eliyau Hallio. The bilingual inscription on the gate (Ladino and Ottoman Turkish) plastered over by the rioters in 1934 was restored in 2007, see, http://tatilname.blogspot.com.tr/2010/10/aynal-cars-canakkale.html. [Accessed 1 June 2014].

43 Arzık, pp. 58–62, 93.

Dağlarca, for instance, resonated with the dramatic Akifesque description of the war as a sacred national struggle against the whole world. For him, 'Gallipoli is the prologue of new Turkey'. Nevertheless, the novel approach to the war came from the intellectuals with leftist tendencies. Nesin, the celebrated satirist, focused on the miserable postwar life of Corporal Seyit – a Gallipoli hero – and questioned the militarist interpretations of the Gallipoli Campaign.[44] Notably, Nazım Hikmet's poems were also republished in the 1960s and his stanzas on the selfless and docile Anatolian were quite influential in the shaping of the popular leftist outlook in Turkey. In a nutshell, war was a function of imperialism – and it was cruel.[45]

History magazines were published with a wide circulation by the 1950s and they portrayed the Gallipoli Campaign as a victory of the weak that came at an extraordinary human cost. Popular articles, embellished with German photographs taken in Gallipoli, revolved around this central theme until the turn of the century. Concurrently, F. Fazıl Tülbentçi narrated the Gallipoli saga on anniversaries in his popular radio talks on history.[46] Turkish people learned about the 'war on Broken Hill' only in 1967 when a history magazine presented the two Muslim assailants, who had killed five civilians in a picnic train, as Turkish holy warriors sabotaging the transportation of ANZAC soldiers.[47] It is notable that the first Turkish film on the Gallipoli Campaign, *The Lions of Çanakkale*, was also shot in 1964 with the logistical support of the Turkish military.[48]

Annual commemorations continued to serve as a diplomatic showcase for Turkey in this period as well. The 50th anniversary of the Gallipoli Campaign was held in 1965 with the participation of a group of German veterans. This

44 Güler, 325–6; Fazıl H. Dağlarca, *Çanakkale Destanı* (Kitap Yay., 1965); Aziz Nesin, 'Koca Seyit', *Bu Yurdu Bize Verenler* (İstanbul: Adam Yay., 2005), pp. 9–23; In his home town Havran Seyit's name was given to a primary school (1967), a mosque (1980), a street (1980), and to his village (1993). A monument was dedicated to him in 1993. The villagers commemorate him every 18 March with Quran and *Mevlid* recitals, see Hasan Mert, 'Çanakkale Savaşının Sonuçları' in Mustafa Demir (ed.), *Çanakkale Savaşları Tarihi V* (İstanbul. Değişim), 2978.

45 For relevant excerpts in English from Hikmet's *Human Landscapes From My Country* see, Kevin Fewster, Vecihi Başarın, Hatice Hürmüz Başarın, *Gallipoli: The Turkish Story* (Allen & Unwin, 2003), pp. 143–6: '. . . Or are the ones in the trenches; Sheep and cattle; Being led to their slaughter by a network of shepherds; Captured not only by their bodies; But also by their minds? . . .'

46 Miyase Koyuncu Kaya-Niyazi Kaya, '1915 Çanakkale Savaşları'nın Aylık Popüler Tarih Dergilerine Yansıması' in *Gelibolu: Tarih, Efsane*, pp. 417–30; Tülbentçi, *Şehitler* (1961), *Türk Zaferleri* (1961), *Tarihe Şan Veren Türk* (1987, 6th edn), *Kahramanlar Geçiyor I-III* (1984, 1987, 8th, 7th, 3rd editions) all published by Inkılap Kitabevi (İstanbul).

47 Ekrem Saltık, 'Anzak Komplosu', Erkan-Fidan, *Osmanlı'nın Son Kilidi Çanakkale 2* (İstanbul: Çamlıca, 2011), pp. 95–121; Feridun Hikmet Es, 'Avustralya'da Harp İlan Eden İki Türk'ün Yarattığı Destan', *Hayat Tarih* 5 (June 1967), p. 6.

48 Written and directed by Nusret Eraslan-Turgut Demirağ.

was perhaps a political gesture on the part of Turkey in gratitude for the German acceptance of Turkish 'guest workers' from 1961. The Cypriot Question has haunted Turkish diplomacy since 1964, leading to diplomatic isolation after the Turkish invasion of the island in 1974. Nevertheless Turkish military officers regularly represented Turkey on Anzac Day all around the world in these difficult years, and the increasing emphasis on 'national unity' found its expression in the establishment of the Gelibolu Peninsula Historical National Park in 1973.[49]

Guarding the state and nation, 1980–2000: whose sacrifice?

A new Turkey emerged in the 1980s, based on 'Atatürk nationalism' under the secularist tutelage of the TAF and the high judiciary. De-politicisation (that is, the suppression of unions, syndicates, and a multitude of associations), toleration of Islamic movements against the leftist threat, and liberalisation of the economy shaped this new national agenda. TAF became the predominant actor in the commemoration ceremonies and fostered its invented role in the making of Turkey in the period 1915–23. Military coups in Turkey always led to a renewed vigour for memorial-building projects in search of legitimacy, but this bordered on absurdity after the 12 September 1980 coup d'état.[50] The single-factor explanation of the victory based on Atatürk turned into something of a craze in the 1980s. Monoliths that usually featured quotations from Atatürk gained popularity as signboards of important battles, places, and events of the Gallipoli war.[51] In accordance with the agreement signed with Australia and New Zealand in 1985, the Arıburnu Cove was renamed as Anzac Cove in violation of Turkish sensitivities, and Atatürk memorials were established in Canberra and Wellington (1990). Rather than representing the Turkish sacrifice at the Dardanelles, they stood for hailing Atatürk.[52]

The Dawn Service held on 25 April was transformed into Anzac Day in the 1990s. The 75th anniversary of the war was an occasion for British Prime Minister Thatcher and the Australian Prime Minister Hawke to visit the Gallipoli Peninsula in 1990 and the next year President Özal paid a visit to New Zealand

---

49 Davis, pp. 289, 31, 271; Arzık, p. 85.

50 There were 12 Atatürk monuments in 1946–60 and 59 in 1960–70, Ü. Aylin Tekiner, *Atatürk Heykelleri: Kült, Estetik, Siyaset* (İstanbul: Iletişim, 2010), p. 171.

51 Esra Özyürek, 'Miniaturizing Atatürk: Privatization of state Imagery and Ideology in Turkey', *American Ethnologist* 31:3 (2004): pp. 374–91; Turkey built more than 20 monuments in the 1980s, see Davis, p. 289; Bobbitt, pp. 51, 68; UNESCO declared 1981 as the Year of Atatürk, Tekiner, pp. 194.

52 The 'Atatürk Garden of Monuments' is located at the northeast end of the Anzac Avenue in Canberra. Port Albany (Western Australia) was the main port of departure for the Australian soldiers in the Great War. One of its entrances was renamed 'the Atatürk Entrance', Davis, pp. 270, 290–1.

and Australia. The establishment of the Gallipoli Peace Park was put on the agenda in the following years. Afforestation of the peninsula with the participation of many university students after the great conflagration of 1994 actually eroded the trenches and battle-sites, but the forest was supposed to be a 'green comforter' for the martyrs. The Gallipoli Peninsula was now a significant tourist venue with tactless monuments.[53]

While the monopolisation of the commemorative services by the state in the 1980s reduced public interest in the event, the Kurdish Question and the Islamist resurgence heightened social awareness in the 1990s. At the 1990 commemoration ceremony the municipal mayor of Çanakkale refused to greet the new President Özal, who had always been loathed for undermining the Kemalist principle of laicism. Secularist apprehensions increased to an alarming level during the coalition government led by the Islamist Erbakan.[54] In the 1990s, history textbooks turned more militaristic and began to praise unequivocally the unavoidable sacrifice as the cost of full independence.[55] The 500,000 Turkish lira banknote featured the Çanakkale Martyr Memorial on its reverse in 1993–2006. Moreover, a gold medal was awarded to the city of Çanakkale on which was depicted the famous wartime dictum, '*Çanakkale Geçilmez'*.[56]

A signal event in the Islamist-secularist confrontation was the public controversy over the documentary aired on the official TRT channel on 18 March 1988. Sponsored by an Islamic bank, the programme made no mention of Atatürk. The matter was debated in the national assembly to soothe public fury.[57] Intellectuals from a wide political spectrum had both reason and freedom to attack the Kemalist establishment, part of which was the reinvigorated cult of Atatürk. Secular Turks and religious conservatives toured the peninsula as separate groups, while intellectuals challenged the usual interpretations of the victory.[58] Official discourse, they asserted, falsified history so as to create the myth of Atatürk.

The bestselling authors with Islamist leanings agreed with some influential leftist intellectuals on the negligible role of Mustafa Kemal in the victory. He

53 Davis, pp. 262, 271, 290–5; Güler, p. 328.

54 Güler, pp. 326–30; Arzık, pp. 82, 103–08.

55 Etienne Copeaux, *Tarih Ders Kitaplarında (1931–1993) Türk Tarih Tezinden Türk-İslam Sentezine* (İstanbul: TTV, 1998), p. 258.

56 *No Way Through Çanakkale* by Necmeddin Sahir was published on 18 March 1922 in the *İkdam* daily: '. . . *The Turk has the power to crush, he is never to be vanquished; Let the world know: Çanakkale is not to be breached!*' [author's translation]; the motto was written in *mahya* (oil-lamp illumination) and strung up between the minarets of the Süleymaniye mosque after the naval victory in 1915 according to Turgut Özakman, *Diriliş. Çanakkale 1915* (İstanbul: Bilgi, 2013 [122nd edn]), p. 181.

57 Özakman, *Vahidettin, M. Kemal ve Milli Mücadele: yalanlar, yanlışlar, yutturmacalar* (Ankara: Bilgi, 2000), pp. 101–02.

58 Tekiner, pp. 187–98; Güler, pp. 328–30.

was merely a divisional commander of the reserve force. His victories were either insignificant or actually belonged to others, and, they argued, his offensives resulted in unnecessary casualties. Moreover, the victory at Çanakkale was perhaps not so crucial as had been alleged as the Allies ultimately occupied İstanbul after the war.[59] The backlash came from the late Özakman, the outspoken 'Atatürk nationalist' immediately after the military memorandum, dated 28 February 1997. The 'postmodern coup' compelled the government to take strict measures against the Islamist upsurge and eventually precipitated the collapse of the Erbakan government. Özakman reasserted the critical role played by Mustafa Kemal during the initial landing at Arıburnu Cove in April and the scramble for Sari Bair in August. He underlined Atatürk's resentment of the German commanders and their defensive plans. For him, Atatürk's saga in the Dardanelles was not a Kemalist invention; the censorship of Enver Pasha, rather, stole the victory and fame from Mustafa Kemal by suppressing his name in the press. He accused the critics of Atatürk of subverting the Republic by way of downplaying or ignoring his accomplishments in the Çanakkale Battles.[60]

Contesting the Republic, 2002–2015: whose memory?

Commemoration ceremonies today continue to be militaristic and triumphalist. They are arranged to present Çanakkale as the birthplace of new Turkey and underline bravery, self-sacrifice and Atatürk's heroic feats. These continuities notwithstanding, Ottoman Islamic cosmopolitanism also gained ground under the AKP rule after 2002. Embedded in this outlook is the desire to create a neo-Ottomanist Islamic cosmopolitanism among the former Muslim subjects of the empire.[61] Completion of the Martyrs' Memorial five decades after its inception is a case in point. The symbolic cemetery adjacent to the memorial has been redesigned three times since 1992. Many transparent Plexiglas plaques with the names of martyrs today represent the districts of the Ottoman Empire so as to create an image of Ottoman Islamic brotherhood. A praying room was also added to the 57th Regiment Memorial.[62] Concurrently, the tombstone of Captain Dmitroyati, a

59 Abdurrahman Dilipak, *Cumhuriyet'e Giden Yol* (İstanbul: Beyan, 1989); Bünyamin Ateş, B. Bozgeyik, Mustafa Kaplan, *Gayri Resmi Yakın Tarih Ansiklopedisi*, 6 vols, (İstanbul: Risale, 1993); Kadir Mısıroğlu, *Lozan, Zafer mi Hezimet mi?*, 3 vols (İstanbul: Sebil, 1992), on the other side of the spectrum are Yalçın Küçük, *Türkiye Üzerine Tezler*, vols 2 & 5 (İstanbul: Tekin, 1987) and Çetin Altan (his various interviews), see *Yeni Yüzyıl* daily, 8 July 1996 and *Aktüel* weekly, issue: 36, 12–18 March 1992).

60 Özakman, *Vahidettin, Mustafa Kemal*, pp. 94–178.

61 Bobbitt, pp. 76, 85; Güler, 320; Arzık, pp. 110–1.

62 İşcen, 'Dinci Kesime Yeni Bir Rant Kapısı; Çanakkale Savaşları . . .', http://www.gallipoli-1915.org/15yetkin.iscen.dini.turizm.htm [Accessed 12 June 2013]; Güler, pp. 334–5.

regimental doctor, which was a very popular spot, was removed from the symbolic graveyard in 2010 on the pretext that no such name existed in the muster roll of the Regiment.[63]

Erdoğan contradicted several times the official view by emphasising that Turks were never left to fight alone in 1915–23. The Gallipoli Campaign, for him, was just another crusade that rallied the Muslims of the Balkans, the Middle East, and Egypt behind the Ottomans. Neo-Ottomanist imagination has the Muslim Senegalese soldiers refusing to fight their Muslim brethren after hearing the call to prayer at Çanakkale.[64] The 'spirit of Gallipoli' was a literary metaphor glorifying the selfless sacrifice of the patriotic solidarity of the religious Turkish soldiers at Çanakkale through the use of religious terminology (i.e. *gazi* [holy warrior] and *şehid* [martyr]). There is a mass of literature that draws heavily on the popular tales about Corporal Seyit and several Sergeant Mehmets. In the neo-Ottomanist reformulation of the concept, by contrast, Islam ceased to be a supportive rallying power and turned into the real and central purpose of the fighting. CHP (founded by Atatürk) protested the Islamist turn and arranged an alternative commemoration at the tomb of Corporal Seyit in 2011.[65] Özakman's *Diriliş* [resurrection], which reclaimed the Kemalist memory of Çanakkale, came out in 2009 and sold more than 200,000 copies.[66]

The course of the 1997 post-modern coup and the aftermath was the driver for the invention of many traditions by the Islamists and secularists alike. Mass participation in the Victory Day as a form of demonstration against the Erbakan government was transformed into the Çanakkale Martyrs Day in 2003, an event modelled on Anzac Day. One of the novel traditions integrated into the commemoration was the re-enactment of the legendary march of the 57th Regiment under Mustafa Kemal to the Chunuk Bair on 25 April. By 2012, 14,000 participants marched along 'the path of Atatürk', leaving a heap of rubbish behind in their wake. Another innovation was the taking of the communal meal that the 57th Regiment supposedly had before the march.[67]

Mevlid recitals in the graveyards have become a Ramadan tradition on Gallipoli. One can even dedicate Quran recitals to the souls of the martyrs via social media. The

---

63 Yüzbaşı Sarkis Torosyan, *Çanakkale'den Filistin Cephesine* Ayhan Aktar (ed.), Gizem Şakar (trans.) (İstanbul: Iletişim, 2012), Ayhan Aktar's introduction: 'Torosyan'ın Adı Yok', pp. 90–92.

64 Aktar, *Yüzbaşı Torosyan Tartışması* [forthcoming]. I thank Aktar for sharing the manuscript with me. Erdoğan's speech, 19 May 2014, http://www.youtube.com/watch?v=q93a42dzlxg [Accessed 5 June 2014].

65 Bobbitt, p. 77.

66 Özakman, *Diriliş*, pp. 551–2.

67 Nevin Yazıcı, 'Lise Müfreat Programlarında ve Ders Kitaplarında Çanakkale Savaşı'nın Öğretimi Üzerine Eleştirel Bir Yaklaşım', *Hacettepe Üniversitesi Eğitim Fakültesi Dergisi* 28/2 (2013), pp. 537–8; İşcen, 'Türsabı Çağıran Çanakkale Şehitleri', http://www.gallipoli-1915.org/03yetkin.iscen.tursabi.cagiran.can.sehitleri.htm [Accessed 12 June 2014].

city of Tokat has got a local symbolic Çanakkale graveyard. Daily trips organised by many municipalities brought hundreds of thousands of trippers to the Peninsula. Students from Georgia, Romania, Libya, Azerbaijan, and north Cyprus are also taken to Çanakkale to visit the tombs of their 'grandfathers'.[68]

Four decades after the affair, the *Kadeş* scandal was revisited with a view to favour religious commemoration over secular ceremonies. According to this simplistic view, the responsibility for the debauchery lies with the corrupt Kemalist youth, who were not so much interested in honouring the fallen as partying aboard the boat. It was against them that the grandchildren of the martyrs had to wage an uphill struggle. Finally, the latter won 'the second Çanakkale victory' and wiped away the *Kadeş* youth.[69] Islamic conservatives consider the Kemalist state as an aberration in Islamic Turkish history. For them, the deplorable loss of many 'Islamists' on the Gallipoli front gave a free rein to Kemalists until the 1950s. They argue that Islamism was a genuine bottom-up intellectual movement, an organic link between the Islamic Ottoman past and the contemporary Muslim Turks.[70]

A survey revealed that 80 per cent of the university students in Çanakkale believed the supernatural stories about the martyrs. Half of them thought one needed to be a Muslim in order to attain martyrdom in the afterlife. Immortal martyrs descended from heaven to fight the enemy according to 66 per cent of respondents.[71] This result is partly explained by the animistic cult of immortal saints, which survived in the Turco-Islamic notions of *dedes* (wise old man) and *ermiş* (saint). Dağlarca, for example, devised the literary character of *Er-dede* in his 'Çanakkale Epic', who rushed to the assistance of the Turkish lads in the Dardanelles.[72] War propaganda literature was replete with extraordinary tales based on real war stories, which the laicist Turkish military has republished

68 Güler, pp. 308, 335, 338–9; Bobbitt, 82; Arzık, p. 112.

69 Mustafa Armağan, 'CHP gençliğinin Çanakkale şehitleri rezaleti', *Zaman* daily, 5 August 2007, http://www.zaman.com.tr/mustafa-armagan/chp-gencliginin-canakkale-sehitleri-rezaleti_787177.html. [8 June 2014]. Arzık, pp. 59–61, 227; Armağan 'İşte CHP'nin Çanakkale rezaletinin belgeleri', http://www.mustafaarmagan.com.tr/iste-chpnin-canakkale-rezaletinin-belgeleri.html [8 June 2014].

70 Armağan, 'Çanakkale'de Gözbebeklerimizi Kaybettik', http://www.mustafaarmagan.com.tr/canakkale-de-gozbebeklerimizi-kaybettik.html [Accessed 8 June 2014]. The interview with the Islamist thinker Ali Bulaç, http://gundem.bugun.com.tr/kozmik-odaya-girdiler-haberi/1145248 [Accessed 19 June 2014]; Esra Özyürek, 'Public Memory as Political Background: Islamist Subversions of Republican Nostalgia', Özyürek (ed.), *The Politics of Public Memory in Turkey* (Syracuse University Press, 2007): pp. 114–37.

71 Abdulvahid Sezen, 'Üniversite Öğrencilerinin Çanakkale Savaşlarıyla İlgili Bilişsel Algı ve Yorumlama Biçimleri', *Dinbilimleri Akademik Araştırma Dergisi* 10:2 (2010): pp. 175–201. Çoban's findings corroborate Sezen's, Çoban, p. 97.

72 İbrahim Kıbrıs, 'Fazıl Hüsnü Dağlarca'nın Çanakkale Destanı'nda Yer Alan Erdede Simgesi' in *Gelibolu, Tarih, Efsane*, pp. 499–515.

several times.[73] After all, the genre was intended to boost public morale and it laid the groundwork for various epics on the Çanakkale saga. Pepeyi, for instance, portrayed in 1936 the Gallipoli battles as a modern epic for the Turkish nation which had fought on alone against the industrial nations.[74] The popular Islamist genre, however, has abused this literature to appropriate the memory of the saga for Islamic cosmopolitanism. Fairy tales, as well as perplexing and often fake stories, are abundant in this literature. Among many themes, one can cite those about the foundation of Israel through a Jewish conspiracy at the Dardanelles; the holy guidance in the laying of the sea mines that sank the Allied ships on 18 March 1915; the reincarnation of the martyrs with green turbans who fought the enemy; and the cloud that mysteriously kidnapped a company of the Royal Norfolk Regiment.[75]

Writing Atatürk out of the Gallipoli front narrative is regarded as essential to wrest the collective memory from the Kemalists.[76] At present, the Islamist mourning for the fallen graduates of religious schools (*medrese*) competes with the secularist consternation over the loss of university graduates at Gallipoli – which allegedly deprived Turkey of the much-needed intelligentsia. Themes such as the unjustifiability of the Allied attack on Gallipoli – a gross distortion of Akifesque anti-imperialism – or the alleged war crimes committed by the Allies against the Ottomans, gained in popularity.[77]

The contest over the collective memory sketched above is not taking place independent of the commercialisation of the Gallipoli Peninsula. Ingrained in 'battlefield tourism' is the danger of trivialisation.[78] Souvenir shops sell cheap magnets depicting war heroes and necklaces made of fake bullets. One of the fabulists, Gençcan, even owns a museum at Çanakkale in which crude dummies

73 *Kahramanlık Destanları*, Genelkurmay X. Şb. (İstanbul Askeri Matbaa, 1938); *Kahramanlık Menkıbeleri* (İstanbul: KKK Yay., 1954); *Çanakkale muharebeleri 75. Yıl Armağanı* (ATASE, 1990).

74 Haluk Nihat Pepeyi, *Çanakkale: Destan* (İstanbul: Yeni Kitapçı, 1936).

75 See, Vakkasoğlu, *Bir Destandır Çanakkale* (İstanbul: Nesil, 2013); Talha Uğurluel, *Çanakkale Savaşları ve Gezi Rehberi* (İstanbul: Kaynak, 2003); Mehmet İhsan Gençcan, *Çanakkale Savaşlarından Menkıbeler* (Çanakkale, 1987); Kemal Erkan-Adem Fidan (eds), *Osmanlı'nın Son Kilidi Çanakkale 1* (İstanbul: Çamlıca, 2011), p. 63; articles published in the *Sızıntı* periodical, http://www.sizinti.com.tr; Halil Ersin Avcı, *Çanakkale Ruhu* (İstanbul: Metropol, 2007); Mustafa Turan, *Destanlaşan Çanakkale* (İstanbul: Papatya, 2005).

76 Cezmi Eraslan, *Unutulmasın Diye II. Abdülhamid'in Çanakkale Savunması* (İstanbul: Yitik Hazine, 2014).

77 Hamit Pehlivanlı, 'Müttefiklerin İnsanlık ve Hukuk Dışı Davranışları', in *Osmanlı'nın Son Kilidi Çanakkale 1*, p. 63; Recep Ş. Apuhan, *Mehmetçik* (İstanbul: Timaş, 1996), p. 76.

78 Bobbitt, p. 80; concerns over the phenomenon of battlefield tourism were raised for the first time in, George L. Mosse, *Fallen Soldiers: Reshaping the Memory of the World Wars* (Oxford, 1980).

of Ottoman soldiers perform daily prayers in the trenches with the Quran being recited at the background. Meanwhile, a religious society fabricated fake pictures of the Çanakkale battles and turned the wrong tomb into a fake memorial for the captain of the legendary mine-layer *Nusret* only to be destroyed after the ensuing scandal in 2007.[79] The primary concern of many visitors seems to be praying in the real or symbolic graveyards rather than engaging in an experiential exploration of the conditions of the battle. The strip cartoons on the Gallipoli Campaign are rife with commonplace superstitions, religious rancour, and jingoism.[80] The patriotic approach to popular culture favours 'our Gallipoli heroes over Tommiks, Texas, and Superman'.[81] An examination of poems composed on the Gallipoli battles confirms that a wide range of issues such as anti-globalisation, opposition to EU membership, and reaction to Hollywood heroes find a place in the genre.[82]

The Islamist upsurge in Çanakkale trips led to the restoration of many religious sites in the vicinity.[83] Reorganisation of the entire region as a centre of pilgrimage is nevertheless distressing for many including Tolga Örnek, whose documentary *Gallipoli: The Front Line Experience* narrated the common fatigue of the both sides. He expressed his concerns that the Islamists attempted to make Çanakkale an alternative site to Atatürk's mausoleum (*Anıtkabir*). Yılmazer, a researcher of the Gallipoli Campaign, disputes the idea of a religion-free commemoration of the war. He, nevertheless, seems to have confused religiosity (of the soldiers and visitors) with the modern political movement of Islamism: in short, the means have been mistaken for the ends.[84]

79 Güler, p. 340; A scale model of *Nusrat* was built in 1982. The ship was re-built on the original plan in 2011; see, İşcen's web page for Islamist trivialisation, http://www.gallipoli-1915.org [Accessed 12 June 2014].

80 Güler, pp. 308, 330–32; Osman Arslan, *Çanakkale Destanı*, issues: 1–15 (Mavi Medya Yay.). Also 'the real stories' strip cartoon series, *Türk Tarihi Gerçek Öyküler Çizgi Roman Dizisi 1–10* by the Turkish military (Ankara, 2007); The Mayor of Manisa published his own strip cartoon (*Çanakkale Destanı*) in 40,000 copies and sold it at a negligible price to middle-school students in 2013, http://www.showhaber.com/canakkale-destani-cizgi-romani-basildi-haberi-646790h.htm [Accessed 8 June 2014].

81 Güler, p. 333; For Çanakkale tales for children see Halil İbrahim Bulan, 'Mensur Eserlerde Çanakkale' in *Çanakkale Savaşları Tarihi V*, pp. 2943–8, 2965–7.

82 Mustafa Duran, 'Cumhuriyet Dönemi Türk Şiirinde Çanakkale Muharebeleri ve Etkileri' (MA thesis, Sakarya Üniversitesi, 2008), pp. 122–3. Turkish novels on Gallipoli (numbering roughly 10) are imbued with superstitions, myths, and triumphalist stories, see Celal Mat, 'Türk Romanında Çanakkale Muharebeleri ve Çanakkale Muharebelerini Konu Alan Romanların Eğitime Katkısı' (MA thesis, Dokuz Eylül Üniversitesi, İzmir, 2006); *Şafakta Yanan Mumlar* [*Candles At Dawn*] (Limelight Press, 2004) by Serpil Ural is an exception.

83 Arzık, pp. 113–6.

84 The interview with Örnek, *Metro Magazine* 153, pp. 86–95; interview with Örnek, daily *Hürriyet*, 19 July 2004; Tuncay Yılmazer, 'Çanakkale Maneviyat Olmadan

Towards pluralism?

The extent to which the Gallipoli commemorations have transformed into a global and cosmopolitan affair is impressive. Turks have joined Melbourne's Anzac Day parade with their own contingent since 1996.[85] Nonetheless, Turkish–ANZAC relations are not free of tension. Turkish authorities in Canberra and Wellington condemned the showing of *All the King's Men* (2000) because of its anti-Turkish flavour. The reading of Atatürk's 1934 statement during Anzac Day services sometimes lead to protests. Consumption of alcohol by tourists and the use of the Gallipoli landscape are the two thorny issues in Turkey.[86] Mysterious events are also noteworthy in the shared memory of Australians and the Turkish nation, such as the 'skull affair' in 2002. The skull of a supposedly Turkish soldier kept by an Australian as a war trophy was returned to Turkey with proper military ceremonies and buried in the symbolic graveyard in the Martyrs' Memorial on 18 March 2003. The Turkish branch of Returned Soldiers' League in Victoria had campaigned for a mausoleum for 'Mehmet's skull' in Australia but to no avail.[87] In 1995 some of the local Turks wanted to dedicate a memorial to the 'holy warriors' of Broken Hill, while the Turkish Embassy at Canberra requested the remains of the assailants.[88] According to the interpretation of Vakkasoğlu, the fabulist, what lay behind the controversy was that the two 'Turkish heroes' inflicted 'hundreds of casualties' on the Australian army and thus created 'the Gallipoli [saga] in Australia'.[89]

Gallipoli has been a 'mythscape'[90] since the 1930s. Despite the top-down approach in the construction of a collective memory, different groups came up with their own interpretations of the meaning of the war in the peninsula.[91] There

Anlaşılmaz', *Zaman,* 3 August 2004, http://www.zaman.com.tr/yorum_canakkale-maneviyat-olmadan-anlasilmaz_76677.html. For a criticism of Yılmazer see, İşcen, 'Gözümüz aydın! Bir Doktor Tarihçimiz Daha Oldu', http://www.gallipoli-1915.org/18yetkin.iscen.doktor.mektup.htm [Accessed 12 June 2014].

85 A local Turk from New Zealand, Akif Keskin, organised the first Anzac Day service to be held in Los Angeles in 1979. Davis, pp. 256, 292; Fewster et al., pp. 139–42.

86 Davis, p. 297, also pp. 30, 59.

87 Fewster et al., pp. 147–8.

88 İşcen, 'Britanya İmparatorluğu'nun 11 Eylülü: Broken Hill Katliamı . . . Ne İlk Şehittiler Ne de Mücahit', *Çanakkale 1915* 6 (August 2010): pp. 32–8.

89 Vakkasoğlu, *Bir Destandır Çanakkale*, pp. 238–49; 'Australian casualties are inflated to 7,416!', see http://www.guncel46.com/gundem/dunyayi-hayrete-dusuren-iki-turk-h2196.html [Accessed 12 June 2014].

90 See Bobbitt for this conceptualisation based on Duncan Bell, 'Mythscape: memory, mythology and national identity', *British Journal of Sociology* 54:1 (2004).

91 Ahenk Yılmaz, 'Bellek Topografyasında Özgürlük: Gelibolu Savaş Alanları ve Mekansal Bir Deneyim Olarak Hatırlama', Leyla Neyzi (ed.), *Nasıl Hatırlıyoruz? Türkiye'de Bellek Çalışmaları* (İstanbul: Türkiye İş Bankası Kültür Yay., 2011): pp. 187–216.

were always Muslim visitors who considered the experience a spiritual pilgrimage. A group of Turkish researchers argue that the commemoration ceremonies had a religious dimension from the beginning. Atatürk had supposedly ordered the recital of Quran and *Mevlid* as well as the distribution of rice *pilav* every year on 10 August before the institutionalisation of the 18 March Victory Day. This resembles the dispute between the secularist views and religious approaches to Anzac Day in Australia.[92] The problem lay not so much in the existence of competing memories as in their mutual exclusivity, which is a reverberation of non-pluralistic Turkish democracy. As a matter of fact the participation of non-Muslims, non-Turks, women, children, and non-Ottoman soldiers in the Gallipoli Campaign does not get nationwide recognition in Turkey.[93] A comparison of the Turkish case with the ANZAC case is again illuminating.

Both in Turkey and Australia women participants on the Gallipoli front are largely ignored in the commemorations despite the participation of many nurses in the campaign on both sides.[94] Some ANZAC veterans rumoured that there were Turkish women snipers at Gallipoli, and indeed there must have been women combatants who fought in men's uniform as suggested by the interview with Mücahide Hatice Hanım (Izmir, injured) and research on Sergeant Zeynep Mido (Kosovo, killed). There were women who fought in Gallipoli against the invasion of their village without masquerading as some other identity.[95]

A survey shows that Kurdish middle and high school students resented the exclusion of Kurds from the mainstream discourse on the Gallipoli war. While students in Çanakkale viewed the war primarily as a Turkish victory, those in Batman and Van considered it as a case of solidarity and brotherhood between Turks and Kurds.[96] Kurdish politicians usually try to capitalise on the Kurdish casualties to enlarge political and civic rights. There is a growing tendency to associate one's own ethnic and religious group with the Gallipoli victory as though participation in the war were licence to equal treatment with the Turks.[97]

The Ottoman 6th Army was a demographic mirror of the empire in terms of the manpower it mobilised. The Balkan Muslims fought in eight 'Kosovo battalions', losing 214 men. Many women accompanied the volunteers from the Balkans to the front and worked in military hospitals and logistics. Death rates increase to 914 for those coming from the modern Middle East and the Arabian Peninsula.

92 Arzık, pp. 59, 119–20; Davis, pp. 4–30, 137.

93 Bobbitt, p. 57.

94 İslam Özdemir, *Çanakkale Muharebelerinde Tekirdağ: cephe gerisindeki bir şehirde yaşananlar* (Istanbul: Akıl Fikir yay., 2012).

95 Davis, pp. 170–1; N. Yazıcı, 'Çanakkale Savaşı'nda Türk Kadınının Rolü', *Akademik Bakış* 5:9 (2011): pp. 245–628; Zümrüt Sönmez (ed.), *Kızıl Toprak Ak Yemeni Savaşın Kadınları* (İstanbul: Yarımada yay., 2008).

96 Çoban, pp. 90–3.

97 Güler, p. 337; Arzık, p. 118.

To this must be added 34 dead from North Africa, the Caucasus, Crimea, Iran, and Afghanistan.[98] Remarkably, Muslims of Kosovo partly share the common memory of the Gallipoli Campaign such as the saga of Corporal Seyit and the feats of Mustafa Kemal. A version of the aforementioned *Çanakkale Türküsü* (folk song) is sung in Macedonian and Albanian lyrics with all listeners rising up on the occasion in respect to the martyrs.[99]

Men with diverse religions, languages, and ethnic backgrounds fought in Çanakkale. New Zealand and Australian forces at the Dardanelles, for instance, had some contingents of Maoris, Aboriginal Australians and Torres Strait Islanders. The Maori contribution was never ignored in New Zealand.[100] Conversely, the Australian Aboriginals were denied voice in commemorations until the 1990s. Davis views this hesitancy as a reflection of 'the contested place of Aborigines in (white) Australian society'. Peter Weir's film *Gallipoli* (1981), for example, depicted the ANZAC as 'white men' who were innocent victims of British imperialism.[101] It should be noted that the All-India War Memorial (Rajpath, New Delhi) had been unveiled in 1931 in honour of 70,000 Indians who died in the British Army. Mihir Bose, a journalist from India, reported in 2002 with dismay that the names of the 4,000 Sikh and Gurkha casualties in Gallipoli were listed haphazardly and only after those of the British and the ANZAC losses in the nameplates of the British war memorials. Nevertheless, the new nameplates removed such complaints.[102]

Battlefield tourism and worldwide ceremonies have the potential to encourage more pluralistic forms of rituals. Monuments still compete with each other in the Gallipoli landscape. Many Turks question the meaning of the ANZAC Monument on top of Chunuk Bair since New Zealand troops had never set foot on this sector of the hill. The 'symbolic invasion' was reciprocated by the building of a bronze statue of Atatürk in 1993 right across the ANZAC Monument.[103] The 'cold war' among the Turkish, Australians, and New Zealanders is best illustrated in the mutual omission of the intrusive monument of the other in the photographs taken; among the visitors 'the notion of contested commemorative space is evident' on 25 April – a day marked by 'separation, distance and respect'.[104] Interestingly enough, refugees from the White Army, who had resided in 1920–21 in Golopole ('bare plain' in Russian), erected their own monument on the peninsula. The

98 Veysi Akın, 'Çanakkale Şehitleri' in *Çanakkale Savaşı Tarihi* V, pp. 2229–49.

99 For the lyrics of the Macedonian version, Sofuoğlu, 'Çanakkale Savaşı'na Kosova'dan Katılanlar' in *Çanakkale Savaşı Tarihi V*, pp. 2368–73.

100 Gary Oakley, 'Ten Renkleri askerlik için çok kolaydı', *Çanakkale 1915* 11 (March 2012): pp. 28–31; Davis, pp. 30, 220, 255–6, 284; Christopher Pugsley, *Gallipoli, The New Zealand Story* (Reed Publishing, 1998).

101 Davis, pp. 21–3, 254, 269. Quotation is from p. 225.

102 Vanthoft, 'Om Bhagwati Nam. Hintli Gözüyle Çanakkale Savaşları', *Çanakkale 1915* 7 (December 2010): pp. 40–6.

103 Özakman, *Diriliş*, p. 662; Uğurluel, p. 386; Bobbitt, p. 53.

104 John McQuilton, 'Gallipoli as Contested Commemorative Space' in Jenny Macleod (ed.), *Gallipoli: Making History* (London: Frank Cass, 2004), p. 153.

desolated memorial rebuilt in 2008 made no mention at all of Tatar soldiers of the White Army.[105]

Although exclusivist claims to memory carries the day, as Davis argues, 'The Gallipoli Anzac Day story had come full circle; from war to peace to memory. Gallipoli was now a shrine to common memories rather than the battlefield of war.'[106]

By the same token, the commemoration ceremonies turned into an appropriate day for protest and self-expression by the 1960s not only in Turkey but also in Australia and New Zealand. Left–right confrontation on 18 March ceremonies had counterparts on Anzac Day ceremonies. Anti-Vietnam campaigners, women demonstrators against war rape, or Maoris' denouncement of the world wars as 'capitalists' war' became usual components of these commemorations.[107]

As for Turkish collective memory, there has hitherto been no space for the recognition of the sufferings of non-Muslim (and non-Turkish; i.e., Arabs) Ottoman subjects in the Gallipoli battles. In 1998, a sensational TV commercial by the rubber tyre producer *Petlas* owned by 'the green/Islamist capital' *Kombasan* distorted a true story. Accordingly, an officer bought the much-needed truck tyres for the army at Gallipoli from a recalcitrant Jewish 'hoarder' with dud notes saying, 'to be paid in blood in Çanakkale'.[108] In reality, many Ottoman Jews had fought in the Ottoman army. The Jewish community of Çanakkale, İstanbul, and İzmir hold religious ceremonies every 29 October (the Republic Day) and commemorate the sacrifice. Memories of protracted wars resonate in Jewish songs as well:[109]

> The Turkish army was commanded by Mustafa Kemal
> We were crying out 'We will save Çanakkale, forward! forward!'
> We lost a lot of our numbers . . . they were martyred screaming liberty
> Pregnant women holding babies in their groins were killed bloodthirstily
> We used to sing the songs of liberty, offering thanks to the saviour Mustafa Kemal Pasha.

---

105 Bülent Bakar, *Esir Şehrin Misafirleri Beyaz Ruslar* (İstanbul: Tarihçi, 2012), pp. 64–71, 120–3; Oya Dağlar Macar-Elçin Macar, *Beyaz Rus Ordusu Türkiye'de* (İstanbul: Libra, 2010), pp. 149–75.

106 Davis, p. 31.

107 Davis, pp. 234–7, 254–6; nationalists students chanted slogans in 1968 such as 'our only leader is the Prophet', 'God Save the Turk', Communists to Moscow', 'Muslim Turkey' and they were expelled from Çanakkale, see Arzık, p. 94.

108 In reality, the Jewish merchant was paid by the authorities. See the commercial at http://www.youtube.com/watch?v=g4EqM3CUD8o. Also told in a book published by the Religious Directorate on the Gallipoli war which is full of Quranic verses and hadiths, Sezgin Çevik, *Çanakkale Unutulmasın. Çanakkale Zaferinin 95. Yılı Anısına* (Ankara: Diyanet İşleri Başkanlığı, 2010).

109 As cited in Tuncoku, 'İsrail'in Kuruluşuna Varan Gelişmeler İçinde Çanakkale Savaşları'nın Önemi', *Buzdağı'nın Altı*, pp. 83–90.

Fortunately, scholarly interest in the composite nature of the imperial army seems to have grown in the last years. Popular history magazines now adopt a more inclusive and pluralistic narrative of the Great War.[110] Suppression of non-Muslim memories is likely to end in the near future; a popular Greek singer, Fedon, told the press that Turkey refused to make him a naval officer although his grandfather was a Çanakkale 'martyr'.[111]

A real breakthrough in Turkish perceptions of Çanakkale, however, occurred after the publication of the war memoirs of Captain Sarkis Torosyan in Turkish in 2012.[112] Graduating from the Military Academy in 1914, Sarkis served in strong batteries at Gallipoli. He was promoted from second lieutenant of artillery to the rank of major on the order of Enver Pasha after sinking a British warship. He later fought in Macedonia, Romania, and Syria with distinction. However, he was then imbued with hatred for the Turks after losing his parents in the death convoys to Syria. His grief became unbearable after the death of his sister, and his beloved Cemile – the adopted Armenian girl of the Ottoman Pasha whose protégé he was – due to illness. He joined the Arab Revolt to avenge the Armenian massacres and vociferously attacked the Ottoman troops in Palestine. After serving in Cilicia under the French for a while, he emigrated to the USA as a broken man. Aktar, who edited the memoirs in Turkish, emphasised that Torosyan fit into neither the Kemalist nor the Islamist narratives of the Gallipoli Campaign. The existence of an Armenian artillery officer in Gallipoli was beyond comprehension for many.[113]

The ensuing 'Torosyan Debate'[114] in Turkey has revolved around a number of matters. The discernible literary threads and tropes permeated the memoirs while there were obvious errors on minute details of military operations, place names and dates. Furthermore, the authenticity of the Ottoman documents published in the memoirs was found questionable. Thus the critics declared Torosyan a liar

110 On Ottoman Jewish soldiers in the Dardanelles, see Sevilay Nihan, 'Son İstirahatgahına Türk Bayrağı ile Uğurlandı', *Çanakkale 1915* 12 (2012): pp. 10–13 and idem., 'Daha Nicelerinin Anısına', *Çanakkale 1915* 11 (2012): pp. 12–15; Kaya-Kaya, '1915 Çanakkale Savaşları'nın', pp. 429–30; Aktar, '18 Mart Zaferi'nin unutulan kahramanları, yahut Çanakkale bir 'Haçlı Seferi' midir', *Taraf* Daily, 18 March 2014, 13 [English version: http://www.ayhanaktar.com/] and Ayşe Hür, '1915 Çanakkale Savaşı: Efsaneler ve Gerçekler', *Öteki Tarih I* (Istanbul: Profil, 2012): pp. 225–41 [published in *Taraf*]; daily *Milliyet* ran an article series by Mehmet Gündem on non-Muslim Ottoman soldiers, 1–4 March 2005.

111 http://www.milliyet.com.tr/2005/03/04/guncel/axgun01.html [Accessed 18 June 2014].

112 Yüzbaşı Sarkis Torosyan, *Çanakkale'den Filistin Cephesine* Ayhan Aktar (ed.), Gizem Şakar (trans.) (İstanbul. Iletişim Yay., 2012) [*From Dardanelles to Palestine: a true story of five battle fronts of Turkey and her allies and a Harem romance*, Boston: Meadow Pub. Co., 1947].

113 Aktar, 'Torosyan'ın Adı Yok', *Çanakkale'de Filistin Cephesine*, pp. 13–93.

114 Refer to http://www.ayhanaktar.com/ for the digitised corpus of the Torosyan Debate.

and his memoirs fraudulent.[115] Aktar faced these criticisms by pointing out that Torosyan suffered from PTSD (post-traumatic stress disorder) and that many war memoirs erred on the minute details. He accused the critics of focusing narrowly on the text at the expense of the historical and contemporary context: the Armenian massacres and the mainstream perception of the Ottoman army as a Muslim and Turkish entity.

Esat Pasha, the commander of the 3rd Army Corps at the Gallipoli front, testified that 3 per cent of the 6th Army was composed of Armenian conscripts and officers some of whom saw active service on the front line.[116] No less than 105 non-Muslim conscripts died in the Çanakkale Battles. Among 215 Ottoman medical officers who were killed between 3 April 1914 and 2 April 1917 there were 75 non-Muslims.[117] Ottoman Jews, for instance, not only served in the auxiliary services but also in the regular army units as conscripts, NCOs, and officers. One can only hope that more war diaries and memoirs by the 'subaltern' members of the Ottoman army see the light of day and enrich our understanding of the Gallipoli realities.[118] It should be noted that *Nar Taneleri* ('pomegranate seeds'), an amateur theatre company, adapted Torosyan's memoirs for theatrical presentation and has performed on the stage several times since its premier on 29 March 2014. The first performance had a dramatic effect on the audience that was largely composed of the Armenian community of İstanbul, as it served as recognition of the Armenian component of the Ottoman army.[119]

Conclusion

Commercialisation of the Gallipoli memories at a popular level[120] contrasts with the dogmatism of Turkish history textbooks. Relevant research has revealed that

115 Y. Hakan Erdem, *Gerçek ve Kurmaca Arasında Torosyan'ın Acayip Hikayesi* (İstanbul: DK, 2012). Turkish General Staff announced that two Armenians bearing the name Sarkis fought in Çanakkale, but none had the surname Torosyan. One of the Sarkis was a first lieutenant of Artillery who was awarded medal after the Krithia battles. http://www.ayhanaktar.com/wp-content/uploads/2014/03/genelkurmay-aciklamasi.pdf

116 Aktar, *Yüzbaşı Torosyan Tartışması* [forthcoming].

117 Şahap Erkoç-A. Kazancıgil, 'Osmanlı Ordusunda I. Dünya Savaşında 3 Teşrinisani 1330–33 Nisan 1333 Tarihleri Arasında (1914–1917) Şehit Olan Sağlık Subaylarının Listesi', *Tıp Tarihi Araştırmaları* 10 (June 2001).

118 Glenda Abramson, *Soldiers' Tales: Palestinian Jewish Soldiers in the Ottoman Army during the First World War* (London: Vallentine Mitchell, 2013), pp. 1–46.

119 http://www.cumhuriyet.com.tr/haber/tiyatro/59217/Kendi_topraginda_tutsak_.html [Accessed 5 August 2014]. Ayhan Aktar also attended the premier night of 'Bir Ezginin Yazgısı' [The Fate of a Melody] at Ataköy Yunus Emre Kültür Merkezi at the invitation of the theatre company.

120 Sinan Cetin, *Çanakkale Çocukları* [Canakkale Children] (2012), tells the story of two brothers with a Turkish-British parentage who fought in opposing armies and killed each other in a bayonet charge. The film was commercially a failure and its pacificism was

history textbooks do not conform to the norms set out by UNESCO and the EU. The narration of the war does not reflect an appreciation of universal peace. There is no recognition of the sacrifice of the 'other'. It, rather, propounds nationalist and antagonistic values which dismiss the contribution of women, children, and the Red Crescent.[121] The 1880-generation, shaped by Hamidian modernisation, made the 1908 Revolution, fought the terrible wars in 1911–22, and finally created modern Turkey.[122] The educated few and the illiterate masses alike constructed conflicting social memories and negotiated their political identities from the very beginning. These were crystallised in the course of time, often interacting with the political life of the country as well as diplomatic affairs. At the time of writing, Turkey is preparing for a set of centennial anniversaries of the landmark developments in 1915–23. Was the year of 2015 to be remembered as a joyful celebration of the Çanakkale saga, or a mournful commemoration of the frozen soldiers of the Caucasus? Will we be told that the sacrifice for the fatherland should compensate for the disgraceful Armenian massacres?[123] Will Gallipoli continue to serve as a battleground for the clashing Kemalist-Islamist perceptions of late Ottoman history? One can only hope that the centennial commemoration will lead to a more lasting acknowledgement of plurality of the past experiences in an imperial setting by all sides.

---

criticised for belittling the Çanakkale saga; Özakman's *Diriliş* was also adapted to cinema by Yeşim Sezgin, *Çanakkale 1915* (2012); Kemal Uzun and Serdar Akar, *Çanakkale Yolun Sonu* [Canakkale End of the Road] (2013) tells the story of a Turkish sharpshooter.

121 Şerafettin Zeyrek, 'Liselerde Okutulan Türkiye Cumhuriyeti ve Atatürkçülük Adlı Ders Kitaplarında ÇK Savaşları' *Ankara Üniversitesi Türk İnkılap Tarihi Enstitüsü Atatürk Yolu Dergisi* 40 (2010): pp. 707–21.

122 Yılmaz calls for a re-evaluation of this forgotten generation, Fikret Yılmaz, *Gelibolu Mektupları, 1912–1915. Ruhum, Sevgili Beyim!* (İstanbul: Bahçeşehir Üniversitesi Yay., 2014), p. 2.

123 Erdoğan released on 23 April 2014 a message of condolence for the forced relocation of Armenians and the ensuing casualties in 1915. This unprecedented move signals a change in Turkish policy regarding the Armenian massacres on the eve of the centennial commemoration of the *Medz Yeghern*, see http://www.bbc.com/news/blogs-echochambers-27151970 [Accessed 6 August 2014].

Chapter 11
Reflections on the Gallipoli Campaign in Turkish literature

Şafak Horzum

When the Turkish war literature after the Second Constitutional Era of the Ottoman Empire in 1908 is examined, it is clear that political and literary societies like 'The New Literature' ('Edebiyat-ı Cedide') felt more comfortable dealing with more 'liberal' subject matters such as local issues, use of native language, and Turkishness compared with Occidentalism. In order to serve the newly flourishing genre, hundreds of new journals, magazines and newspapers were published with the purpose of preventing the collapse of the empire, and there were a variety of novel movements to save the regime from the philosophical paralysis it had been languishing in for decades. Despite these attempts, Turkish war literature was limited to a small number of writers, poets and dramatists at the beginning of the twentieth century and has remained so in the contemporary era. This limited range in the literature also affected the representation of both the defeats and the victories of the Battle of Çanakkale.[1] The Turkish literary works on the Gallipoli Campaign comprise mostly poems, short stories, novels and a handful of plays. Among these genres, poetry is at the forefront as everyone, from sultans to peasants, was genuinely interested in writing, citing, and reading poetry in the Ottoman Empire until the dissolution period. For that reason, the aim of this chapter is to articulate the general scope and themes of the Turkish war literature and to analyse some Turkish poems written in the period of the campaign and the contemporary age in a comparative manner.

The Ottoman Empire fought on several fronts during the First World War. Çanakkale was the turning point in the history of the war and for Europe as the most significant theatre of the Great War for 14 months – a 259-day struggle to decide the fate of the Ottoman Empire – but also because it was an assault by the Allied forces on the Dardanelles that was planned with the strategic objectives to end the reign of sultans, to get Russia off the hook of the Bolsheviks, and to rule over trade routes via controlling İstanbul and the straits.[2] Peoples of both

1 In this chapter, the Battle of Çanakkale is interchangeably used with its various names as 'the Gallipoli Campaign', 'the Battle of Gallipoli', and 'the Dardanelles Campaign' depending on the context.

2 Yavuz Bülent Bakiler, *Ölümünün 50. Yıldönümünde Mehmet Âkif Ersoy* [Mehmet Akif Ersoy in the 50th Death Anniversary] (Ankara: Kültür ve Turizm Bakanlığı, 1986), p. 7.

sides were gathered from a great variety of regions and across the social strata, and brought to Gallipoli so as to realise these strategic goals. So much so that the profile of those who fought against Turkish soldiers in Çanakkale appeared unusual; they were not the one type of enemy whose members were gathered under the umbrella of one ideology, or religion, or purpose prior to the war. Yet they were amassed for only one formal purpose, namely, to triumph under the command of the Allies. There were also several individual motives such as individual heroic emulation, to support one's family members financially by means of joining the war, and to fulfil the elevation of a national or ethnic identity. The Allies had united many nationalities, ethnicities and religions: foreign legions, the Zouaves from Africa, the Gurkhas and the Sikhs from India, the employee battalions from Greek and Eastern Jewish workshops, French and British sailors; English, Scottish, Welsh and Irish troops; Australian and New Zealand (ANZAC) contingents, as well as Arabs from the Middle East and Northern Africa.[3] Turkish soldiers' profiles are unusual too when the education levels and occupations of the soldiers are taken into account: the medics, the madrasans, and the jurists.[4] All their efforts at Çanakkale enabled the Gallipoli Campaign to become the 'preface' of the Republic of Turkey.[5] Thereafter, literary people have attempted to elevate this preface with special and selected accounts composed during and after the war.

A close look at the narratives of the Battle for Gallipoli, focusing closely on the bitter realities of what happened, according to the grim experiences of the participants, shows that nonfictional documents such as letters, diaries and administrative papers are actually abundant and easily accessible. Despite the multitude of these historical accounts, the victory of the Turks at Gallipoli has not been widely represented in the fictional works of Turkish literature, whereas the situation in Australian and New Zealand literatures is the opposite. Yahya Kemal Beyatlı, the representative of Parnassianism in Turkish poetry,[6] states the situation in one of his essays as follows:[7]

> One day, after the Great War, I saw one eximious, bibliophilic ex-frontline soldier of ours holding a famous French writer's work on our Çanakkale epic: he

3 Yalçın-Çelik, 'Ay Bedir Halindeydi', pp. 85–6.

4 Zeki Taştan, '*Çanakkale Mahşeri ve Uzun Beyaz Bulut – Gelibolu* Romanlarında Çanakkale Savaşları'na Gönüllü Katılan Aydınlar [Voluntary Intellectuals Joining the Çanakkale Battles in 'The Armageddon of Gallipoli' and *The Long White Cloud – Gallipoli*]', *İlmi Araştırmalar* 19 (2005): p. 122.

5 Turgut Özakman, 'Çanakkale . . .', *The Turkish Yearbook of Gallipoli Studies* 8, No. 8–9 (2010): p. 9.

6 İnci Enginün, *Yeni Türk Edebiyatı: Tanzimat'tan Cumhuriyet'e (1839–1923)* [New Turkish Literature: From the Tanzimât to the Republic (1839–1923)] (İstanbul: Dergâh, 2006), p. 620.

7 All Turkish to English translations from both primary and secondary sources are done by the author of this chapter.

> had quite a number of works similar to that one about us in French. Having seen this, I felt a pain in my heart. I said we were doomed to read in French even the accounts of blood we shed. The thousands of phrases about our war fronts have already been non-existent in our literature. That means, over the years, these campaigns will also be forgotten just like our ancient wars. There is a reason for this: war memories are not a clear genre in our literature.[8]

Beyatlı actually articulates his discomfort, which is still valid today: that of reading one's own accounts in different languages and through different filters, all of which are foreign to that culture, traditions and experiences of that society, and not from the narratives completed by the people from the society in question. Ahmet Mithat Efendi, a prolific early Turkish novelist, and Nihad Sâmi Banarlı interpret the situation in a more patriotic way by saying that the Turks had enough time to create epics, but not to write them (quoted in Koçak 2013).[9] Alongside these interpretations, the loss of almost all the literate and well-educated Turkish youth in the war affected the production of literary representations in every sense in the Republican period, while political, social, and economic problems affecting contemporary Turkey have altered society too quickly for writers to meditate on the past victories of the nation.

Although there were administrative deficiencies in the ministries of the Ottoman Empire that led to the dissolution of the state in the First World War, the Ministry of War participated in the work of literary circles and endeavoured to make use of the arts and literature as a means to encourage people to enlist into the army. This was because 'the whole state and nation must coalesce into one in order to remain standing in this war for which millions of people had been mobilised and to propel more soldiers to the front lines'.[10] In addition to providing encouragement for recruitment, the administrators were also conscious that literature mirrors the recollections of a society. Furthermore, it also 'witnesses the transformation [and] modification of the future and facilitates those recollections so as to be spread among and accepted by the readers of that society and to be transferred on to future generations via codes placed in the written accounts'.[11] War literature elucidates that conflicts are not only made up of battles on the front lines but also deeply

8 Yahya Kemal Beyatlı, *Edebiyata Dair* [On Literature], 2nd edn (İstanbul: İstanbul Fetih Cemiyeti, 1984), pp. 148–9.

9 Koçak, 'Savaşı Şiirden Okumak', p. 468.

10 Mustafa Selçuk, 'Birinci Dünya Savaşı Sürecinde Harbiye Nezareti'nin 'Çanakkale Kahramanlığını Yaşatma' Amaçlı Faaliyetleri [The Activities of the Ministry of War 'for Cherishing the Heroism of Gallipoli' during the First World War]', *Avrasya İncelemeleri Dergisi* 1, No. 2 (2012): pp. 196–7.

11 Yadigar Türkeli-Sanlı, 'Edebiyat; Toplumsal Hafızanın, Geleneğin Kaybında, İnşasında Ne Kadar Etkilidir? [How Important is the Literary Texts to Construct, Loss of the Social Memory, Tradition?]', *Çankırı Karatekin Üniversitesi Sosyal Bilimler Enstitüsü Dergisi* 2, No. 2 (2011): pp. 163.

influence people due to their sorrows, cruelties, exoduses and deaths as well as through their defeats and victories. Literary works, therefore, are 'irreplaceable', and, through close examination, help us to comprehend the humane dimensions of the matter.[12]

Within this framework, the Ministry of War of the Ottoman Empire decided to gather a committee of artists and literary men from various branches of the arts and announced that volunteers would visit the Gallipoli front to compose works so as to increase enlistments, to support fighting Turkish soldiers morally, to gain the support of the people, to keep alive the spirit of resistance, and to relieve the beloved families of those at the front. The Ministry would also publish the literary works in its military journals which would then be delivered throughout the country in an attempt to maintain the faith in victory and to inspire those fighting on the front lines as well as their families and friends supporting them on the home front.[13] The literary men who formed the majority of the committee, which was seen as a call to duty and a national service, gathered in a warlike atmosphere to create their war literature.[14] The committee set off on its journey on the morning of 11 July 1915 (28 June 1331) from the Sirkeci Station, İstanbul and arrived at the front on 15 July.[15] They were welcomed in Gallipoli by the commanders and generals and immediately set about to observe the battle areas as well as the emergency hospitals behind the lines. İbrahim Alaattin Gövsa, one of the writers in the committee, gave an account of the conditions at the front in this period:

> I walked into the trenches closest to the enemy and saw how our soldiers defended strongly the land under the harsh and deplorable conditions against the excellent and preponderant instruments of assault, and how they fought against iron and fire with their tenacity and faith. The graveyards of martyrs, as wide as cities, and corpses, as numerous as armies, which had not been buried yet, left me with unforgettable suffering. I witnessed what a catastrophic, lofty madness is a war.[16]

Having seen such traumatic scenes at Gallipoli, some of the committee members left the area on 19 July, and some on 22 July.[17] The literary men who witnessed the miserable conditions of soldiers at the Gallipoli front wrote poems and stories

---

12 Halûk Harun Duman and Salih Koralp Güreşir, 'Yeni Türk Edebiyatı'nın Kaynakları: Savaş ve Edebiyat (1828–1911) [The Sources of Modern Turkish Literature: War and Literature (1828–1911)]', *Turkish Studies* 4, No. 1-1 (2009): p. 73.

13 Selçuk, 'Harbiye Nezareti', pp. 197–8.

14 Ibid., pp. 200–01.

15 Ibid., pp. 203–04.

16 İbrahim Alaattin Gövsa, *Çanakkale İzleri: Anafartaların Müebbet Kahramanına* [Traces of Çanakkale: To the Eternal Heroes of the Suvla] (Ankara: Atatürk Kültür Dil ve Tarih Yüksek Kurumu 1989), p. 12.

17 Selçuk, 'Harbiye Nezareti', p. 209.

which were published in the special journals like *Harp Mecmuası* [War Journal] produced as 27 issues between November 1915 and June 1918.[18]

The victory at Gallipoli was employed in many poems, short stories, novels and few dramas; however, the quantity and quality of these works, dissimilar to the multitude of news and photographs from papers, have not, according to the Turkish critics, been able to represent the victory gloriously enough[19] though the sincerity and truth about and respect for the war has been reflected to an indisputably high standard.[20] Turgut Özakman, a well-known Turkish dramatist and novelist, especially criticises the contents of the works because 'they recite the Battle of Çanakkale as a ball of superstitions'[21] rather than employing the crucial scientific, political and social facts, losses and achievements. Just like historians David Hume and Edward Gibbon, he suggests that writers should be careful in blending the historical realities and the imaginative elements for the composition of historiographically designed works. For that reason, bringing some ossified historical fallacies into question by means of correct, historically scientific research[22] is an approach promoted by the modern authors. Peyami Safa, a productive Turkish author, satirises the committee taken to Gallipoli by the Ministry of War:

> Our war literature is completely empty. They shuttled some of our poets and publishers to Çanakkale. Their highnesses, the honourable litterateurs, who were not even allowed to enter the danger zone as foreign war journalists did, watched how their brothers' eyes were closed by the enemy bullets forever while smoking the cigarettes which are reserved for administrative tycoons. After they got tired of this view, they returned to İstanbul with a stock of shallow and subtle impressions just enough for two or three essays from each one of them.[23]

It seems that these inadequacies and incapacities did not affect the production of a few works though. Turkish commanders' knowledge, Turkish officers' leadership, and Turkish soldiers' bravery, patriotism, self-devotion and self-confidence were all reflected in some certain journals and newspapers.

---

18 Ibid., p. 213–15.

19 Koçak, 'Savaşı Şiirden Okumak', 47; Turgay Anar, 'Türk Edebiyatında Edebiyat Kanonu: Kanon, Kanona Girmek ve Kanona Müdahale [Literary Canon in Turkish Literature: The Canon, Acceptance by the Canon and the Anti-Canon]', *FSM İlmî Araştırmalar İnsan ve Toplum Bilimleri Dergisi* 1 (2013): pp. 70–71.

20 Koçak, 'Savaşı Şiirden Okumak', pp. 469, 470.

21 Özakman, 'Çanakkale . . .', p. 11

22 Alev Baysal [Karaduman], '18. Yüzyıl İngiltere'sinde Tarih Yazım Kuramları ve Tarihi Roman [Theories of Historiography and the Historical Novel in 18th-century England]', *Littera* 17 (2005): pp. 73–4.

23 Peyami Safa, *Objektif 2: Sanat – Edebiyat – Tenkit* [Objective 2: Art – Literature – Criticism] (İstanbul: Ötüken, 1990), pp. 116–17.

Ideologies of the era inevitably reveal themselves in the publications of works based on the Battle of Çanakkale. As Karaduman asserts, '[the literature] is held within ideology, but also manages to distance itself from it, to the point where it permits the reader to 'feel' and 'perceive' the ideology from which it springs.'[24] The interwoven ideological approaches of the authors direct the readers intentionally or unwittingly towards related journals. *Harp Mecmuası* was the journal established and ever supported by the Ministry of War and it enabled the members of the committee to publish their war narratives after their visit to the Gallipoli front. *Türk Yurdu* [Journal of Turk Land] was one initial example of these journals and it amalgamated this aim with the idea of nationality, that is to say, Turkishness. *Sebilü'r-Reşad* [Journal of True Path] was another pioneer media organ emphasising Islamic unity and religious values. *Servet-i Fünûn* [Journal of the Wealth of Knowledge] and *Sabah* [The Morning Newspaper] were two other significant publications in favour of Occidentalism.[25] These were four all-important prints and they represented the main movements within the Second Constitutional Era. For further studies, representative poets of the time, who are not the core matter of this chapter, include Yusuf Ziya Ortaç, Hamdullah Suphi Tanrıöver, Enis Behiç Koryürek, Mehmet Emin Yurdakul, İbrahim Alaattin Gövsa, Abdülhak Hamit Tarhan, Rauf Yekta, Mehmet Ziya Gökalp, Fâik Ali Ozansoy, Fazıl Hüsnü Dağlarca, Faruk Nafiz Çamlıbel, and private Mustafa son of Ömer from Boyabat.[26] In the poems of these poets, the themes generally consist of spirituality during the wartime, the love of one's country and religion, the elevation of Turkish identity, the victories of Turkish history, the Turk's aid to the Europeans in the past and the Europeans' betrayal to the Turk in the present, and Turkish soldiers' bravery against the heavily armed enemies before the Dardanelles. Among all the male poets, one woman poet appears, Salime Servet Seyfi. In the Ottoman Empire, girls were permitted to attend secondary and high schools to take up vocational education in the nineteenth century, whereas, due to the Islamic tenets, only primary or private education was possible for them in the previous age.[27] Salime Servet Seyfi is one prominent woman poet who guides the soldiers with her poetry published in *Donanma Mecmuası* [Navy Journal] and encourages

24 Alev Karaduman, 'The Changing Social Scene in 19th-century England: The Victorian Novel Revisited in terms of Marxist Ideology' in *Batı Edebiyatında İdeoloji – Ideology in Western Literature*, eds Ertuğrul İşler et al. (Denizli: MacArt, 2012), p. 24.

25 Koçak, 'Savaşı Şiirden Okumak', p. 469.

26 Ibid., pp. 470–71, 475.

27 Burçin Erol, 'Tanzimat'tan Cumhuriyet'e Türk ve Batı Kadını [Turkish and Western Women from the Tanzimât to the Republic]' in *Kastamonu'da İlk Kadın Mitingi'nin 75. Yıldönümü Uluslararası Sempozyumu Bildiri Kitabı* [Proceedings of the International Symposium of the 75th Anniversary of the First Women's Demonstration in Kastamonu] (Ankara: Atatürk Araştırma Merkezi, 1996), pp. 149–51.

them to accept martyrdom rather than returning home in defeat.[28] By fostering the stoic masculinity of soldiers, she gives them the support of the Anatolian women with enthusiasm and excitement in her poems.

After so many poets, it is requisite to look through the prose authors and their works, too. Ömer Seyfettin, who was a committee member commissioned by the Ministry of War and was a successful nationalist short story writer, has four significant short stories entitled as 'Bir Çocuk: Aleko' [A Boy: Aleko], 'Müjde' [Good News], 'Çanakkale'den Sonra' [After Gallipoli] and 'Kaç Yerinden' [How Many Wounds][29] which are directly related to the battles in Gallipoli and revolve around themes of heroism and valour. Since attention to drama only started in the early twentieth century in the Ottoman Turkey,[30] one can only find two plays directly related to the Dardanelles Campaign. One of them is *Yirmisekiz Kânunuevvel* [December 28] by Mithat Cemâl Kuntay. The play employs the conflict of the time as the struggle for freedom and the hopelessness of trying to win the battles. The Gallipoli front is depicted on the stage in a vivid way in order that the play arouses the emotions of the Turkish audience by perpetuating their efforts for independence from the imperial powers. The other play is *Pâyitaht'ın Kapısında* [At the Door of the Capital] by Fâik Ali Ozansoy. Also here, the pro-war ideas are interwoven through characters and settings as it strives to serve the purpose of saving the nation.[31]

In terms of fiction, the main interest in writing novels about Çanakkale flourished in the last quarter of the twentieth century; in that sense, it resembles the historical process of the Turkish–Greek relationships that were affirmatively starting to be dealt with in the literary and cultural works of that period. The first example of the novel form is the . . . *Ve Çanakkale* (*1 Geldiler*; *2 Gördüler*; *3 Döndüler*) [. . . And Çanakkale (1 They Came; 2 They Saw; 3 They Returned)] trilogy by Mustafa Naci Sepetçioğlu in 1989. This is regarded as the first historical novel on Gallipoli, which multiplied in later years with a similar focus on religion, motherland and nation.[32] The novel concentrates on the wartime difficulties that stemmed from first 'economic misery' on account of manpower poverty, second, 'human misery' due

28 Betül Coşkun, 'Savaşlar Çağında Yetişmiş Bir Kadın Yazar: Salime Servet Seyfi [A Woman Writer in the Age of Wars: Salime Servet Seyfi]', *Turkish Studies* 7, No. 2 (2012), p. 264.

29 Melih Erzen, 'Cihan Harbinin Karanlığında Aydınlığı Hatırla(t)mak: Ömer Seyfettin'in Kaleminden Kahramanlara Dair [Remembering/Reminding the Daylight at the Darkness of World War I: About Heroes from the Pen of Ömer Seyfettin]', *Gazi Akademik Bakış* 7, No. 14 (2014), p. 296.

30 Alemdar Yalçın, *II. Meşrutiyette Tiyatro Edebiyatı Tarihi* [History of Theatre Literature in the 2nd Constitutional Era], 2nd edn (Ankara: Akçağ, 2002), pp. 37–9.

31 Yalçın, *Tiyatro Edebiyatı Tarihi*, pp. 157–60.

32 Celal Mat, 'Çanakkale Muharebelerini Konu Edinen Romanlar Üzerine [On the Fictions Concerning the Battles of Çanakkale]', *Balıkesir University Journal of Social Sciences Institute* 10, No. 17 (2007), p. 98; Taştan, 'Gönüllü Katılan Aydınlar', p. 121.

to the exhaustion of Anatolian people, and third 'administrative misery' because of both problems in the management of the state and the army, and disputes that arose between the administrators and official institutions.[33] Mehmed Niyazi Özdemir's *Çanakkale Mahşeri* [The Armageddon of Gallipoli] (1998) was another significant historical novel that portrayed a forging of victory by Turkish soldiers for the sake of the freedom of their beloved country and families.

All those historical narratives pay homage to the victories of the Turkish ancestors and great commanders who strove against the Allied forces in Gallipoli. They all utilise historical and documental accounts derived from the original memoirs, letters and experiences of the soldiers that had been in the war as well as the official archives of the related countries. The two most authentic fictional accounts came one after the other in 2000 and 2001: respectively, Serpil Ural's *Candles at Dawn* and Buket Uzuner's *The Long White Cloud – Gallipoli.* Ural's youth fiction *Candles at Dawn* employs the encounter of two young girls in today's world whose grandfathers fought on different sides, and it questions the concepts of war, peace and freedom. The novel emphasises the vain ideals of imperialism and the futility of enmity, but the importance of humane values between two once-conflicting identities. However, Ural is unrighteously criticised by partisan, 'politically catalyst', prejudiced commentators[34] since she supposedly did not write it in a manner appropriate to the historical facts[35] and her work was condemned as hack. Buket Uzuner, another woman writer and author of *The Long White Cloud – Gallipoli* fuses two seemingly different identities – Turks and Australians – into one and examines the credibility of the past and attempts to settle with the traditional notions, doctrines and narratives. Following these works, Turgut Özakman produced another historical and documental novel in 2008: *Diriliş – Çanakkale 1915* [Resurrection – Çanakkale 1915].

As stated above, poetry rather than drama and novel enables one to track the effects of the war from the early twentieth to the twenty-first century. One of the most significant poems written through the inspiration of Çanakkale is 'The Imperial Ghazal'[36] of five couplets by Sultan Mehmed V Reshad in 1916. In the

---

33 İsmail Çetişli, 'Türk Milletinin Çanakkale Savaşı Günlerinde Yüz Yüze Kaldığı Yokluk ve Yoksullukların . . . *Ve Çanakkale* Romanına Yansımaları [The Reflections of the Poverty that the Turkish Nation Encountered in the Çanakkale War, in the Novel ". . . And Çanakkale"]', *Erdem Dergisi* 17, No. 49 (2007), pp. 186–7, 190, 193.

34 Ali Gültekin, 'Türk Çocuk ve Gençlik Edebiyatında Eleştiri Kültürüne Örnek Olarak Serpil Ural'ın *Şafakta Yanan Mumlar'ı* [An Example of Literary Criticism on Turkish Children's and Youth Literature: Serpil Ural's *Candles at Dawn*]', *Burdur Eğitim Fakültesi Dergisi* 6, No. 11 (2006), pp. 55–6.

35 Gültekin, 'Türk Çocuk ve Gençlik Edebiyatında', pp. 46–52.

36 'Two strong enemies of the Muslims united and attacked Gallipoli by both land and sea. However, Allah helped our army on time and each of our soldiers became a steel castle. In the end, the enemies abased themselves after having seen the determination of our

ghazal, the sultan accepts the tough conditions the Empire was in compared to 'Two strong enemies of the Muslims' and addresses the men fighting on the front line as 'our soldier sons' by embracing them like a father. As the 35th Ottoman Caliph in Islam, he proves the importance of absolute faithfulness in Allah that 'helped [the Turkish] army' and thus made them victorious. This ghazal actually shows itself as a sign of thankfulness to God, and it is seen that it is simply written in a clear scheme, with the use of plain language. The gratitude of the sultan was 'praised by the courtiers' and the high-ranking officials close to the Dolmabahçe Palace. Nevertheless, he was also 'criticised with regard to his lack of administrative capacity and failure' in the *tahmises*[37] by the contemporary poets.[38]

Among all the works about the Battle of Gallipoli, one poem emerges as a supremely well-developed composition, namely 'To the Martyrs of Çanakkale' (1924) by Mehmet Akif Ersoy. Ersoy's poem is a part of the 'Asım' chapter in his book *Safahat* that eternises the Epic of Çanakkale from the Turkish point of view in 84 lines. 'To the Martyrs of Çanakkale' is designed with a rhyme scheme in the arud prosody similar to *Masnavi* (1258–73) by Jalāl ad-Dīn Muhammad Rumi. For a better analysis, the poem is divided into three sections. At the beginning, Ersoy describes the grand scale of 'This Dardanelles war – without equal in the world / Four or five mighty armies are pressed and are hurled / To reach the Sea of Marmara by hill and pass / So many fleets have surrounded a small mass . . . . '.[39] Immediately after, he describes both sides: the enemies of the Turks as rapist 'Europeans' of 'what dishonourable assemblages'[40] resembling 'braying hyenas, released from their reeking cages' along with 'The Old World and the New World, all have come this way, / Bubbling like sand, like a flood, or like Judgement Day; / The seven climes of the world stand opposite you / Australia, beside which observe Canada too!' He criticises the quasi 'civilisation' of the Europeans whose main drive for the Great War was for imperial and colonial benefits.[41] The

soldier sons. [The opponents] who came to capture the heart of Islam [İstanbul] swallowed their honour and ran away off the shores. Reshad! Prostrate for the sajdah of thankfulness, and pray Allah to render the Islamic countries safe all the time'. The Imperial Ghazal's prose translation from Turkish to English by the author of the chapter. For Turkish prose translation, see, Enfel Doğan and Fatih Tığlı, 'Sultan V. Mehmed Reşad'ın Çanakkale Gazeli ve Bu Gazele Yazılan Tahmisler [The Lyric Poem of Sultan V. Mehmed Reşad about the Çanakkale Wars and the Tahmises Written on This Poem]', İstanbul Üniversitesi Türk Dili ve Edebiyatı Dergisi 33 (2005), p. 46.

37 Tahmis is a kind of 'quintet' in Turkish poetry.

38 Doğan and Tığlı, 'Sultan V. Medmed Reşad', pp. 49–50, 51.

39 Mehmet Akif Ersoy, 'To the Martyrs of Çanakkale', trans. S. Tanvir Wasti, accessed June 18, 2014, http://www.canakkale.gen.tr/eng/poetry/po2.html.

40 Mehmet Akif Ersoy, 'To the Martyrs of Çanakkale', trans. Michael R. Burch, The HyperTexts, accessed June 18, 2014, http://www.canakkale.gen.tr/eng/poetry/po2.html.

41 Ahmet Kolbaşı,'Çanakkale Şehitlerine' İsimli Destanda Yer Alan Tarih ve Medeniyet Olguları Üzerine Bir Değerlendirme [An Evaluation of the Facts of Civilisation

Ottoman Empire had not only been a border-neighbour for Europe, but was also seen a rich, ever-coveted and immense reserve for the Western colonialists. This centralisation of attraction for Turkish lands had begun in the sixteenth century after the conquest of Hungary by the Ottoman Empire.[42] After the second half of the nineteenth century, which corresponds to the dissolution period of the Ottoman Empire, the attitude of the European travellers, writers and politicians towards Anatolia altered and became 'sarcastic, despising and pejorative'.[43]

Thus, Ersoy addresses the colonial practices planned to be carried out by the Allied imperial forces. The Turks, who lacked the materials sufficient to accomplish victory on the war fronts, clung tightly to the spirituality they found in their Islamic religion, according to Ersoy.[44] Praising the courage shown by the Turkish soldiers, he likens them to Kilij Arslan I of the Seljuk Sultanate of Rum, who was victorious in the Peasants' Crusade[45] and the Crusade of 1101,[46] and to Saladin of the Ayyubid dynasty who successfully defeated the Third Crusade and was able to construct a strong national will. Here, Ersoy resembles the Allied forces to the Crusaders who sacked Anatolia and the Middle East for the sole cause of their economic prosperity. The poet, who was 'in doubt and pessimism' about the future of the country and nation because of 'the bitter news from Çanakkale', desires only victory at the end.[47] The ethnic variety of the belligerents, the siege of the straits, the tough conditions and skirmishes during the battles are described in the poem as the poet is particularly loyal to the historical facts of the Battle. In the middle section of the work, the cinematographic action is built and animated with the use of intense visual and audio elements from the close combat scenes[48] in the following fictionally, yet realistically, narrated lines: 'Lightning severs horizons! / Earthquakes regurgitate the bodies of the dead! / Bombs' thunderbolts explode brains, / Rupture the breasts of brave soldiers. / Underground tunnels writhe like hell / Full of the bodies of

---

and History in the Epic entitled 'To the Martyrs of Çanakkale', in *Türk Epik Ənənəsində Dastan* (Bakü: Azərbaycan Milli Elmlər Akademiyası Folklor İnstitutu, 2010), pp. 30, 32.

42 Himmet Umunç, 'Türkiye'de Hollandâlı Bir Seyyah: Cornelis de Bruyn ve Gözlemleri [A Dutch Traveller in Turkey: Cornelis de Bruyn and His Observations]', *Belleten* 266 (2009), p. 150.

43 Alev Karaduman, '*Eothen*: İngiliz Seyyah Alexander Kinglake'in Osmanlı Türkiyesine Ötekileştirici Bakışı [*Eothen*: English Traveller Alexander Kinglake's Othering View of Ottoman Turkey]', *Hacettepe Üniversitesi Türkiyat Araştırmaları Dergisi* 19 (2013), pp. 96, 97.

44 Yalçın-Çelik, 'Ay Bedir Halindeydi', pp. 91, 92–3.

45 Jill N. Claster, *Sacred Violence: The European Crusades to the Middle East, 1095–1396* (Toronto: University of Toronto Press, 2009), p. 45.

46 Steven Runciman, *A History of the Crusades: The Kingdom of Jerusalem and the Frankish East, 1100–1187*, vol. 2 (Cambridge: Cambridge University Press, 1951), pp. 22–4.

47 Yalçın-Çelik, 'Ay Bedir Halindeydi', p. 89.

48 Yalçın-Çelik, 'Ay Bedir Halindeydi', pp. 92–4.

burn victims. / The sky rains down death, the earth swallows the living. / A terrible blizzard heaves men violently into the air. / Heads, eyes, torsos, legs, arms, chins, fingers, hands, feet . . . / Body parts rain down everywhere. / Coward hands encased in armour callously scatter / Floods of thunderbolts, torrents of fire. / Men's chests gape open, / Beneath the high, circling vulture-like packs of the air'.[49] Thus, the onomatopoeic alliteration in the original Turkish version provides the sounds from the battlefield. In these two sections, it can be deduced that a binary opposition is constructed and placed in the texture of the poem by putting the blood(shed) of the Turks in contrast with the modern weaponry of the quasi-civilised Allies. In the final section, Ersoy refers to the martyrs by glorifying them: 'Outstretched he lies there, shot right through his spotless brow, / For this Crescent O Lord, what suns are setting now. / O soldier, for this earth's sake fallen to the dust, / If your heavenly forbears kissed your brow, "'twere just" '.[50] The poet metaphorically prepares a mausoleum for these brave soldiers. The mausoleum is of the Kaaba 'to be built on the site' as the monument and the sky as the dome of the tomb which will be embellished with the Pleiades, the constellation of the Seven Sisters. Herein, the dynamism in the fight sections gives way to the silent respect for the deceased who sacrificed themselves for the sake of what they believed in. The speed of wording, accounting and scenes in the poem 'raises the inner rhythm, affectivity, and critical thought provocation'.[51] Thus, the poem in memoriam of the martyrs of Anatolia comes to a conclusion by uniting Turkishness and Islam as a war epic. The poem points to a hope that it will trigger national feelings in hard times, and trust in the future generations for whom all these lines were gifted, with the intention of transferring to them the savagery of 'civilised' Europe through the strength of their ancestors despite all the misery they endured.

Having examined the patriotic poem of Mehmet Akif Ersoy, it is better to look at a contemporary poem written towards the end of the twentieth century so as to comprehend the changing mindset of the Turks, through the example of 'Gallipoli – A Postwar Epic' (1988) by Bülent Ecevit. The poet, who was the five-times former prime minister of the Republic of Turkey, expresses the importance of fraternity by means of dialogues between an anonymous Mehmet of Anatolia, an ANZAC soldier and a 15-year-old English war drummer, and recites the consolation to the members of several nations' martyrs, and the current condition of Gallipoli: 'Gallipoli now abounds / with gardens full / with nations full / of burial grounds[.] / a paradise on earth Gallipoli / is a burial under the ground / those who lost their lives in fighting / lie there mingled in friendly compound'.[52] The people

49 Mehmet Akif Ersoy, 'To the Martyrs of Çanakkale', trans. Michael R. Burch.

50 Mehmet Akif Ersoy, 'To the Martyrs of Çanakkale', trans. S. Tanvir Wasti.

51 Yalçın-Çelik, 'Ay Bedir Halindeydi', p. 97.

52 Bülent Ecevit, 'Gallipoli – A Postwar Epic', DurYolcu.com, accessed June 18, 2014, http://www.duryolcu.com/default.asp?m_id=3&c_id=382&title=%C7anakkale%20-%20B%FClent%20Ecevit.

who died for different purposes at the Battle of Gallipoli now gather to discuss the validity of these ideals against the beauty they created with the blood they shed by 'leaving aside their antagonistic and solipsistic manner'.[53] These representative soldiers' voices recount their longing for their homelands, their memories before the war and their present condition, which led to the erasure of their 'names' and 'identities' off the earth. It becomes clear that the once-antagonistic identities try to find a salvation from this enmity by getting to know one another, realising the benefits of the imperialist 'great civilisations' which affected them so directly. The poem written by a prime minister of a country also matters on the grounds that he represents his national ideas as well as changes in international relations.

In conclusion, the liberal atmosphere that sprang up following the Second Constitutional Era of the Ottoman Empire led to three main movements: the Islamist perspective, trying to gather the Muslim nations under the realm of the Ottoman state; the ideal of Turkishness, which sought to unify the Anatolian population together with all the other Turks in Asia in order to assert themselves among the imperial powers; and the Occidentalist approach that argued the Ottomans had fallen behind the other European countries and cultures and that reform was essential for the sake of the development of the state. All the movements brought their own perspectives into the literary works written on behalf of the Battle of Çanakkale, the Turkish martyrs fallen in Gallipoli, and their families who endured emotional and economic misery in Anatolia. Sultan Mehmet V Reshad's 'The Imperial Ghazal' is, therefore, an early example of the attempt to encompass all the Islamic, Turkic, and Western perspectives. Despite individual and ministerial attempts, Turkish war literature at the beginning of the twentieth century remained limited because educated youth had been wasted on the front lines to protect the nation against the multi-national enemy forces. One can also see that the Turkish national poet Mehmet Akif Ersoy's poem 'To the Martyrs of Çanakkale' has been regarded as a 'national' masterpiece on the Turkish Epic at Gallipoli by all the literary circles to the extent that no other author has attempted to compose a new work which would be compared to Ersoy's. The satires upon the limited, or lack of, interest in the glorious victory at the Dardanelles, obviously did not have much effect on later generations until the 1980s.

'Gallipoli – A Postwar Epic' by Bülent Ecevit, an important ex-political figure in the Republic of Turkey brought a new dimension into the relationships between the Turks and the other nations who fought in the Dardanelles. After the emergence of historical novels in the late 1980s, which concentrate upon historically factual accounts collected during the battles, *Candles at Dawn* and *The Long White Cloud – Gallipoli*, respectively by Serpil Ural and Buket Uzuner, take the readers to the conclusion that identities that once were in conflict are now blended into one. It is clear that the Turkish perspective of the Battle of Çanakkale, and understanding of the concept of the enemy, have come to an 'accommodationist' point through the national education and global experiences of the twenty-first century.

---

53 Alev Karaduman, 'Recognising the Other: Identities in Conflict at Gallipoli'. *Hacettepe Üniversitesi Türkiyat Araştırmaları Dergisi* 15 (2011), p. 146.

Index